CliffsNotes®

Praxis II Biology Content Knowledge (0235)

D1319404

CliffsNotes®

Praxis II Biology Content Knowledge (0235)

by
Glen Edward Moulton, Ed.D.

WILEY

John Wiley & Sons, Inc.

About the Author

Glen Moulton has served 36 years in public education in such diverse roles as middle school science and mathematics teacher, high school chemistry and physics teacher, high school administrator, central office science supervisor, and adjunct professor. His teaching experience includes an inner-city setting in Chicago as well as rural-suburban Maryland. His diverse experiences as a student and teacher have shaped his understanding of the process of education to include all learners. His philosophy is often summarized in one of his quotes, "Your students cannot be the problem!"

Included among Dr. Moulton's work is The Complete Idiot's Guide to Biology and Professional Teaching Knowledge, an on-line course for preservice teachers including a series of videos and podcasts designed to help first-year teachers. Most recently, Dr. Moulton drew upon his experience in working with Special Education and troubled learners to produce Express Biology, a high school biology curriculum for reluctant learners, and Express Earth and Space Science, a secondary Earth Science curriculum also for reluctant learners.

Author's Acknowledgments

Thanks to my Lord, Jesus Christ, for preparing me to write this text and helping me every day.

Editorial

Acquisition Editor: Greg Tubach

Project Editor: Kelly Dobbs Henthorne

Copy Editor: Catherine Schwenk

Technical Editors: Kenneth Crawford and Michael Yard

Composition

Proofreader: Tricia Liebig

John Wiley & Sons, Inc., Composition Services

CliffsNotes® Praxis II Biology Content Knowledge (0235)

Published by:
John Wiley & Sons, Inc.
111 River Street
Hoboken, NJ 07030-5774
www.wiley.com

Copyright © 2012 John Wiley & Sons, Inc., Hoboken, NJ

Published by John Wiley & Sons, Inc., Hoboken, NJ
Published simultaneously in Canada

Library of Congress Control Number: 2011945568
ISBN: 978-1-118-07497-8 (pbk)
ISBN: 978-1-118-22260-7; 978-1-118-23004-6; 978-1-118-23016-9 (ebk)

Printed in the United States of America

10 9 8 7 6 5 4 3 2 1

Table of Contents

PART I: SUBJECT AREA REVIEWS

Chapter 5: Ecology

Chapter 6: Science, Technology, and Society

PART II: FULL-LENGTH PRACTICE TESTS

Practice Test 1

Practice Test 2

Introduction

Do you want to pass the Praxis II Biology Core Content Knowledge (0235) exam the first time you take it? Do you need help remembering the similarities between photosynthesis and cellular respiration? Are you up-to-date with the latest information describing your immune system? How much do you really remember about the vascular system of plants? Would a refresher on mitosis and meiosis help fill in some memory gaps?

If your answer to any of these questions is yes, you've come to the right place. This test preparation guide is designed to help first-time test-takers pass the Praxis II Biology Core Content Knowledge (0235) exam the first and only time they take it! Every topic on the test is covered in detail with scaffolding, illustrations, and examples for the more difficult concepts. Sample test questions cover each topic and are similar in style, content, and degree of difficulty as the ones you will encounter on the Praxis exam. The answers to the sample questions are provided along with thorough explanations for the correct answers as well as explanations about why the incorrect answers are wrong. Lastly, the language is straightforward, crisp, to the point, and with minimal trivia.

This text is written by a former public school teacher, high school administrator, and central office supervisor, and contains insights that reveal useful techniques and classroom strategies.

Reasons to Take the Praxis II Biology Core Content Knowledge (0235) Exam

A number of reasons exist for preservice and classroom teachers to take the Praxis II Biology Core Content Knowledge (0235) exam. An increasing number of states are requiring a passing score on Praxis II Subject Area Tests for certification and employment. Some teachers complete the Praxis II Biology to strengthen their resumés for new opportunities and options. Colleges and universities often require successful scores on the Praxis examinations for completion of the teacher education program and certification in that state. Increasingly, entry into top-notch graduate programs and sophisticated specialized training events may also require a passing score on a Praxis assessment. Finally, many professional associations and organizations require passing scores as a criterion for credentials and professional licensing.

About the Exam

The Praxis II series of assessments has been developed by the Educational Testing Service (ETS) to measure knowledge in specific subject areas and general teaching skills. The Praxis II: Biology Core Content Knowledge (0235) exam is designed to assess whether you have the knowledge and competencies that are expected of a successful biology teacher in a secondary school.

The Praxis II Biology Core Content Knowledge (0235) exam consists of 150 multiple-choice questions, which are to be completed within the two-hour time limit. The questions cover topics that are fundamental to an introductory college biology course and reflect national standards as established by the National Science Education Standards (NSES). The questions range from easy definitions to more challenging applications of concepts and analysis of events. The content categories, approximate number of questions, and approximate percentage of questions are organized in Table I-1.

Table I–1		
Content Categories	**Approximate Number of Questions**	**Approximate Percentage of Questions**
Basic Principles of Science	12	8%
Molecular and Cellular Biology	38	25%
Classical Genetics and Evolution	23	15%
Diversity of Life, Plants, and Animals	45	30%
Ecology	22	15%
Science, Technology, Society	10	7%

Scoring the Test and Interpreting the Results

Hopefully you will get all 150 questions on the test correct. In the event that you don't, your score will be based on the total number of questions that you answer correctly. There are several editions of the test, all of which conform to the test parameters found in the preceding table. Some of the questions will be easy for you, and some may take more time. Is there a penalty for guessing? In a word, no. There is no subtraction for wrong answers, so an incorrect answer whether you guessed or not simply subtracts from the total correct.

You will receive a score report within six weeks, longer if you fill out the grid sheet incorrectly. Your score report will tell you the following:

- Whether you passed or not
- Your score
- The range of possible scores
- The raw points available in each category
- The range of the middle 50 percent of scores on that test
- Your Recognition of Excellence Award status, if you qualify

Additional information is available at the ETS website: www.ets.org.

How to Use This Study Guide

This book is a test preparation guide. The goal is to pass the test the first time you take it. The contents of this guide provide all of the factual information needed along with questions to assess how well you have integrated the knowledge commensurate with Praxis expectations.

There are many proven ways to use this book. One method is to start at the beginning and methodically work through each section of this book. Working section by section is a good technique because the Praxis exam covers a wide range of topics. However, remember to concentrate on all topics, but keep in mind the weighting of the categories as described in Table I–1 of a previous section. Remember that each category is weighted differently. You may want to adjust your study time to meet those requirements. When you feel comfortable with the content, take one of the practice tests at the end of the book. Based on your results, either take the Praxis test ASAP or return to selected sections and review the material. When finished, take the other form of the test found at the end of the book. Decide whether you are ready for the Praxis test or need to review a different category.

Another method is to take one of the practice tests at the end of the book. If you answer the questions correctly, take the Praxis exam. If not, analyze the category or categories that gave you the most problems. Not all categories carry the same weight. Locate your weakest categories in the text and work through them, keeping in mind the type of questions that were asked. When you have mastered the content, take the other practice exam. Decide whether you are ready for the Praxis test or need to review a different category.

PART I

SUBJECT AREA REVIEWS

Chapter 1

Basic Principles of Science

Scientific Method and Processes Involved in Scientific Inquiry

The **Scientific Method** is a logical problem-solving technique that requires reasoning, skepticism, and direction. Scientists use the Scientific Method to discover the truth by confirming or rejecting hypotheses, thoughts, and ideas. Most researchers agree on the main steps of the Scientific Method:

1. **Observation**—The discovery of an unexpected event or phenomenon; often as a result of intriguing or discrepant experiments conducted by other researchers.

2. **Research**—A review of relevant literature including related studies and experiments to predict the cause and effect for the observed phenomenon: What is it? What caused it?

3. **Hypothesis**—A prediction that proposes the cause (independent variable) and effect (dependent variable) for the observed phenomenon. The hypothesis predicts the cause and effect relationship regarding the observed phenomenon. Often a hypothesis is written in the "If (independent variable), then (dependent variable)" format. However, the **null hypothesis** is more sophisticated because it states that the expected cause (independent variable) has no effect on the outcome (dependent variable). The null hypothesis places the investigator in a position to construct experiments and pose ideas to prove the null hypothesis incorrect. The null hypothesis minimizes experimenter bias. Well-tested, scrutinized, and supported hypotheses may form a strong conclusion. A **conclusion** is a statement that confirms or rejects the hypothesis and is based on the data collected for that experiment. Conclusions that successfully withstand the intensive scientific scrutiny, review, and experimentation over time may become a theory. A **theory** is a statement of understanding based on accumulated evidence that has been challenged by multiple peer researchers that have confirmed and never rejected the statement of understanding. The main difference between a theory and a hypothesis is that a hypothesis is a specific testable prediction and a theory is a scientifically supported explanation for a given concept based on a broader range of data.

4. **Test of hypothesis**—A controlled scientific experiment that compares the effect of the independent variable using an experimental group and a control group to determine if there is a significant effect on the dependent variable. The **independent variable** is the factor that is being tested. The **dependent variable** is the factor being measured. Measuring the change in the dependent variable provides evidence of an effect caused by the independent variable. The **control** (controlled group or controlled variable) is the specific group that does not receive any treatment and is used for comparison. The results of the experimental group (receives the treatment prescribed by the independent variable) are compared to the control group to determine if there is a difference in the data. If there is no difference between the results obtained by analyzing the data from the control and treatment group, then the independent variable had no measurable effect on the dependent variable. If the results of the control and treatment groups are different, then the effect noted by the dependent variable is likely due to the independent variable (or experimental error). For instance, if the independent variable tests the effect of green light on the growth of plants, then the dependent variable is the amount of plant growth. How do you determine if the growth was only due to the green light? In other words, maybe the plants would have grown at the same rate or size in normal light. A control is used to compare the results of the experimental group (those plants receiving only green light) to the control group (those plants receiving normal light). If there is a difference in the growth of the plants, then the growth can be attributed to the green light. It is important to note that all factors or potential confounding independent variables that may influence an experiment must be accounted for and controlled. For instance, all plants in the control and treatment groups are grown under identical conditions, such as the same amount of light, water, temperature, and humidity level. Scientific experiments minimize bias and experimental error to execute a fair test of the hypothesis.

5. **Analysis of data**—The data is evidence that either supports or rejects the hypothesis. If the data supports the hypothesis, then a conclusion follows. If the data rejects the hypothesis, the data may be used as research information to help construct a new hypothesis for testing. Charts and graphs enable the researcher to see vast amounts of data in an organized format. The independent variable is always on the *x*-axis (abscissa) and the dependent is on the *y*-axis (ordinate); for a table or chart, the independent variable is on the left of a vertical chart or the top of a horizontal chart and the dependent variable is on the right or bottom.

If data supports hypothesis, state a conclusion.

If data does not support the hypothesis, go back to step 2.

6. **Conclusion**—States the acceptance or rejection of the hypothesis. Additional commentary may be added which reviews the data leading to the conclusion.

7. **Communication**—All data from a well-designed scientific experiment is useful to other researchers who may be completing their own research into a similar question. Communication elaborates on the experimental procedure for further scrutinizing experiments by other independent researchers. Models are created to increase the understanding of the event or phenomenon. Conclusions become concepts, and, upon scientific review, may become theories which may become natural laws or facts after they have been tested and scrutinized by other leading scientists and found to consistently be correct over time. This process may take decades or centuries, such as the theory of evolution. Scientific knowledge is confirmed by the continual scrutinizing of what is "known." The process of science builds upon the proven discoveries of previous scientific experiments.

The following figure is a model of the Scientific Method.

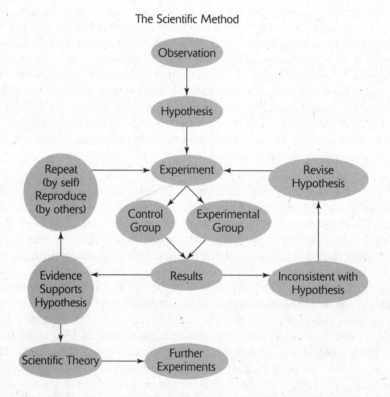

The Scientific Method

The use of the Scientific Method by the researcher is designed to encourage skepticism and a level of uncertainty without allowing the possibility of researcher bias. Several characteristics of researchers underlie the Scientific Method:

- **Skepticism**—Scientists are trained to treat new data with doubt. In reproducing another scientist's experiment or analyzing their data, scientists always look for the hidden uncontrolled variable that may have influenced the experiment and confounded the data. High standards in the judging of evidence and skepticism of one's own work are the mark of a good scientist. The Piltdown Hoax is a common example of the gullibility of the scientific community. The "discovery" of the missing link between man and ape in an archaeological site in England in 1908 and 1912 turned out to be a fake.

- **Tolerance of Uncertainty**—Researchers often discover that their data produces a piece of the puzzle but not in the anticipated order. Productive research is similar to assembling a jigsaw puzzle. Scientists are trained not to ignore data that does not fit into their preconceived ideas or training. The discovery and understanding of micro-RNA was delayed because of unexpected data.

- **Researcher Bias**—Scientists sometimes become so convinced that their hypothesis is correct that they overlook a flaw or misread the data to prove that wrong is right. The process of independent scientific investigation exposes researcher bias. Conclusions become increasingly valid as independent researchers confirm or deny results. To date, the "cold fusion" phenomenon has not been successfully reproduced by independent researchers although many have tried.

History and Landmark Events in Biology

The advancement of scientific knowledge is based on extending prior understandings through scientific experimentation and continual scrutiny and repetition of the procedure by independent researchers. Scientific knowledge advances in small steps through scientific inquiry. Occasionally, a researcher or research team makes a larger leap which opens more fields of inquiry, greater understandings, and more questions.

Some of the landmark events in biology are listed chronologically here. Earlier dates are approximate.

400–450 B.C.E.—Democritus described the atomic hypothesis.

400–430 B.C.E.—Thucydides proposed the immune system.

1020—Avicenna's *The Canon of Medicine* marked the beginning of experimental medicine and ushered the discovery of the contagious nature of infectious diseases.

1242—Ibn al-Nafis described pulmonary circulation and parts of the circulatory system.

1543—Vesalius pioneered research into human anatomy.

1628—William Harvey described blood circulation.

1669—Jan Swammerdam discovered that species breed true.

1675—Anton van Leeuwenhoek created the microscope and observed microorganisms.

1753—Carolus Linnaeus created the binomial nomenclature system for classifying species.

1770—Jan Ingenhousz discovered photosynthesis.

1790s—Edward Jenner invented the smallpox vaccine.

1796—Georges Cuvier established extinction as a fact.

1802—Jean-Baptiste Lamarck proposed teleological evolution.

1805—John Dalton described the atomic theory.

1830—Charles Lyell wrote *Principles of Geology,* which supported James Hutton's concept of **uniformitarianism,** the belief that Earth was formed by forces that are still in effect today; influenced Charles Darwin.

1831—Robert Browne identified the nucleus.

1833—Anselme Payen isolated the first enzyme, diastase.

1838—Matthias Schleiden stated that plants are made of cells.

1846—William Morton discovered anesthesia.

1848—Lord Kelvin described absolute zero temperature (Kelvin scale).

1858—Rudolph Virchow stated that cells can only arise from pre-existing cells.

1859—Charles Darwin and Alfred Wallace proposed the theory of evolution by natural selection.

1860s—Louis Pasteur developed pasteurization (killing of harmful microorganisms) and the germ theory of disease.

1865—Gregor Mendel discovered the basics for genetics and laws of inheritance.

1869—Paul Langerhans described the histology of the pancreas.

1879—Walther Flemming observed cell division in animals; Eduard Strasburger independently identified cell division in plants.

1884—August Weisman identified sex cells.

1886—Several scientists discovered cell differentiation which led in later years to stem cell research; these scientists also discovered mitochondria.

1903—William H. Bayliss and Ernest Starling discovered the function and coined the name "hormone."

1913—Neils Bohr proposed a revised model of the atom (Bohr model).

1928—Alexander Fleming discovered penicillin.

1935—Arthur George Tansley described ecosystems and promoted environmental science.

1937—Hans Krebs identified the process that cells use to convert sugars, fats, and proteins into energy, known as the Kreb's Cycle.

1943—Oswald Avery proved that DNA is the genetic material in the chromosome.

1951—George Otto Gey propagated HeLa, the first cancer cell line.

1953—James Watson and Francis Crick described the helical nature of DNA based on work by Rosalind Franklin and began the field of molecular genetics.

1970s—Donald Johanson and his team discovered "Lucy," the skeletal remains of an extinct, perhaps oldest hominid species, *Australopithecus afarensis*.

1977—Carl Woese discovered *Archaea*.

1983—Luc Montagnier and Robert Gallo discovered the HIV virus, the cause of AIDS.

1984—Kary Mullis invented the polymerase chain reaction (PCR) that promoted molecular biology.

1997—Roslin Institute cloned Dolly the sheep.

2001—International Human Genome Sequencing consortium and J. Craig Venter Institute released the first draft of the human genome.

2010—J. Craig Venter Institute created the first synthetic bacterial cell.

Mathematics, Measurement, and Data Manipulation

Mathematics is a foundational tool for all sciences. Every branch of science uses one of the many functions of mathematics for measuring, comparing, calculating, or presenting data to the scientific community. Mathematics quantifies scientific concepts for manipulation, expansion, and increased understanding of the natural and physical world.

Student performance in mathematics is among the areas tested by the Third International Mathematics and Science Study (TIMSS). Both the American Association for the Advancement of Science's (AAAS) "Benchmarks for Science Literacy" (Project 2061, 1993) and the "National Research Education Standards" (NSES, National Research Council, 1996) measure students' ability and understanding of measurement skills.

SI Units

Measurement in science is fundamental. Measurements in science are expressed in **SI Units** and are usually metric. SI is the abbreviation for System International unites, French for the International System of Units. All weights and measures are linked through international agreements supporting the International System of Units.

The SI is built upon base units that define the unit absolutely and do not require referencing other units. There are numerous SI units, but the most common biological base units are listed in the following table.

SI Units		
Base Unit	**Unit Symbol**	**Measures**
meter	m	distance
kilogram	kg	mass
second	s	time
Kelvin	K	temperature
mole	mol	amount of substance
candela	cd	light intensity

Derived SI Units		
Base Unit	**Unit Symbol**	**Measures**
joule	j	energy
degrees Celsius	°C	temperature
katal	kat	catalytic activity

The base units are then combined with SI Prefixes to make the unit of measure smaller or larger. For instance, a kilometer is the best unit for measuring long distances, such as miles. However, to measure the same distance in millimeters would create an enormous number. Likewise when measuring a microscopic organism, micrometers may be the best fit. Measuring a microorganism in kilometers would also create a very small number.

Name	Symbol	Factor
mega	M	10^6
kilo	k	10^3
hector	h	10^2
deca	da	10^1
deci	d	10^{-1}
centi	c	10^{-2}
milli	m	10^{-3}
micro	μ	10^{-6}
nano	n	10^{-9}

Precision and Accuracy

Precision and accuracy are often misused. **Precision** refers to how close several measure values are to each other. **Accuracy** is how close the measured values are to the true or actual value. Imagine a dartboard with all of the darts clumped in the bull's eye. In this case, the precision and accuracy are both high. If the darts are spread all of the board, the precision and accuracy are low. Look at the graphic that follows and discover that it is possible to be precise but not accurate.

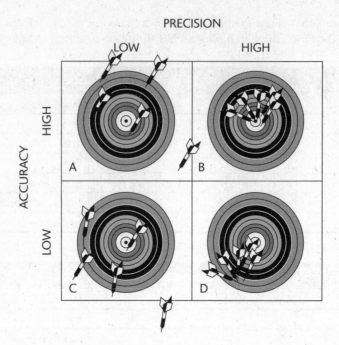

An unfortunate example of precision and accuracy occurs in research. For example, a consistent decimal point error will give precise but very inaccurate results.

Measuring in the Science Laboratory

Measuring solids and liquids is a common activity in the science laboratory. Whether as a teacher you are measuring liquids to make a solution or massing solids to compare results, measurement is important.

Measuring liquids is more difficult than measuring solids. Liquids form a meniscus when resting in a container. The **meniscus** is the curve that forms the upper surface of a liquid. Normally the meniscus of aqueous solutions is concave with the curve pointing down. When reading a liquid measurement, the eye must be level with the top of the liquid to read the bottom of the meniscus.

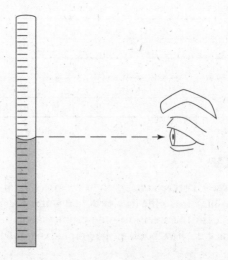

Measuring solids may involve an electronic balance or triple beam balance. Note that a **balance** measures mass and a **scale** measures weight. It's important to tare a balance prior to use. The **tare** is the unwanted mass that may come from the mass of the container or a maladjusted balance. Electronic balances make life easy. Normally a tare button does the work for you. Once the unit is tared, the object's mass is displayed automatically.

A **triple beam balance** is cheaper and more hands-on than an electronic balance so teachers often prefer them for classroom use. A triple beam balance has a balancing area or pan that is counterbalanced by masses on three rider bars. Once the tare is finished, placing an object on the balancing pan lifts the masses on the other side. To balance and thus determine the mass of the object, the operator must carefully slide the weights along the bars until the object is balanced. Each of the three bars or riders has a different amount of mass. Typically the largest mass is 100 g, the next rider has a 10 g mass and the final rider has a 1 gmass. The 1 gram mass can be moved right or left on the bar to determine tenths of a gram. The effect of the masses increases as you move them further away from the balancing pan. The 100 g mass can balance up to 500 g because there are five slots moving away from the pan on the rider. For an object larger than 500 g, the middle rider balances another 100 g because there are 10 locations for the 10 g mass. The smallest mass can add another 10 g of balancing power. The total mass of an object is the sum of the masses on each rider. For instance, the total mass that can be measured by a triple beam balance is usually 610 g. Check the mass on the following object. Can you determine the mass?

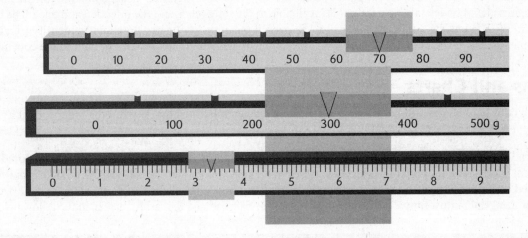

The mass of the object is 373.3 grams: 300 + 70 + 3.3 = 373.3 g (3 bars, 3 masses).

Significant Figures

Significant figures are critical to an accurate measurement. **Significant figures** tell the reader how well you could actually measure your data. Not examining the quality of the data numbers creates an experimental error. Four rules guide significant figures:

1. *All* nonzero numbers are always significant (1,2,3,4,5,6,7,8,9).
2. *All* zeros between significant numbers are always significant (809).
3. *All* zeros at the right of the decimal point and at the end of the number are always significant (89.00).
4. *All* zeros to the left of a decimal point and in a number greater than or equal to 10 are significant (501.98).

Note: If you get confused about rule # 3 and # 4, convert the number into scientific notation. If you can get rid of the zeros, they are not significant.

Scientific Notation

Scientific notation is a short way to express large numbers. The numbers in scientific notation are made up of three parts: the coefficient, the base, and the exponent. Examine this scientific notation example:

$$5.01 \times 10^{13}$$

The "5.01" is the coefficient.

The base is always 10.

The exponent is 13.

5.01×10^{13} is scientific notation for 50,100,000,000,000.

The rules for writing in scientific notation are simple:

1. The coefficient must be greater than or equal to 1 and less than 10.
2. The decimal always goes after the first number in the coefficient.
3. The base must be 10.
4. The exponent is the amount of decimal places that the decimal needs to be moved to convert into standard notation. A negative exponent moves the decimal to the left.

Interpreting Results

Interpreting results is one of the most important steps in a scientific investigation. The assimilation of the raw data into a meaningful and understandable format is invaluable to the researcher and the intended audience. The careful presentation of data enables a reader to interpret the overall meaning of the raw data and to identify trends, patterns, or omissions. Eye-catching data displays that are simple to interpret connect the raw data to the conclusion.

Graphs and Charts

Organizing data onto charts and graphs helps to visually display relationships between the independent and dependent variables.

Charts refine raw data into an organized format. Consider the experiment that measures the effect of colored light (independent variable) on the growth of carrots (dependent variable). Note that the **independent variable** is the variable manipulated by the researcher and is always recorded on the top of a vertical chart and on the left of a horizontal chart. Organizing data into a simple chart provides a visual confirmation of the results as seen in the following chart.

Colored Light and the Average Growth Rate of Carrots cm/21 Days				
Red	**Green**	**Blue**	**Yellow**	**Control**
13.6	6.6	7.9	14.1	14.4

A simple analysis of this chart makes it is easy to rank in order the light colors that provide the most or least amount of growth for carrots. Graphing the same data provides a better visual cue as seen here:

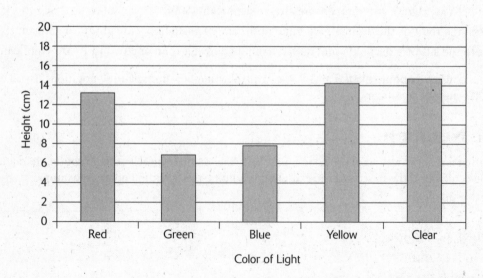

Average Growth Rate of Carrots

This graph is easy to analyze. When the data is more extensive and complicated, graphing helps to interpret and present the data. Note that all **graphs** have a title, labeled axes, equal intervals, and are easy to read. The best titles relate the independent and dependent variables.

What are the most common types of graph used in biology? Three graph types are the most common: line, bar, and pie.

Line graphs compare data that shows continuous change. Line graphs are often used to show the changes in the independent variable over time, or as a function of temperature as dependent variables. Line graphs are not used when the data are discrete points. The following line graph shows the continuous relationship between the number of whales spotted per year.

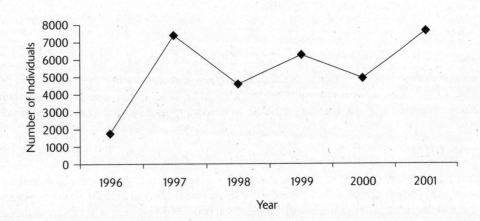

Number of Whales Spotted 1996–2001

Bar graphs represent discrete blocks of data that are not continuous. Bar graphs are most useful in showing the rank order of several different treatments or trends. It is easy to analyze the following bar graph and discover the favorite classes.

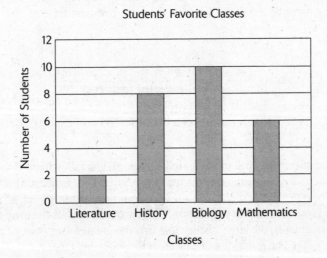

Students' Favorite Classes

Pie graphs are designed to show the component parts of a whole. Pie graphs are often based on percentages or percent composition. The following pie graph makes it easy to read and determine the percentage of students who take each mode of transportation.

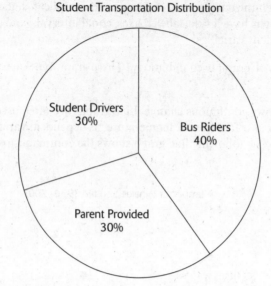

Student Transportation Distribution

Graphs are useful in making predictions. Trends established and recognized on a graph can be extended beyond the data. **Extrapolation** is the process where an investigator estimates values beyond the graphed data. **Interpolation** is the process where values within the graphed data are estimated. Interpolation usually occurs between graphed points.

Chi-Square (X^2)

Chi-square is a statistical test often used in biology to compare observed data with expected data for a particular hypothesis to determine the goodness of fit for the data. Chi-square is used to identify data discrepancies that may be the result of something other than the independent variable. For instance, if you were expecting 50 of newborn offspring to be male and in fact 34 were male and 72 remove percent were female, is that a chance event or were other uncontrolled variables involved? The researcher decides how much deviation from the expected outcome is acceptable before considering that another factor beyond the hypothesis may be contributing an unexpected effect. The chi-square is always testing the null hypothesis that states that there is no difference between the observed and expected results against an alternative research hypothesis. Note that the chi-square must use numbers, not percentages and must be a discrete variable (for example, gender).

The formula for chi-square is

$$X^2 = \text{sum of } \frac{\left(\text{observed frequency} - \text{expected frequency}\right)^2}{\text{expected frequency}}$$

Chi-square is the sum of the squared difference between the observed and expected data divided by the expected data in all categories.

So how does the chi-square statistical test work in a research situation? The following is a simple example that employs the chi-square statistic. Suppose that an investigator was testing the effect of a new drug on the treatment of a disease in fruit flies. The disease is known to kill 50 percent of untreated fruit flies within 1 week of exposure. After carefully selecting a random sample of 100 flies from the population, the researcher applies the drug to the treatment group. (Note, as in all statistical measurements, the larger the sample size, the greater the power of the statistic; chi-square is more effective in sample sizes > 20.) The results are displayed in the following table.

Survived	Died	Total
45	55	100

Using the chi-square test, the researcher can determine the effectiveness of the new drug as seen here:

$$X^2 = \frac{(45-50)2}{50} = -5^2 = 25$$

$$\frac{25}{50} = 0.5$$

The results of the chi-square are then compared to the chi-square tables, which shows that the probability of obtaining results as large or larger than 0.5 is about 50 percent. This is a fairly high number, which indicates that the treatment has limited value beyond the normal survival rate of the fruit flies.

A more sophisticated chi-square problem is depicted in an analysis of fish caught in the Snake River. The South Fork of the Snake River is divided into three sections: Upper, Middle, and Lower. Fish caught in each section are from four species: Rainbow Trout (RBT), Yellowstone Cutthroat Trout (YCT), RBT-YTC hybrids, and Brown Trout (BT) in the numbers represented on the following table.

Trout Harvest in the South Fork of the Snake River			
	Upper	Middle	Lower
RBT	24	22	18
YCT	23	28	19
RBT-YCT	18	27	29
BT	16	21	23

The null hypothesis states that the fish species are evenly distributed throughout the river. In this particular experiment, the degrees of freedom (df) are 6; the chi-square is 9.743; and the probability is 0.1359. The chi-square statistic in this case does not support the null hypothesis. This means that the fish are not evenly distributed throughout the three sections of the South Fork.

Percent Error

Percent error is similar to the chi-square. **Percent error** compares experimental results with a known or expected value. The formula for calculating percent error is

$$\% \text{ Error} = \left| \frac{\text{Theoretical value} - \text{Experimental value}}{\text{Theoretical value}} \right| \times 100$$

Why is it important to calculate percent error? Among other things, percent error indicates the presence of some form of experimental error, but also includes biological variability (not every organism responds identically to an independent variable). Note that experimental error occurs in most student experiments and compromises the concept of a fair test of the hypothesis.

Experimental Error

When interpreting the results, it is important to remember that every experiment has sources of experimental error. In well-designed experiments, the experimental error may be minimized to insignificance. In flawed tests, the experimental error allows for confounded data.

Sources of experimental error include the following:

- **Human error**—Either through inexperience or a blunder
- **Instrument limitations**—The width of the calibrations on graduated cylinders and metric rulers affect the reading

- **Manipulation**—Handling an animal or inserting a thermometer into a liquid affects the test
- **External influences**—Contaminated chemicals or change in air pressure affect the test
- **Poor experimental design**—It is not a fair test or controlled scientific procedure
- **Sampling**—Random samples may not be random or typical

Laboratory Procedure and Safety

The science laboratory is integral to the study of all sciences. The science laboratory presents an opportunity for students to engage in meaningful activities and experiments that confirm their understanding and extend their ideas in a hands-on, minds-on learning environment. The science laboratory is also a location of great danger. Accidents happen! The role of the teacher is to provide a learning environment that is safe, productive, and orderly. Teachers as well as the building administration and related central office personnel are legally responsible for maintaining a safety-first workplace. Students are expected to conduct themselves in a manner consistent with established and recounted safety rules.

Safe Preparation, Storage, Use, and Disposal of Laboratory and Field Materials

The greatest concern usually involves the safe use, storage, and disposal of chemicals.

The safe use of a chemical begins with an understanding of the properties of that chemical and its use in the activity. Each laboratory should have the **Material Safety Data Sheet (MSDS)** on file for each chemical. They can also be located on the Internet. The MSDS sheets document the features for a particular chemical.

An inventory of all chemicals is essential. Each chemical should be dated upon arrival and all out-of-date chemicals should be properly disposed. Inventories should also list the storage location for each chemical.

Following are several general guidelines for safe chemical storage:

- Store all chemicals in a well-ventilated, secure location and limit access.
- Use OSHA– or NFPA–approved storage cabinets for acids, flammables, and explosives.
- Store acids (6M or greater) in a clearly labeled and OSHA– or NFPA–approved Acid Cabinet; nitric acids must be stored separately.
- Use explosion-proof refrigerators; do not store food or flammables.
- Store all chemicals at eye level and below and in compatible family groups.
- Store chemical clean-up supplies (that is, neutralizers, absorbents) in the chemical storage area.
- Limit the quantity of flammable, combustible, and hazardous chemicals to a one-year supply, so that none are left over.
- Order and use small lecture-type bottled gases and store in an upright position away from flammable sources.

Dispensing chemicals provides an opportunity to model safety features:

- Microscale chemicals whenever possible.
- Measure out chemicals in student-approved containers ahead of time.
- Label all containers.
- Never return chemicals to the stock solution; correctly dispose of all leftover dispensed chemicals.
- Bond and ground flammable liquid containers.

Knowing the five common chemical hazards in the science laboratory can prevent problems. These hazards are flammables, corrosives, oxidizers/reactives, toxins, and mercury:

- **Flammables**—Substances which produce vapors that catch fire readily and burn in air. The **flashpoint** is the minimum temperature needed to vaporize enough liquid to create an ignitable mixture with air. The ignition temperature is the minimum temperature needed to initiate self-sustained combustion without a heat source.

- **Corrosives**—Substances that can cause bodily injury and metal corrosion by direct exposure. The major classes of corrosives substances includes: **strong acids** (nitric, sulfuric, hydrochloric, hydrofluoric); **strong bases** (sodium hydroxide, potassium hydroxide); **dehydrating agents** (sulfuric acid, sodium hydroxide, phosphorus pentoxide, and calcium oxide); **oxidizing agents** (hydrogen peroxide, chlorine, bromine).

- **Oxidizers/reactives**—Include chemicals that can explode, violently polymerize, form explosive peroxides, or react violently with water or air. An **oxidizer** or **oxidizing agent** is any chemical that initiates or promotes combustion in other materials, either by causing a fire or by releasing oxygen or other combustible gases. **Reactives** are chemicals that are pyrophoric or flammable solids, are water reactive, form explosive peroxides, or undergo violent polymerizations.

- **Toxins**—Chemicals that can injure living tissue. Toxins include carcinogens, asphyxiants, neurotoxins, irritants, and allergens.

- **Mercury**—Along with its organic and inorganic compounds—is a health hazard. Mercury is found in thermometers, barometers, batteries, and manometers. The use of mercury should be avoided.

One of the best ways to control preparation, use, storage, and disposal problems is to only order chemicals that are on the approved list for your school and in the smallest quantities possible.

Spills and breakage happen. Preventing and cleaning up afterward are important safety concerns. There are several general rules for spill cleanup:

- Contain spills and clean them up immediately.
- Remove students from the area.
- Dispose of waste properly.
- Dry mop floor after cleaning dry to remove chemical micro traces and to reduce slippage.

General rules for spills that may create a fire hazard:

- Extinguish all flames immediately and turn off all electrical devices.
- Stop all experiments and activities.
- Vacate the room until the situation is stabilized.

General rules for other spills:

- Wear rubber gloves and use a brush and dustpan. Thoroughly clean the area and then mop dry.
- Absorb aromatic amine, carbon disulfide, ether, nitrile, nitro-compound, and organic halide spills with cloths, paper towels, or vermiculite and dispose of the cloths in suitable closed containers.
- Use an absorbent material to neutralize a liquid.
- Select absorbent materials that are specific for the type of spill:
  - for acids use powdered sodium bicarbonate
  - for bromine use limewater or 5–10 percent sodium thiosulfate solution
  - for organic acids, halides, nonmetallic compounds, or inorganic acids, use slaked lime and soda ash
  - for general spills use commercial absorbents or spill kits, clay absorbents (kitty litter), or vermiculite

Waste disposal is also a part of laboratory safety. Before using a chemical, the teacher should know the proper use and disposal of that chemical. MSDS sheets and the chemical origination provide this information. All activities involving chemicals create waste chemicals. Some waste must be professionally incinerated, other waste can be deposited in designated landfills, or neutralized and disposed of in normal waste disposal systems.

Follow these suggestions to help with waste removal:

- Substitute a benign chemical for a hazardous or toxic chemical.
- Perform microscale experiments.
- Consider classroom demonstrations that utilize less chemicals than whole-class experiments.
- Plan with other teachers to coordinate the use of a chemical.
- Store waste in a central area with approved closed containers that are labeled with the chemical and date of use.
- Segregate waste to avoid reactions and ensure cost effective disposal.
- Acids above pH 3 and bases below pH 8 can be flushed if the sewer leads to a waste treatment facility.
- Flushed chemicals should be followed with 100 times their volume in water.

The use and disposal of field materials and nonchemical substances is important for the biology teacher. In biology it is important to differentiate between infectious and noninfectious waste. Please keep the following guidelines in mind:

- **Noninfectious biological**—Materials are not a "communicable" hazard and may consist of biological samples free of parasites and contagious pathogens, and household substances. Noninfectious biological waste can be disposed of by double bagging in plastic trash bags secured by metal wire twists; these wastes can then be added to the materials headed for the public landfill in accordance with state and local regulations.
- **Infectious biological materials**—Consist of all communicable biological materials including all body fluids, contagious microorganisms, parts of microorganisms (bacteria, viruses, DNA), and disposable equipment that has been exposed to infectious materials. Infectious materials require decontamination before removal from the site by on-site incineration or decontamination.
- **Release of nonindigenous species (plant and animal)**—Is unlawful in most areas. The release of indigenous species must be approved by the State Department of Natural Resources.

Legal Aspects of Laboratory Safety

The classroom teacher is ultimately responsible for the safety of the students. However, the state, school district, school board, superintendent, and school administration all share the liability for student safety. The classroom teacher bears the responsibility for actions related to the concept of **negligence** including:

- Exercising good judgment in the planning, conducting, and supervising of the instruction
- Maintaining laboratory and safety equipment in good working order to carry out the instruction safely
- Documenting that appropriate safety instruction has taken place

What constitutes a negligent act? Legal action against a teacher presumes that the teacher is the expert in the laboratory and, as such, has the responsibility to ensure that exercises and activities carried are carried out in a prudent and safe manner. **Liability** exists to the extent that an injury can be shown to be the result of an action or inaction on the part of the teacher.

- A teacher may be deemed negligent if the teacher allows a foolish or imprudent act to be committed; is careless in performing a demonstration; neglects a pre-existing unsafe condition; or neglects to warn of any hazards associated with the activity, operation, or demonstration.
- A teacher may be found fully, partially, or no fault at all depending on how the court judges culpability among the following:
  - The degree to which the teacher is judged to be able to foresee or prevent the results of the action
  - The student's injuries were the result of the student's own actions
  - The accident came about as a result of circumstances over which the teacher had no control or could not reasonably have been able to foresee
  - The extent to which the teacher's actions were reasonable and prudent

Negligence also exists in **tort law.** Four elements must exist for a liability tort to be brought:

- A teacher's duty to protect the students in their charge
- A breach of this duty existing between two parties
- Personal injury or monetary damages directly caused by the breach in legal responsibilities
- Legal breach of responsibilities judged to be the cause of the injury or damages

Such a breach may arise in one of three ways:

- **Misfeasance:** the defendant acts in an imprudent manner
- **Nonfeasance:** the defendant did not act at all when the defendant had a duty to act
- **Malfeasance:** the defendant acted with a bad motive or to inflict deliberate injury

The following items are recommended to avoid negligence:

- Provide prior warning of any/all hazards associated with the instruction
- Demonstrate the essential parts of the instruction to make the activity and its risks understandable and avoidable
- Provide active supervision
- Maintain all equipment in good working order
- Gain/update sufficient safety training and have appropriate safety equipment available
- Ensure the safety of the environment

Documentation of all safety-related items is critical and may include:

- Student signed rules agreement
- 100 percent passing of safety test and retention of test by teacher
- Pre-laboratory tests and quizzes that include safety questions
- Notations in lesson plans that indicate the review of safety procedures
- Direct teaching of visually displayed instructional safety rules
- Safety rules visually displayed and copied into notes by the students
- Safety rules written into each laboratory activity

Established safety and emergency procedures prevent problems and minimize teacher liability. Knowing what to do and having the students know what to do in a crisis situation may save injuries, property damage, and a day in court. There are several items that help teacher become more prepared for emergencies:

- Have a visually displayed plan and back-up plan for emergency evacuation including clearly marked pathways, maps, and emergency escape/exit routes; practice having the students walk in an organized fashion to the assembly area for attendance.
- Label and orient the students to all safety equipment; maintain the safety equipment in good working order.
- Know the location and limit the access to emergency gas, water, and electricity shut-off valves.
- Know the emergency school code words that indicate an emergency and how to use the intercom or room phone to access the main office and neighboring teachers.
- Manage the instruction to accommodate students with disabilities.
- Do not use a fire extinguisher on a person; help the student stop, drop, and roll to smother the fire or, in more serious cases, plunge the student into the deluge shower—do not use the fire blanket if clothing is on fire.
- For small classroom fires, the teacher must take prompt action to extinguish the fire with fire extinguishing equipment; small fires such as in a vessel can be smothered by replacing the lid or covered with the fire blanket.

- For larger fires or explosions, evacuate the room via the emergency evacuation plan, sound the fire alarm, shut off the gas and electricity, and close all doors and windows if possible. Most school fire alarms automatically ring the local fire department; when they arrive prepare to hand them your list of chemicals, where they are stored, and the storage pattern—especially for any flammable or hazardous materials.

- Eye wash fountains should be accessible to all students in no more than 10 seconds (ANSI.Z, 358.1–1998) from any student location; hands free operation that drenches both eyes; students should be shown how to hold their eyelids open and allow the water to flood their eyeballs; eye wash stations should be tested annually, recorded, and witnessed by school or district authorities; portable eye washes are not recommended.

- Learn the school first-aid plan for stabilizing accident victims until emergency help arrives and develop one for your classroom including a first-aid station stocked according to your school plan and instant access to the school nurse and main office.

- Utilize safety shields to protect students working nearby and minimize any fire or explosion expansion.

- A deluge-type safety shower should be available in every laboratory so that no student is more than 10 seconds away with a minimum flow rate of 30 gallons per minute (ANSI.Z, 358.1–1998); drench showers remove harmful chemicals and put out fires and provide a continuous flow until shut off at the valve; deluge showers should be annually tested, recorded, and witnessed by school or district authorities.

- Chemical splash safety glasses should be worn at all times by teachers, students, and visitors in the laboratory setting; eye protectors should meet the standards of the American National Standards Institute Z87.1–1989; safety glasses should be sanitized between each use; face shields do not replace safety glasses.

- Require that laboratory aprons be worn when using chemicals and are recommended to be worn at other times; plastic aprons should be avoided due to static buildup around flammable materials.

- Wear safety gloves when handling warm or cold materials, corrosive chemicals, sharp or rough objects, or whenever surface protection is needed; gloves should be examined routinely and periodic glove replacement is necessary due to the buildup of residues and possible punctures.

- Know that soft contact lenses can absorb some vapors, however removing them may cause a vision problem; if an eye splash occurs, remove the contacts as soon as possible.

- Stock each laboratory with spill kits and ensure the teacher knows how to use them.

- Provide adequate ventilation for each activity; in the case of hazardous or noxious vapors, place the substance in a fume hood.

- Prohibit loose fitting or highly flammable clothes, sandals, open-toed shoes, or canvas shoes. Restrain long hair and loose jewelry, and alert students that chemicals can sometimes get under finger rings and other jewelry and cause problems.

- Contact the main office as soon as possible for any and all emergency events; write down your version of the events as soon as possible; post emergency phone numbers in a conspicuous place in case the main office is unreachable.

The selection and appropriate use of laboratory equipment is fundamental. The proper use and maintenance of laboratory equipment is essential for laboratory safety. You may want to consider the following suggestions:

- Use the correct type of glassware:
    - when heating: always use borosilicate glassware (Pyrex or Kimax) to prevent breaking and explosive shattering
    - for measuring volume: pipettes, graduated cylinders, burets, and volumetric flasks
    - for storing solids and liquids: vials and bottles
    - for containing reactive substances during experiments: beakers, test tubes, test plates, flasks, and watch glasses
    - for transferring liquids and gases: glass tubing and funnels
    - for measuring temperature: thermometer (not mercury)
    - for measuring air pressure: barometer (not mercury)
- Clean all glassware before each use to remove all residue; use laboratory grade detergents.
- Check all glassware before use for cracks, chips, or residue; discard all rejects.
- All glass tubing should be fire polished.

- Do not attempt to separate "frozen" glass; discard.
- Follow the procedure for inserting glass tubing into rubber stoppers.
- Demonstrate and have the students demonstrate the correct technique for operating the heat source, especially a burner.
- Never heat a closed container.
- Never pour water into acid.
- Routinely inspect all electrical cords, outlets, and equipment; assume all circuits are on and working.
- Use a bulb to draw a liquid into a pipette—never use your mouth.
- Inspect and test the centrifuge ahead of use; never touch a spinning centrifuge.
- Forbid student handling of nonflammable cryogenics such as dry ice and liquid nitrogen; liquid nitrogen is extremely dangerous and should be avoided unless the teacher is well trained in its use and properties.
- Understand that compressed gases present dangers through toxicity, reactivity, and flammability; an improperly used gas cylinder can become an indoor rocket; use only in a well-ventilated area.
- Keep compressed gas away from electrical lines and heat sources.
- Always keep the work area and aisles free of clutter.
- Do not place any apparatus on the floor.
- Avoid any activity, chemical, or apparatus you are unfamiliar with.
- When in doubt, do not do it.

Chapter 2

Molecular and Cellular Biology

Chemical Basis of Life

Chemistry is the study of matter and its changes. Chemistry unlocks an understanding of life processes. **Biochemistry** is the union of biology and chemistry, and integrates the changes in matter that support the life processes of all organisms.

Basic Chemical Structures

Matter is made of atoms. All **atoms** are made of three subatomic particles: electrons, protons, and neutrons. Protons and neutrons exist within the atomic nucleus while electrons orbit the nucleus in defined energy levels or orbitals. Protons and neutrons are a stable form of hadrons or composite particles made from quarks. Up to this time, quarks have never been found in isolation but always within hadrons.

Atoms

Atoms are spherical in shape with a small and dense nucleus that has a positive (+) charge provided by the positive **proton(s)**. **Neutrons** are considered neutral and add no charge to the nucleus. The nucleus accounts for 99.97 percent of the atomic mass and only $\frac{1}{10,000}$ of the volume. Atoms have an overall electrically neutral charge because of the balance between the positively charge nucleus and the negatively charged electron cloud.

The **electron(s)** provide a negative (–) charge characteristic of the atom's electron cloud. The electron cloud is made by fast moving electrons that orbit the empty space around the nucleus in well-defined energy levels. The energy levels are concentric rings of increasing energy moving out from the nucleus and are numbered accordingly. Energy level 1 is located closest to the nucleus and contains the least amount of energy and when filled contain the smallest total number of electrons: two. Electron levels further from the nucleus contain more energy (remember the balancing forces that define an atom) and when filled, more electrons. The electron cloud accounts for most of the size of an atom, but contains almost no mass and varies in size and shape depending on the element. Note the following graphic.

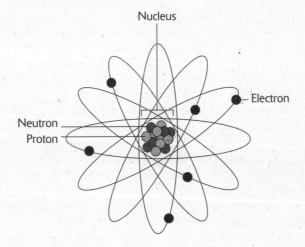

Each atom is held together by a balance of forces. Like a magnet, the opposite charges within the protons and electrons draw the electrons toward the nucleus. This attractive force is counteracted by the energy contained within the electron, which powers its movement away from the nucleus. The electron's orbit or energy levels around the nucleus is defined by the proton-electron attraction and is balanced by the energy of the electrons.

To date, there are 118 different types of atoms, and it's likely that more radioactive, man-made atoms will be added in the near future. Atoms differ in their number of protons, neutrons, or electrons. Each specific atom represents a different element. The number of protons in the nucleus, called the **atomic number,** determines the type of atom. Atoms with the same atomic number constitute an **element,** such as gold. Atoms with the same atomic number represent the same element; and atoms with a different atomic number represent a different element. For instance, gold atoms and silver atoms contain protons, neutrons, and electrons, but in different amounts, so their atomic numbers are different. Atoms are listed in order by their increasing atomic number on the Periodic Table of Elements.

Periodic Table of Elements

An **element** is a pure substance that is made of one type of atom that cannot be broken down and still retains its identity. The **Periodic Table of Elements** organizes elements by their atomic number. The simplest element, hydrogen, is also the simplest atom and contains 1 proton. Hydrogen is located in the upper left of the Periodic Table. The most complicated, Ununoctium with 118 protons, is located in the lower right. The periodic table also provides additional information about each element including: the name of the chemical, such as hydrogen; the atomic number, 1; the chemical symbol, H; and the average atomic mass, 1.008. Note the organization of increasing atomic numbers from left to right on the Periodic Table.

1 H Hydrogen 1.01																	2 He Helium 4.00
3 Li Lithium 6.94	4 Be Beryllium 9.01											5 B Boron 10.81	6 C Carbon 12.01	7 N Nitrogen 14.01	8 O Oxygen 16.00	9 F Fluorine 19.00	10 Ne Neon 20.18
11 Na Sodium 22.99	12 Mg Magnesium 24.31											13 Al Aluminum 26.98	14 Si Silicon 28.09	15 P Phosphorus 30.97	16 S Sulfur 32.06	17 Cl Chlorine 35.45	18 Ar Argon 39.95
19 K Potassium 39.10	20 Ca Calcium 40.08	21 Sc Scandium 44.96	22 Ti Titanium 47.90	23 V Vanadium 50.94	24 Cr Chromium 52.00	25 Mn Manganese 54.94	26 Fe Iron 55.85	27 Co Cobalt 58.93	28 Ni Nickel 58.71	29 Cu Copper 63.55	30 Zn Zinc 65.38	31 Ga Gallium 69.72	32 Ge Germanium 72.59	33 As Arsenic 74.92	34 Se Selenium 78.96	35 Br Bromine 79.90	36 Kr Krypton 83.80
37 Rb Rubidium 85.47	38 Sr Strontium 87.62	39 Y Yttrium 88.91	40 Zr Zirconium 91.22	41 Nb Niobium 92.91	42 Mo Molybdenum 95.94	43 Tc Technetium (99)	44 Ru Ruthenium 101.07	45 Rh Rhodium 102.91	46 Pd Palladium 106.42	47 Ag Silver 107.87	48 Cd Cadmium 112.41	49 In Indium 114.82	50 Sn Tin 118.69	51 Sb Antimony 121.75	52 Te Tellurium 127.60	53 I Iodine 126.90	54 Xe Xenon 130.30
55 Cs Cesium 132.91	56 Ba Barium 137.34	57 La Lanthanum 138.91	72 Hf Hafnium 178.49	73 Ta Tantalum 180.95	74 W Tungsten 183.85	75 Re Rhenium 186.21	76 Os Osmium 190.2	77 Ir Iridium 192.22	78 Pt Platinum 195.09	79 Au Gold 196.97	80 Hg Mercury 200.59	81 Tl Thallium 204.37	82 Pb Lead 207.19	83 Bi Bismuth 208.98	84 Po Polonium (210)	85 At Astatine (210)	86 Rn Radon (222)
87 Fr Francium (223)	88 Ra Radium (226)	89 Ac Actinium (227)	104 Rf Rutherfordium (257)	105 Db Dubnium (260)	106 Sg Seaborgium (263)	107 Bh Bohrium (262)	108 Hs Hassium (265)	109 Mt Meitnerium (266)									

Lanthanides

58 Ce Cerium 140.12	59 Pr Praseodymium 140.91	60 Nd Neodymium 144.24	61 Pm Promethium (147)	62 Sm Samarium 150.35	63 Eu Europium 151.96	64 Gd Gadolinium 157.25	65 Tb Terbium 158.93	66 Dy Dysprosium 162.50	67 Ho Holmium 164.93	68 Er Erbium 167.26	69 Tm Thulium 168.93	70 Yb Ytterbium 173.04	71 Lu Lutetium 174.97

Actinides

90 Th Thorium (232)	91 Pa Protactinium (231)	92 U Uranium (238)	93 Np Neptunium (237)	94 Pu Plutonium (242)	95 Am Americium (243)	96 Cm Curium (247)	97 Bk Berkelium (247)	98 Cf Californium (251)	99 Es Einsteinium (254)	100 Fm Fermium (257)	101 Md Mendelevium (258)	102 No Nobelium (259)	103 Lr Lawrencium (260)

The Periodic Table of Elements also provides additional information about each element. Elements located within the same vertical row are classified in **groups** or **families.** Elements in the same group have similar reactivity characteristics caused by their electron distribution. For instance, each element in Group 1 has one valence electron in its outermost energy level. **Valence electrons** are loosely held and are easily donated or shared to form chemical bonds. Atoms react chemically by donating, accepting, or sharing electrons to reach a more stable energy level where their outermost energy level is completely filled with electrons. For most Main Group (Groups 1A–8A) atoms this arrangement of electrons is called the "stable octet". All members of Group 1, hydrogen (H), lithium (Li), sodium (Na), potassium (K), rubidium (Rb), cesium (Cs), and francium (Fr), are very reactive because they tend to be anxious electron donors and are looking to donate one electron—a characteristic of alkali metals. Likewise, elements in Group 2, known as the alkali earth elements are slightly less reactive because they have two valence electrons which they are ready to donate. Elements in Group 7, called the **halogens,** include fluorine (F), chlorine (Cl), bromine (Br), iodine (I), and astatine (At). Group 7 elements have seven valence electrons, which give them a similar reactivity profile. Group 7 elements need one more electron to reach the electron stability found in the atoms of Group 8. Because it's easier to gain one electron than lose seven, elements on the right side of the Periodic Table are electron accepters—a characteristic of nonmetals. The **noble gases,** or **inert elements** are mostly nonreactive elements located in Group 8. Their chemical stability is due to the filled valence electron energy levels. Inert elements do not need to add, share, or subtract valence electrons to become more energetically stable.

Elements on the Periodic Table are also organized in horizontal rows called **periods** or **series.** Moving from left to right, the number of protons (and atomic number) increases by 1 up to the last element in that period. The last element, called a noble gas, or inert element contains the optimum number of electrons to fill its outermost energy level of electrons. Inert elements are chemically stable and do not want to react because they do not want to gain, share, or lose electrons. The next period begins when another proton is added and continues as protons are added, thereby creating new elements until the inert element stability is reached. The reactivity characteristics of the elements change when moving from left to right within a series. Atoms on the left tend to be electron donors, whereas atoms on the right, except for the inert elements, tend to be electron acceptors and form ionic bonds. Elements in the middle tend to share electrons and form covalent bonds.

Ions

Recall that in a neutral or uncharged atom, the number of protons and electrons is equal. An atom with a charge is called an **ion.** An ion is formed when a neutral atom gains or losses an electron(s). Ions can be either positive or negative.

A **positive ion** forms when an atom loses one or more of its electrons. Losing an electron from an atom means the neutral atom now has one more positive charge than negative charge, giving the atom an overall positive charge. Therefore the loss of electron(s) creates a positive ion or cation. Recall from the Periodic Table that the metallic elements found in Groups 1 and 2 are likely to form positive ions because they readily lose electron(s).

A **negative ion** is formed when an atoms gains one or more electrons. Gaining an electron changes the electrical balance in a neutral atom to a negative atom, or ion. Gaining electron(s) creates a negative ion. Groups 6 and 7 readily gain electron(s), so they are likely to form negative ions or anion. Remember that atoms are identified by the number of protons, so creating ions does not change the name of the atom. For instance a platinum atom becomes a platinum ion, not a new element.

Chemical Bonds and Molecules

A **chemical bond** is the force that holds atoms together. The two main types of chemical bonds are ionic bonds and covalent bonds. In both cases the bonds are the result of the interaction of valence electrons. The nucleus is not involved in a chemical reaction; nuclei join (fusion) or break apart (fission) in nuclear reactions. A compound is formed when ionic bonds join one or more atoms; a covalent bond forms a molecule.

Ionic bonds are formed between ions. When an atom donates an electron to a receiving atom, both atoms are left with a charge; one is +, the other is –. The opposite charges hold the atoms together in much the same way that the protons and electrons are held together. Opposite charges attract. The following graphic shows a sodium atom donating a valence electron to a receiving chlorine atom. Both atoms result in a full outermost energy level, making them more stable.

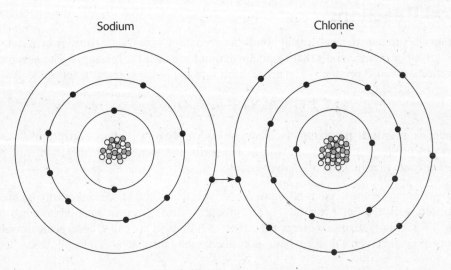

Sodium   Chlorine

Covalent bonds form when atoms share their valence electrons to provide a stable outermost energy level for both atoms. Covalent bonds form because neither atom is strong enough to pull the electrons away from the other atom. The atoms are held together because the electron cloud is now enveloping both atoms. A molecule is formed when two or more atoms are covalently bonded. For instance, elements in Group 4 have four valence electrons. To reach the stable octet, they can gain, lose, or share four electrons. In most cases, it is more energetically efficient to share the electrons. Often, elements like carbon bond with themselves forming extremely long molecules. Carbon-to-carbon bonds form the basis for all biologically important organic molecules and organic chemistry.

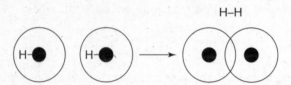

Polar covalent bonds are a hybrid between ionic and covalent bonds. Polar covalent bonds vary in their degree of ionic and covalent nature depending upon the atoms involved. Note that a polar covalent bond forms a partial positive and a partial negative charge on the resulting molecule. The most common biologically important polar covalent molecule is water.

Examine the following graphic that depicts a polar covalent bond to form water. Note that the electrons are depicted closer to the oxygen atom, thereby creating a partial (–) charge on the oxygen end of the molecule and a partial (+) charge on the hydrogen end. The resulting water molecule is considered a polar molecule, which allows it to attract other water molecules to create surface tension; attract and dissolve ionic compounds as a universal solvent; and form acids and bases. All biochemical reactions in living organisms take place in a water environment. The polar nature, which allows water to dissolve polar and ionic substances, also has biological importance through promoting membrane permeability and the transmission of nerve signals.

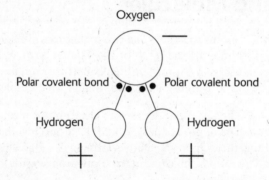

Biochemical Reactions

A **chemical reaction** is a process where chemical bonds between atoms are formed and/or broken to produce a new product(s). The starting or raw materials that begin a reaction are called the reactants. The new product(s) or results of the reaction are called products. The generalized formula for a chemical reaction is:

REACTANTS → PRODUCTS

Thousands of chemical reactions are taking place in your body right now that are converting a variety of reactants into the array of products that maintain your homeostasis (well-being), provide growth and repair of cells, digest foods, provide energy for movement, and lots more.

In chemical reactions, energy is absorbed or released. A chemical reaction that releases energy is called an **exergonic** or **exothermic** reaction, such as cellular respiration. The products of an exergonic reaction have less energy than the reactants. Chemical reactions that absorb energy from their environment are called **endergonic** or **endothermic** reactions. The products of an endergonic reaction have more energy than the reactants, like photosynthesis.

Activation energy is the amount of energy needed to start a chemical reaction. The activation energy needed to start a biochemical reaction can be in the form of heat or chemical energy. Biological catalysts, or enzymes, lower the amount of activation energy needed to start a reaction. **Enzymes** are mostly proteins and catalyze most of the biochemical reactions in your body. Enzymes speed up the rates of biochemical reactions that would either not occur without them or would occur at rates too slow to support life.

The following list details the five common types of biochemical reactions:

- **Synthesis reactions**—A biochemical reaction that forms a product from two or more substances: A + B → C. Photosynthesis is a synthesis reaction that combines water and carbon dioxide to make carbohydrates in an endergonic reaction that requires photons of light energy to power the reaction.

- **Decomposition reactions**—A reaction where a large molecule is broken down into smaller molecules: C → A + B. An example of a decomposition reaction is the breakdown of foods into component molecules, such as the decomposition of table sugar (sucrose) into glucose and fructose. Decomposition reactions are the opposite of synthesis reactions.

- **Oxidation or Combustion reactions**—Oxygen combines with other substances in a variety of ways. Cellular respiration is a slow exergonic oxidation of foods to release stored energy: food + oxygen → energy (ATP) + waste products (water and carbon dioxide).

- **Neutralization reactions**—A neutralization reaction occurs when an acid and base of equal strength and volume combine to form a salt and water with a neutral pH: acid + base → salt + water. On occasion, you may take a pill that neutralizes stomach acid to relieve an upset stomach.

- **Condensation reactions**—Condensation reactions are a type of synthesis reaction: two smaller organic molecules combine to form a more complex molecule, releasing a molecule of water in the process. Carbohydrate subunits, or monomers, are chemically bonded in a series of condensation reactions that release water and form large carbohydrate molecules (e.g., glucose combines to form starch [plants] or glycogen [animals]).

pH

pH is the negative logarithm of the hydrogen ion (H^+) concentration. The pH scale measures the acidity or alkalinity of a solution. Acidic solutions have a pH range of 0–7 (the lower the number, the stronger the acid). Basic or alkaline solutions have a pH range of 7–14 (the higher the number the stronger the base). A pH of 7 is considered neutral.

An **acid** is a chemical that releases hydrogen ions (H^+) when dissolved in water such as hydrochloric acid. **Bases,** like sodium hydroxide, donate hydroxide (OH^-) ions when dissolved in water. The pH of a solution can be changed by adding more acid or base. Equal volumes of equal concentrations of acids and bases neutralize each other. Buffers affect the ability of acids and bases to change pH.

Buffers

A **buffer** is a special type of solution that resists change in pH when an acid or base is added. Chemically, a buffer is a solution containing a weak acid and its conjugate base, or, a weak base and its conjugate acid. Acids are neutralized by bases when the H^+ ions react with the weak base to form water. Bases are neutralized when the OH^- ions react with the weak acid to form water. Buffers work by "absorbing" or reacting with the H^+ or OH^- ions to form water. Some biologically important buffers include phosphate, bicarbonate, and protein, which resist changes in pH in biological fluids.

Biologically Important Molecules

Living organisms are mostly composed of organic compounds and water. Recall that organic compounds contain carbon. Organic molecules are involved in every biochemical reaction that occurs in you and every other living organism. Interestingly, all biochemical reactions must take place in water. Four biologically important organic compounds include proteins, carbohydrates, lipids, and nucleic acids. I should also mention one biologically significant inorganic compound: water.

Proteins and Enzymes

Proteins are organic, polymer molecules that are made by joining amino acid monomers together in a specific order. Properly functioning proteins exist as a folded three-dimensional structure. Changes in the three-dimensional structure of a protein alters their function and extreme changes in structure lead to denaturation. Changes in temperature, pH, pressure, salinity, free radicals, or exposure to excessive radioactivity may result in changes in the three-dimensional structure of a protein.

Surprisingly, only 20 **amino acids** function as the organic subunits or monomers for all proteins! Amino acids have the four bonds of a central carbon atom connected to an amino group (NH_2), a carboxyl group (COOH), a hydrogen atom (H), and a side chain (R) of variable complexity. Observe the amino acid components in the following graphic.

$$H_2N-\underset{\underset{H}{|}}{\overset{\overset{R}{|}}{C}}-COOH$$

Amino acids combine in a **condensation reaction** forming a peptide bond between the amino group of one amino acid and the carboxyl group of another amino acid with the release of water. **Peptides** are formed when amino acids are linked together; **dipeptides** are a linkage of two amino acids; **polypeptides** are multiple linkages.

Proteins have four biologically significant functions: enzymes, transport, structure, and hormones.

An **enzyme** is a reusable specialized protein that speeds up metabolic reactions without being changed. Enzymes are biological catalysts that lower the activation energy for a reaction.

How are enzymes so specific in the reactions they catalyze? An active site on the enzyme chemically binds to a unique receptor site on a substrate, forming an enzyme-substrate complex. The specificity of the **enzyme-substrate complex** is often referred to as a "lock and key." The enzyme-substrate complex lowers the activation energy. Enzyme names generally indicate what they catalyze and end with suffix *–ase*. For instance, the enzyme maltase catalyzes the reaction where maltose (substrate) is broken down into two glucose molecules (product).

Enzyme-Substrate Complex

Some enzymes require nonprotein **cofactors** to bind with the active site to facilitate the binding with the substrate. Inorganic cofactors include metal ions, like iron; organic cofactors are more commonly called **coenzymes** and include vitamins. **Prosthetic groups** are cofactors that are chemically bonded to the protein. **Inhibitors** are substances that attach to the active site of an enzyme thereby preventing the catalyzing of a reaction. Heavy metals are poisonous because they are noncompetitive inhibitors that attach to the enzyme (by definition noncompetitive inhibitors bind at sites other than the active site, competitive inhibitors bind at the active site and are typically homologous to the normal substrate) and prevent enzyme functions. **Transport proteins** moves smaller particles throughout the body and through cell membranes. Hemoglobin is a protein found in red blood cells that carries oxygen to the cells.

Structural proteins form materials that cells use for structural purposes such as proteins of the cytoskeleton (actin and tubulin). Structural proteins give cells their shape. Collagen is the structural protein that makes up skin, fur, hair, feathers, wool, fingernails, hooves, ligaments, tendons, and parts of bone.

Hormones are chemical messengers that are made in one gland but travel via bloodstream to influence an action in another part of the body. Some hormones are protein or partly protein, such as insulin. An overabundance of sugar in the blood stimulates the release of insulin from the Islets of Langerhans in the pancreas. Insulin triggers the uptake of blood glucose by the liver, muscles, and fat tissue. Diabetes mellitus results when the pancreas does not secrete any insulin (type 1 diabetes); or the when the pancreas secretes an insufficient amount of insulin or the body is resistant to the insulin produced (type II diabetes). The four groups of hormones (based on structure) are amino acid derivatives, peptides, steroids, and eicosanoids.

Carbohydrates

Carbohydrates are the most important source of energy for your body. Sugars and starches are common carbohydrates. Your body digests carbohydrates into **glucose** (blood sugar) that fuels the cellular respiration reaction that releases energy as needed to the cells in your body. Excess glucose is stored as **glycogen** in your liver and muscles.

Carbohydrates are easily identifiable because they are made from carbon, hydrogen, and oxygen only. Carbohydrates are "hydrates of carbon" which makes remembering their general formula easier: CH_2O. The ratio of hydrogen to oxygen is always 2:1 in a hydrate of carbon. Carbohydrates contain multiple hydroxyl groups (–OH) and a carbonyl (C=O) functional group. Carbohydrates range in size from a single monomer, like glucose, to large polymers made from thousands of monomers, like cellulose.

Carbohydrates are divided into three classes based on their complexity: monosaccharides, disaccharides, and polysaccharides. **Monosaccharides** are often called the simple sugars. The simplest carbohydrate, **glucose**, is a monosaccharide or "1-sugar" often given intravenously to hospital patients. Other common examples of monosaccharides include galactose and fructose. Fructose is known as "fruit sugar" because it is the most common carbohydrate in most fruits. Glucose and fructose are **isomers** because they both have the same formulas ($C_6H_{12}O_6$) but different atom arrangement; glucose and galactose are **stereoisomers** because the hydrogen and hydroxyl groups are oriented differently around one carbon atom. Notice that monosaccharides have a carbonyl group ($HOCH_2$) on one carbon atom and hydroxyl groups on most of the other carbon atoms.

Monosaccharides

When monosaccharides are in solution, they exist in the open chain and closed ring structure as seen in the previous graphic. The cyclic, or closed ring, structures are more stable at equilibrium.

Disaccharides are formed when two monosaccharides are chemically bonded together in a condensation reaction which liberates a molecule of water. The most common disaccharide is **sucrose,** also recognized as common table sugar. Sucrose is formed by the condensation between the monosaccharides fructose and glucose. Lactose, or milk sugar, is formed by the condensation of glucose and galactose.

Polysaccharides are complex carbohydrates that are polymers formed by the condensation of many monosaccharides. Glycogen is a common polysaccharide that is composed of glucose subunits. Glycogen functions as stored energy and is kept in the liver and muscles of humans and other animals. Starch and cellulose are common polysaccharides composed of glucose and made by plants. **Starch** is a water-insoluble molecule used to store energy, similar to glycogen in animals. Cellulose is also water-insoluble but is used as a structural component for forming rigid cell walls, such as the cell walls found in wood.

Glycogen, starch, and cellulose are composed of glucose monosaccharides but the chemical bonds between them are oriented differently so that humans can digest glycogen and starch, but not cellulose. The cellulose that you consume in fruits and vegetables is indigestible and scours through your digestive system as dietary fiber or roughage.

Lipids

Lipids are large nonpolar organic molecules composed of carbon, hydrogen, and oxygen. Lipids are unlike carbohydrates because the ratio of hydrogen to oxygen is always greater than 2:1. Also, lipids are not polymers.

Lipids have four major functions: long term energy storage (fats), structural components of cell membranes (phospholipids), a water barrier (waxes), and various bodily functions such as homeostasis (steroids, vitamins, and hormones).

Triglycerides are a type of lipid formed when three fatty acid molecules bond with a glycerol molecule. Fatty acids are long chains (12–20 carbon atoms) carboxylic acids with a general formula of RCOOH. Saturated fatty acids have no double bonds but instead are "saturated" with hydrogen atoms. Unsaturated fatty acids have one or more double bonds. Triglycerides can be either a solid (fats) or liquid (oils).

Glycerol   A "free" Fatty Acid

Triglyceride

When energy molecules are abundant, fat cells store the excess energy as triglycerides. Enzymes in cells break down triglycerides when energy is required. Interestingly, soap is made in a process called saponification: a strong base is added to triglycerides to form molecules that have a polar (charged) and nonpolar end. The nonpolar end bonds with dirt and oils while the polar end is water soluble and rinses the entire mess away.

A typical cell membrane is a **phospholipid bilayer** in which the nonpolar tails of the fatty acids are pointed inward and the polar heads pointing to the outside surface. This lipid bilayer acts as a barrier allowing the cell to regulate what enters and exits through the membrane.

Waxes are lipids that are formed by combining a fatty acid with a long-chain alcohol. Plants and animals make waxes to prevent water loss, for protection, and for structural purposes. Ear wax catches harmful particles and protects the inner ear. The wax coating on some plant leaves prevents water loss and honeybees make wax to build honeycombs.

Steroids are lipids that are made of multiple closed ring (cyclic) structures and do not contain fatty acid chains. The sex hormones, cholesterol, and vitamin D are common examples of steroids. The sex hormone estrogen is made in the ovaries. Estrogen controls the development of secondary sex characteristics in females and regulates the menstrual cycle. Testosterone is synthesized in the testes and controls the development of secondary sex characteristics in males, such as facial hair, muscle mass, and deeper voices. Sadly the use of anabolic steroids by athletes to increase muscle mass for performance enhancement is well documented.

Nucleic Acids

Nucleic acids are nitrogen-containing organic polymers that store and transmit genetic information. **Deoxyribonucleic acid (DNA)** and **ribonucleic acid (RNA)** are the two types of nucleic acids. Both DNA and RNA are polymers composed of nucleotide monomers.

Nucleotides have three parts: one to three inorganic phosphate (PO_4) groups, a 5-carbon monosaccharide (pentose) sugar, and one of four nitrogenous bases. Nucleotides form a phosphodiester bond that connects the sugar of one nucleotide to the phosphate of an adjoining nucleotide to create a characteristic sugar-phosphate backbone for DNA and RNA. The sequence of the nitrogen bases forms the genetic code for all living organisms. The following model shows a nucleotide monomer.

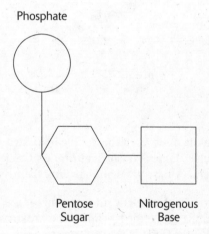

Phosphate

Pentose Sugar

Nitrogenous Base

DNA contains the unique genetic code for life. The structure of DNA is a twisted double helix of nucleotides. The **sugar-phosphate backbone** is on the outside of the DNA molecule and the nitrogen bases are chemically joined by hydrogen bonds (a type of polar covalent bond) in the middle. The nitrogen bases look like stair steps inside of a spiral staircase.

DNA contains four different **nitrogenous bases**: **adenine (A), thymine (T), cytosine (C),** and **guanine (G)** that are sequenced to form the genetic code. The nitrogen bases are like letters of the alphabet. Their specific sequence in the DNA molecule represents the master plan for the organism. The sequence of nitrogen bases is different in every sexually reproducing individual organism! Asexual organisms and clones have the same sequence of nitrogen bases, making them identical to the parent.

Adenine and guanine are **purines,** or double-ringed structures that always bond with the single ring structure **pyrimidines,** thymine, and cytosine. Bonding occurs in a specific pairing: adenine to thymine, and cytosine to guanine. **Chargaff's Rule** states that the number of purines is equal to the number of pyrimidines in a nucleic acid. Chargaff's Rule makes sense because purines and pyrimidines bond to each other, although Chargaff did not know that at the time. The complementary bases pairs A-T and G-C are formed to optimize the number of hydrogen bonds that can form between them. A-T is a double hydrogen bond, but G-C is a triple hydrogen bond.

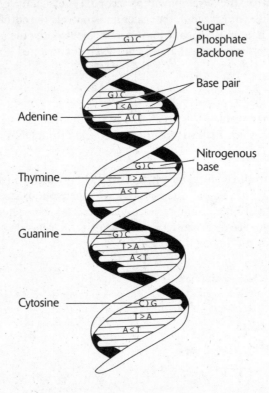

Through crystallography **Rosalind Franklin** discovered the double helix structure and the sugar-phosphate backbone on the outside of the DNA molecule. **James Watson** and **Francis Crick** completed the DNA structure by placing the nitrogen bases in complementary base pairs and creating the twisted structure we now know as DNA.

The function of DNA is to store and convey the genetic information for the cell. DNA is stored in the nucleus of eukaryotes and loosely arranged within the cell in the less advanced prokaryotes. Before the cell divides, the DNA is copied so that all daughter cells receive the same DNA as the parent cell. RNA is similar to DNA but differs in three characteristic ways: RNA is a single strand; RNA contains uracil (U) instead of thymine (T); the sugar is ribose in place of deoxyribose.

The function of RNA is to convey the genetic code from the DNA to the ribosomes for correct construction of proteins. In a process called **transcription,** the DNA is enzymatically copied producing messenger RNA (mRNA). The mRNA is small and packaged to move out of the nucleus through the nuclear membrane and into the cytoplasm. Ribosomes, mostly made of ribosomal RNA (rRNA) facilitate the process of **translation** where the genetic code carried by the mRNA is read by the transfer RNA (tRNA). Each tRNA molecule carries a specific amino acid. The mRNA **codon** matches the tRNA **anticodon** and inserts its amino acid, which bonds with and becomes part of the growing peptide chain as prescribed by the original DNA. For more on DNA and RNA, see "Structure and Function of the Nucleic Acids," later in the chapter.

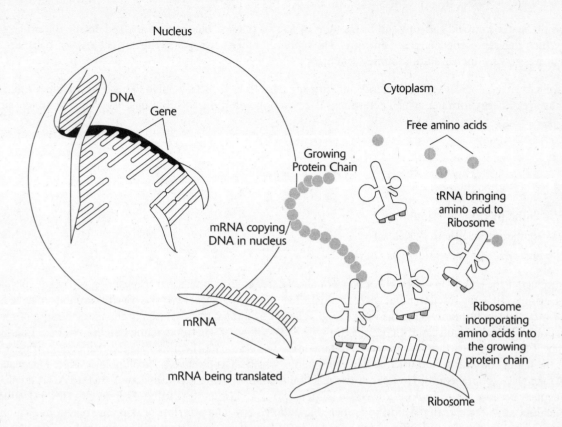

Recent research has identified micro-RNA. Micro-RNA may function to block, cover, or uncover parts of DNA to activate or deactivate the function of that segment of DNA. Stay tuned for more research discoveries.

Thermodynamics and Free Energy

Energy is the power to move or change matter. For biological purposes, the solar energy of the sun is absorbed by plants and through the process of photosynthesis converts light energy into chemical energy. The chemical energy is used within the plant or transferred to animals for use in powering their life processes.

Biological thermodynamics is concerned with the energy controlled biochemical pathways such as the hydrolysis of adenosine triphosphate (ATP), membrane diffusion, DNA stability, and the rate of enzyme controlled reactions. In any chemical reaction, such as DNA bonding, the total amount of energy involved does not change. However, the total amount of usable energy always decreases. In thermodynamic terms, the amount of energy capable of doing work in any chemical reaction is quantitatively calculated by the change in **Gibbs Free Energy.**

The **First Law of Thermodynamics** states that energy is interchangeable but energy cannot be created or destroyed. This law is often referred to as the "conservation of energy" law. Building on the preceding concept, **Hess's Law** states that the heat (energy) requirement for any reaction is constant and independent of the manner in which the reaction takes place. For biological systems this means that regardless of the number of subreactions that may occur, or whether heat is required (endergonic) or released (exergonic), the total heat exchange will be equal as if it were summed as a single reaction. One important component of Hess's Law is the significance of the calorimeter, an instrument used to determine the calories of heat energy contained in a substance or chemical reaction. For biological systems, the calorimeter may be used to determine the amount of energy that enters an animal's body as food. Typically these energy or heat values are measure in calories and displayed as kilocalories because of their magnitude in human and other diets.

The **Second Law of Thermodynamics** states that no natural reaction or process can occur unless it is accompanied by an increase in entropy. The Second Law of Thermodynamics references whether a given biochemical reaction will occur...or not. **Entropy** is a measure of the randomness of the universe. Entropy also tells how much energy is not available to do work. Entropy can be thought of as two piles of blocks: one stacked nicely; the other, scattered. Which one represents increased entropy? The scattered blocks scenario is the correct answer, because nature moves toward increased randomness or entropy.

For simplicity, in biological systems, energy and entropy tend to be directly related. This relationship establishes the **Gibbs Free Energy** formula, which determines if a reaction will proceed spontaneously. The formula is simple:

$$G = H - TS$$

Where:

G = Gibbs Free Energy

H = enthalpy (SI unit = joules)

T = temperature (SI unit = Kelvin)

S = entropy (SI unit = joules per Kelvin)

To be succinct, if the change in Gibbs Free Energy or simply, free energy, is negative, the reaction will occur spontaneously; if positive, then the reaction is not spontaneous. Note that in biological reactions several reactions may be linked together in a stepwise fashion. As per the First Law of Thermodynamics, the total energy change is the sum of all of the reactions. This calculation can then be applied to the Second Law of Thermodynamics and Gibbs Free Energy to determine if the overall reaction will proceed spontaneously. The classic biochemical reaction that demonstrates this point is the joining of glucose and fructose to create sucrose, which has a positive 5.5 kcal/mole G value. This reaction will not take place spontaneously. However, if this reaction is coupled with the conversion of ATP to ADP, it will occur spontaneously because the ADP-ATP conversion has a negative 7.3 kcal/mole G value. Therefore the total G value is −1.8 kcal/mole, so the overall reaction will proceed spontaneously. The principle of coupling reactions to alter the change in Gibbs Free Energy is significant in understanding the enzyme reactions that occur in the biological reactions in all living organisms. Note how the following paired reactions allow the formation of sucrose.

$$\text{glucose} + \text{fructose} \rightarrow \text{sucrose} = +5.5 \text{ Kcal/mole}$$
$$\text{ATP} \rightarrow \text{ADP} = -7.3 \text{ Kcal/mole}$$
$$= -1.8 \text{ Kcal/mole}$$

Cellular Bioenergetics

Bioenergetics is the expression of the energy flow through living systems. In a biochemical reaction, energy is absorbed (**endergonic**) or released (**exergonic**) when chemical bonds are broken or created. **Metabolism** is the term that describes all of the biochemical reactions that occur within an organism. Cells, like yours, receive most of their energy from the metabolism of their food.

An endergonic biochemical reaction is not spontaneous and requires an input of energy before the reaction will occur, indicating a positive G or change in free energy. Endergonic reactions tend to be **anabolic** as in the building up of complex food molecules, such as the glucose created during photosynthesis. An exergonic reaction is a spontaneous reaction that releases energy and is therefore thermodynamically favored. Exergonic reactions tend to be **catabolic** as complex molecules are broken into smaller molecules, such as the energy released as food is broken down by cellular respiration. The energy lost from the breaking and reforming of chemical bonds releases energy which gives an exergonic reaction a negative G or change in free energy.

Photosynthesis

Simply speaking, **photosynthesis** is the **synthesis reaction** that green plants, algae, and some bacteria perform to produce glucose. Photosynthesis uses light energy to join carbon dioxide (CO_2) molecules with water (H_2O) molecules to create glucose ($C_6H_{12}O_6$) and the waste gas oxygen (O_2).

The generalized formula is $CO_2 + H_2O + \text{light} \rightarrow C_6H_{12}O_6 + O_2$.

Interestingly the generalized formula for photosynthesis is the exact opposite of the generalized formula for **aerobic cellular respiration**, a **decomposition reaction.**

Photosynthesis is the process that produces energy for most life forms. Photosynthesis is divided into light and dark reactions:

The first stage of photosynthesis is called the **light reaction** or **photolysis.** A better title would be "light-dependent reaction" because the process is endergonic and will not proceed without the input of light energy:

1. **Photons** of light energy are captured by the chlorophyll pigment molecules located in the disk-shaped **thylakoids** located within the chloroplasts of green plants.

2. The thylakoids transfer the light energy to electrons which "excites" or raises the electrons to a higher energy level. Excited electrons jump to other active sites in the thylakoids membrane which move the excited electrons down an electron transport chain consisting of a series of molecules that remove some of the energy from the excited electrons to create the energy-rich ATP and **nictotinamide adenine dinucleotide phosphate (NADPH)** molecules.

3. The vacancy created by the exit of the excited electrons is filled by electrons from water molecules. Water molecules are split by enzymes in the thylakoids into hydrogen and oxygen. The hydrogen ions (H^+) become very concentrated inside of the thylakoid membrane, creating a concentration gradient that allows hydrogen ions to diffuse through the membrane into an electron transport chain of specialized carrier proteins that catalyze a reaction where a phosphate group is added to **adenosine diphosphate (ADP)** to create the higher energy compound **adenine triphosphate (ATP).** The ATP created is used to power part of the dark reaction of photosynthesis. A second electron transport chain creates NADPH, a molecule that carries high energy electrons needed to create the carbon to hydrogen (C-H) bonds in the dark reaction of photosynthesis. The remaining oxygen atoms are given off as a waste product. The light reaction is a decomposition reaction which decomposes water into hydrogen and oxygen with the help of excited electrons. The light dependent part of photosynthesis is summarized in five steps:

1. Chlorophyll and other pigment molecules located in the thylakoids of the chloroplasts absorb photons of light energy.

2. The energy is transferred to create excited high energy electrons that move through one of two electron transport chains in the thylakoid membranes.

3. Excited electrons are replaced by electrons created by the splitting of water by enzymes.

4. Oxygen atoms created by the splitting of water join together to create waste oxygen gas which is given off to the environment.

5. Hydrogen ions build a concentration gradient inside of the thylakoids that provides the energy to make ATP and NADPH.

The following graphic shows how the chloroplast functions to produce glucose, which then is metabolized by the mitochondrion to produce energy for life.

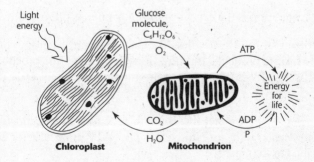

The second stage of photosynthesis is called the **dark reaction.** A better title would be "Light-Independent Reaction" of photosynthesis because the "dark reaction" can and does happen during daylight. This spontaneous reaction is light independent because it is exergonic with a negative G or change in free energy.

The ATP and NADPH made in the light dependent stage of photosynthesis are used to link carbon dioxide molecules together to form glucose and other organic compounds in the light independent stage.

The most common method of carbon fixation is described by the **Calvin cycle.** The Calvin cycle occurs in the stroma of the chloroplasts and is a series of enzyme-assisted biochemical reactions that ultimately produce a 3-carbon sugar. The enzyme Rubisco (ribulose biphsophate carboxylase) catalyzes the first step of the Calvin Cycle by attaching an atmospheric carbon dioxide molecule to the 5-carbon sugar RuBP (ribulose biphosphate). Rubisco is one of the slowest enzymes and creates a rate-determining stage of photosynthesis. Interestingly Rubisco is the most abundant protein on Earth. The Calvin cycle can be summarized in three steps:

1. Carbon dioxide molecules are enzymatically fixed (added) to existing 5-carbon, RuBP molecules. The resulting 6-carbon molecule splits into two 3-carbon molecules.

2. The 3-carbon molecules are turned into 3-carbon sugars by the addition of phosphate groups from ATP (light reaction) and high energy electrons from NADPH (light reaction).

3. One of the 3-carbon sugars is used to make other organic compounds, like sucrose and starch, as a form of stored energy. The remaining 3-carbon sugar is fed back into the Calvin cycle.

Photosynthesis is an endergonic reaction that requires 686 kcal of light energy to produce 1 mole of glucose. Why is photosynthesis an endergonic reaction? Breaking the bonds within the water molecules and carbon dioxide molecules requires 3,564 kcal/mol of energy because the bonds are polar covalent with high bond energies and therefore are difficult to break. The resulting bonds between the glucose molecules and oxygen molecules are lower energy covalent bonds that release 2,878 kcal/mol. Photosynthesis is not a spontaneous reaction because the free energy (G) of photosynthesis is +686 kcal/mol, indicating a need for considerable help from light energy to proceed. In photosynthesis, the solar energy from the sun is captured by the chlorophyll in the chloroplast of a green plant and stored as the chemical bond energy that may then be converted into mechanical, heat, or light energy by the various life forms as they proceed with their unique life functions.

Cellular Respiration

Cellular respiration is a **combustion reaction** whereby cells harvest the energy of organic compounds, like glucose. Most organisms, whether plant or animal need oxygen to perform **aerobic cellular respiration.** However, simpler life forms, usually microscopic, **undergo anaerobic cellular respiration,** which is a type of respiration that uses electron acceptors other than oxygen. Although oxygen is not used as the final electron acceptor, the process still uses an electron transport chain (without oxygen). Aerobic respiration occurs in the mitochondria of eukaryotes and the cell membrane of prokaryotes. Aerobic cellular respiration releases tremendous amounts of usable energy for the cell; anaerobic cellular metabolism releases much less energy. As an example the aerobic oxidation or burning of glucose creates ATP (usable energy) and the waste products water and carbon dioxide. The general formula for aerobic cellular respiration is: glucose + oxygen yield carbon dioxide, water, and ATP.

$$C_6H_{12}O_6 + 6O_2 \rightarrow 6CO_2 + 6H_2O + ATP$$

Interestingly, aerobic cellular respiration is the exact opposite formula as photosynthesis.

Cellular respiration is the oxidizing of food molecules, like glucose or fatty acids, to release energy (ATP) and create water and carbon dioxide as waste products. But how does this occur? The process of aerobic respiration can be broken down into three steps: glycolysis (the splitting of glucose), the Krebs cycle or citric acid cycle, and the electron transport chain.

Glycolysis is a multiple enzyme-controlled, anaerobic chain of reactions that occurs in the cytoplasm of a cell. Glycolysis requires two ATP molecules to begin but releases four ATP molecules for a net gain of two ATP molecules. Glycolysis can be described in four steps:

1. Two ATP molecules attach to a glucose molecule.

2. Enzymes break one 6-carbon molecule into two 3-carbon molecules, each with a phosphate group and with the release of hydrogen atoms.

3. Some of the hydrogen atoms are transferred to an electron acceptor, NAD$^+$, forming two molecules of the electron carrier NADH.

4. Each 3-carbon molecule is converted to a 3-carbon pyruvate ion, producing four ATP molecules.

The steps of glycolysis are represented in the following graphic.

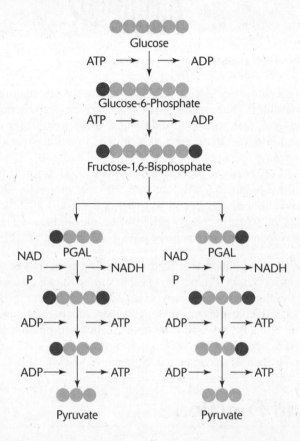

Following glycolysis, cellular respiration may continue as aerobic or anaerobic, depending upon the availability of oxygen.

The **Kreb's cycle,** also known as the **citric acid cycle** or Tricarboxylic Acid cycle (TCA), begins the process of aerobic cellular respiration. The Kreb's cycle occurs in the matrix of the cell's numerous mitochondria. Overall, the Kreb's cycle produces electron carriers that temporarily store the chemical energy from the food.

The Kreb's cycle breaks down the 3-carbon pyruvic acid molecules created during glycolysis to form the electron carriers NADH, FADH$_2$, ATP, and the waste gas carbon dioxide. The Kreb's cycle produces NADH and FADH$_2$, which contain much of the energy that was originally stored in the glucose molecule. The NADH and FADH$_2$ then enter the electron transport chain.

The **electron transport chain** is a series of heme (iron-containing) molecules that are locate on the cristae or inner membranes of the mitochondria. Electrons donated by the NADH and FADH$_2$ are passed along heme molecules in the electron transport chain. Their energy is used to pump the hydrogen ions out of the mitochondrial matrix to the space between the inner and outer mitochondrial membrane (intermembrane space). As the concentration gradient increases on the outside of the inner membrane, hydrogen ions diffuse back across the membrane via a carrier protein that uses some of the electron's energy to add a phosphate group to an ADP creating ATP. The electron transport chain ends with the hydrogen ions, electrons, and oxygen atoms combining to form the waste product water, which is normally exhaled by humans. The electron transport system generates the most ATPs per turn of the cycle, a total of 32 ATP molecules are created for every oxidized glucose molecule.

Examine the following graphic, which shows how the **mitochondrion** transforms the glucose into usable energy.

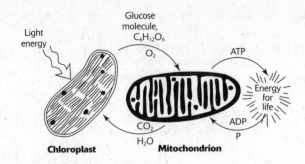

Aerobic cellular respiration is an exergonic biochemical reaction that releases 686 kcal/mol of energy. Why is aerobic cellular respiration an exergonic reaction? The covalent bonds in a glucose molecule require 2,182 kcal to break them, plus the six double covalent bonds of oxygen require an additional 696 kcal for a total of 2,878 kcal to break all of the bonds in the reactants (glucose and oxygen). On the products side, the formation of 6 moles of carbon dioxide requires 2,244 kcal to form the 12 double polar covalent bonds, each with a bond energy of 187 kcal/mol; plus the 6 moles of water requires the formation of 12 O-H bonds, each requiring 110 kcal/mol for a total of 1,320 kcal. Summing the kcal released by the bond formation of the products gives a total of 3,564 kcal. Subtracting 3,564 kcal released by the formation of the products from the amount of energy needed to break the bonds of the starting reactants, 2,878 kcal gives a –686 kcal, which represents the G or free energy change for 1 mole of glucose. The negative G or change in free energy indicates that the reaction is spontaneous and energy is removed from the system.

Fermentation is the anaerobic cellular respiration that occurs when there is no oxygen present to accept the spent electrons exiting the electron transport chain. Prokaryotes perform more than a dozen different types of fermentation. But the general formula states that two 3-carbon pyruvic acid molecules (made in glycolysis) are usually broken into either lactic acid, $C_3H_6O_3$, (which causes muscle fatigue, pain, and evencramps) or ethyl alcohol, C_2H_6O (as per adult beverages). The amount of energy released in anaerobic cellular respiration is considerably less than the amount of usable energy released by aerobic cellular respiration. Interestingly, lactic acid fermentation is use by some microorganisms to live, and by people to commercially prepare some types of cheese and yogurt.

Cell Structure and Function

The **cell** is the basic unit of life that is capable of all life functions. Cells are small but highly organized units with a thin membrane that creates an internal environment that is separate and different from the external environment. Although the basic structure of cell is the same, cells come in all shapes and sizes and levels of complexity. The longest cells are nerve cells that may measure up to a meter in length or small, like a bacterium sometimes less than 1 micrometer. Most cells fall within the 0.5–100 micrometers in diameter range. Unicellular organisms, like a paramecium, are made of one cell and perform all of the life functions as do multicellular organisms. Humans contain 100 trillion cells, give or take a billion or two.

Most cells are too small to see with the unaided eye which postponed their discovery until **Robert Hooke** used a simple microscope to observe thin slices of cork. In 1665, Hooke wrote the book *Micrographia,* in which he described his microscopic observation of plant cells. He called the squares that he saw "cells" supposedly because they reminded him of the small rooms that monks lived in at the time. A decade later, **Anton van Leeuwenhoek** used an improved microscope to observe small creatures that he called "animalcules" or tiny animals swimming in a sample of pond water. The animalcules turned out to be microorganisms that are still common in most freshwater ponds.

About 150 years later, in 1838, **Mattias Schleiden** stated that cells compose plants and **Theodore Schwann** concluded that cells also make up animals. In 1858 **Rudolph Virchow** determined that cells come from pre-existing cells. Summed together, the discoveries of these men became known as the **cell theory:**

- All cells arise from pre-existing cells.
- All living organisms are composed of one or more cells.
- Cells are the basic unit of structure and function in organisms.

Interestingly the size of the cell determines it ability to function efficiently. Because food and water must enter the cell and wastes must exit the cell through its membrane, the ratio of membrane surface area to cell volume is important. If the membrane surface area to cell volume ratio is too low, then substances may not be able to enter and leave the cell fast enough to meet the demands of the cell. Therefore, small cells have a greater exchange rate than larger cells. Check out the arithmetic on the following graphic.

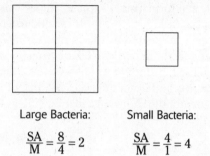

Large Bacteria:

$$\frac{SA}{M} = \frac{8}{4} = 2$$

Small Bacteria:

$$\frac{SA}{M} = \frac{4}{1} = 4$$

Membranes, Organelles, and Subcellular Components of Prokaryote and Eukaryote Cells

The two basic types of cell are prokaryote and eukaryote. **Prokaryotes** are evolutionarily older than eukaryotic cells and therefore less complex. **Eukaryote** cells are often part of a multicellular organism and have specialized functions whereas a prokaryote cell is always unicellular and is unable to perform specialized functions.

Prokaryote cells are small, simple, and are only found in unicellular organisms and bacteria. Some prokaryote cells have a **cell wall** that gives them shape and protection as well as a cell membrane that surrounds the cell. Surprisingly, some prokaryotes are enveloped by a polysaccharide capsule that allows them to stick to almost anything like your food, your teeth, or your friends. The cytoplasm of prokaryote cells has no dividers so the ribosomes, enzymes, and single circular DNA float in the cytoplasm of the cell. Prokaryote cells have no nucleus or membrane-bound cellular structures. Some prokaryotic cells do have a form of locomotion called a flagellum or in some cases, flagella. A **flagellum** is a long whiplike structure that protrudes from the cell surface and waves in a liquid medium to propel the prokaryote.

Plants, animals, fungi, you, your neighbor, algae, and protozoa, are eukaryotes. Eukaryotic cells are characterized as having a membrane-bound nucleus which is an internal cellular organelle that houses and protects the cells' DNA or genetic information. Eukaryotic cells have compartments and membrane-bound organelles that allow for specialized functions, such as a nerve cell conducting electrical transmissions. An elaborate system of membrane channels connect most cellular organelles and provide a means for the distribution of substances. Although most eukaryotes use flagella for locomotion, some also use cilia for movement. **Cilia** are short hairlike structures that may surround the organism and wave in unison to propel the organism. Eukaryotic cells also have a **cytoskeleton** made of an intricate network of protein fibers that serves as an internal framework to maintain shape, (actin fibers); to transport information, such as RNA, from the nucleus to the cellular organelles, (microtubules); and to provide a location for ribosomes and enzyme attachment (intermediate fibers).

The eukaryotic cell has numerous cellular organelles that provide unique functions for the cell:

- The **cell membrane** or **plasma membrane** is a flexible, selectively permeable covering that only allows certain substances from the cell exterior to pass through or internal substances to move out of the cell. The structure and selective permeability are provided by the phospholipid bilayer structure of the membrane. The **phospholipid bilayer** is composed of two layers of lipids that are arranged so that their nonpolar tails are oriented toward the interior of the membrane while the polar heads face either the interior or the exterior of the cell. The polar heads attract the polar water molecules while the nonpolar tails repel water. This keeps the water pressure constant within the cells and helps to contain needed ions, sugars, and proteins inside of the cell. Membrane proteins embedded within the cell membrane serve many functions. **Marker**

proteins are attached to the cells surface and may include a carbohydrate attachment that functions like an address sign. For instance a marker protein may signal that this is a muscle cell for easy identification for hormones, medicines, and some diseases. **Transport proteins** with the help of membrane enzymes move certain substances through the membrane that would ordinarily be repelled by the polar head. Most cells use endocytosis and exocytosis to ingest and secrete large macromolecules. With **endocytosis** the membrane depresses, surrounds the particle, and then pinches away from the membrane on the inside of the cell. The membrane-bound macromolecule can form a small vesicle (**pinocytosis**) or a larger vesicle (**phagocytosis**). In receptor-mediated endocytosis, specialized proteins form specific receptors which allow the cell to select what materials will pass into the cell. In **exocytosis,** the contents of a vesicle are released outside of the cell when the vesicle fuses with the cell membrane. **Microvilli** are projections of the cell membrane that extend into the cells' environment to increase the amount of absorptive surface area. Microvilli are common in the lining of the intestines where nutrients and water are absorbed from food. Examine the cross section of a typical phospholipid bilayer cell membrane shown in the following graphic.

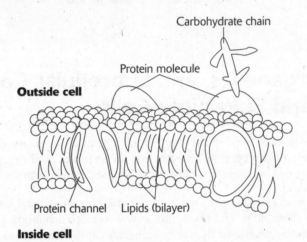

- Substances can move across a cell membrane by diffusion, facilitated diffusion, osmosis, or active transport. **Diffusion** is the random movement of particles from an area of higher concentration to an area of lower concentration until the concentrations are equal. Diffusion does not require energy but satisfies the thermodynamics of increasing the entropy of a system. **Facilitated diffusion** is like diffusion in that it does not require energy, but it does require specialized transport proteins. **Osmosis** is the movement of water through a permeable membrane from a solution of low solute (or salt) concentration to a solution of higher solute concentration. The movement of water (osmosis) continues until the concentration of the solute is the same on both sides of the membrane. It is sometimes said that "water follows salt" as a way to remember osmosis. Osmosis does not require energy but is of strategic importance in maintaining the internal water concentration of the cell. **Active transport** uses the energy of ATP to push substances against a concentration gradient with the help of transport proteins.

The components of cells are known as the cell's organelles. The following list highlights each type of organelle found in an eukaryotic cell as well as the organelle's function:

- The **nucleus** is thought of as the "brain" of the cell because it controls the functions of the eukaryotic cell. It is usually the predominant and easily identifiable cellular organelle. The nucleus is enclosed by a lipid bilayer **nuclear membrane,** or nuclear envelope that protects the DNA and separates the nucleus from the surrounding cytoplasm. The nuclear membrane contains many small channels called nuclear pores. **Nuclear pores** provide a selective passage way for substances, like messenger RNA (mRNA), to move from the nucleus into the cytoplasm. The **nucleoplasm,** a gel-like substance, surrounds, supports, and protects the genetic information for that cell, **deoxyribonucleic acid (DNA).** DNA normally exists as chromatins which are long thin strands made of histones, proteins and DNA that condense to form chromosomes when a cell is ready to divide. The **nucleolus** is a prominent sphere within the nucleus where ribosomal RNA (rRNA) is synthesized.

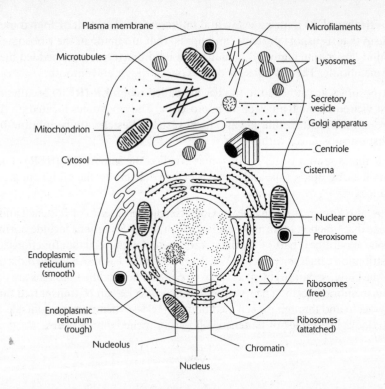

- **Ribosomes** are the site of protein synthesis. Ribosomes are made of rRNA and dozens of different proteins. Like prokaryotes, some of the ribosomes found in eukaryotes are **free ribosomes** that float in the cytoplasm and make proteins that are used and retained within the cell such as structural proteins that build or repair cellular organelles.

- **Attached ribosomes** are connected to the endoplasmic reticulum (ER) and make specialized proteins for use outside of the cell. The following graphic shows a typical ribosome making a protein in the process called **translation.**

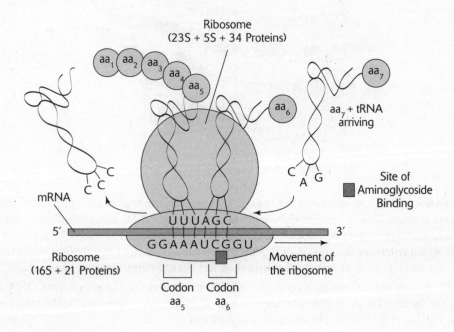

- The **endoplasmic reticulum (ER)** is an extensive and interconnected system of folded membranes and tubules within the cytoplasm that transport proteins (and lipids) that are made in the ribosomes throughout the cell. The intracellular "interstate highway" is made of a lipid bilayer with embedded membrane proteins similar to the cell membrane. The ER consists of two parts: rough and smooth.

  The areas where ribosomes are attached to the ER are called **rough ER (RER)** because this area looked "rough" when first viewed through an electron microscope. The ribosomes located on the RER create proteins that pass through the RER membrane and form vesicles. **Vesicles** are membrane-bound sacs that are used to safely transport substances within cells.

  The part of the ER that does not contain ribosomes is called the **smooth ER (SER).** The SER has several functions including making lipids, fats, and steroids before delivery to the Golgi apparatus, and breaking down toxic substances.

- The **Golgi apparatus,** also known as **Golgi body** or **Golgi complex,** is a series of flattened and folded membranes and stacked cisternae that function to form the secretions for a cell. Secretions include hormones, enzymes, and antibodies. The Golgi apparatus is part of the membrane system with a cell that functions to serve as the storing, packaging, and distribution center for proteins. Vesicles made in the ER move through the cytoplasm and are modified inside of the Golgi apparatus by specialized enzymes. The modified proteins are then repackaged when an area of the Golgi membrane forms a new vesicle. The new vesicles can be transported throughout the cell by the ER or may migrate to and through the cell membrane to release their packages outside of the cell. Note that the Golgi apparatus looks like a stack of flattened balloons or melted dinner plates.

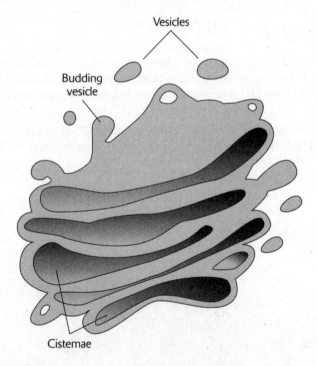

Vesicles

Budding
vesicle

Cisternae

- The **mitochondria** are the "powerhouses" of the cell because they are the location of aerobic cellular respiration, the process where the cell harvests the energy of food to make ATP. Mitochondria are enclosed by a double membrane with a greatly convoluted inner membrane called cristae. The folds of the cristae increase the surface area which enhances the process of aerobic cellular respiration, or metabolism. Cells that require more energy, like muscle cells, have more mitochondria than less energy-requiring cells, like skin cells.

  Interestingly, mitochondria have their own circular DNA that is similar to prokaryote DNA and acts separately from the nuclear DNA. A common theory states that mitochondria may be the result of a primitive prokaryote, like bacteria, living symbiotically inside of a eukaryote.

- **Lysosomes** are membrane structures that are the "clean-up" crew for the cell. **Lysosomes** contain digestive enzymes that break down worn out or damaged cell parts and recycle the contents for additional usage.

Plant cells have three unique features that distinguish them from animal cells:

- The **cell wall** that surrounds and protects the cell membrane of a plant and some bacterial cells is composed of proteins and carbohydrates, like the polysaccharides cellulose and lignin. The function of the rigid cell wall is to provide structure, protect the cell, allow the cell to store massive amounts of water, and permit the cell to connect to adjoining cells.. The following graphic shows how the cell wall determines the shape and maintains the structure of a plant cell.

Plant Cell Wall

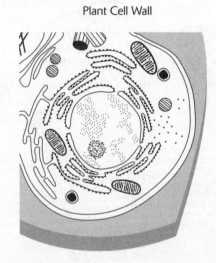

- **Chloroplasts** are the cellular organelle that contains the **thylakoid** stacks in **grana** that provide the location for photosynthesis. Chlorophyll captures the sun's energy needed to combine carbon dioxide and water to make carbohydrates and release oxygen as a waste gas. Chlorophyll pigments within the chloroplasts give them their characteristic green color but auxiliary pigments like red, purple, orange, or yellow color (think fall leaf colors) are able to capture different wavelengths of light than the green chlorophyll. Like mitochondria, chloroplasts are surrounded by a lipid bilayer membrane, contain their own DNA, and are thought to be the result of a prokaryote invasion and subsequent symbiotic relationship with a eukaryote cell. The following graphic shows a cut away view of a chloroplast.

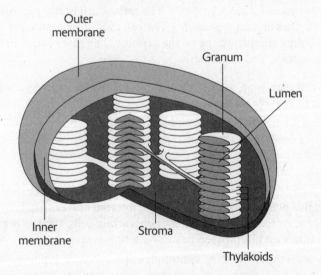

- The **central vacuole** stores water and other substances for the cell. The central vacuole is enclosed by a **tonoplast** or integrated membrane formed from the Golgi apparatus and endoplasmic reticulum. The central vacuole is the dominant feature in plants representing most of the volume. The contents of the central vacuole, called **cell sap** is mostly water but also contains selectively absorbed and interesting substances like colorful flower pigments and plant wastes that may taste bitter to certain herbivores. The **turgor pressure** of the cell is related to the turgor, or fullness of the central vacuole. The rigid shape of a plant cell is partly due to the turgid (full of water) shape of the central vacuole. Wilting occurs when the central vacuole is flaccid, or empty, which causes the cell to collapse on itself. Note the size of the central vacuole in the following graphic.

Plant Cell Central Vacuole

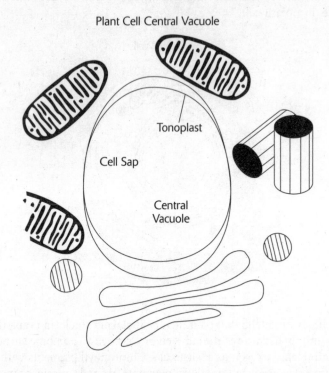

Note that animals also contain membrane-bound vacuoles that serve a variety of purposes. They are much smaller and serve specific purposes like engulfing and expelling unwanted substances from the cell.

Cell Cycle and Mitosis vs. Meiosis

The **cell cycle** describes the life cycle of a eukaryote cell. The cell cycle describes an ordered set of events that includes normal cell functions, growth, and replication. The cell cycle culminates in the cell dividing into two identical daughter cells each with a complete copy of the genome. The three stages in the cell cycle are interphase, which includes G_1, S, and G_2; mitosis; and cytokinesis.

1. **Interphase stage**—The cell spends up to 90 percent of its lifetime in the interphase stage. **Interphase** is a collective term that describes three phases:

   ■ **First growth (G_1) phase** is when the cell is rapidly growing and synthesizing its structural proteins and enzymes. This might be considered the normal phase because cells spend most of their time in this phase performing their normal functions. During the G_1 phase each chromosome consists of a single strand of DNA and its associated histone proteins.

   The G_1 phase is also a critical checkpoint in the normal cell cycle to make sure conditions are correct for cell division. During this phase, the cell monitors the internal and external environment to assure preparedness before beginning the S phase. Interestingly certain cells, such as nerve cells, do not reproduce or regenerate because they do not proceed beyond the G_1 phase.

   ■ **Synthesis (S) phase** is when the cell's DNA is faithfully copied thereby doubling the number of chromosomes. By the end of the S phase, each chromosome consists of two identical chromatids attached to a centromere.

   ■ **Second growth (G_2) phase** is the final preparation phase before beginning mitosis. Protein fibers called **microtubules** organize themselves into an array of fibers called the **spindle.** The spindle helps move the chromosomes during mitosis. The G_2 phase is also a critical checkpoint in the normal cell cycle to make sure conditions are correct before proceeding to mitosis.

2. **Mitosis (M)**—Defined as the process where nonsex cells are duplicated to form two identical diploid daughter cells. Diploid means two sets of chromosomes, one from each parent. Mitosis is asexual reproduction and is used by simpler organisms to reproduce, like binary fission. Mitosis is also the method of asexual reproduction that more complex animals use to grow and repair cells. Mitosis creates daughter cells with the exact DNA complement. For instance, if the parental cell is haploid (one set of chromosomes), then the daughter cells are haploid. Most of the DNA duplication in your body is a result of mitosis. Mitosis can be divided into four stages: prophase, metaphase, anaphase, and telophase. Mitosis is a continuous cycle in which cells spend varying times in each phase of the cycle.

- **Prophase**—Takes place when the chromosomes condense to form visible threads. At this point two copies of each chromosome exist as two identical chromatids that are joined at their centromere. Microscopic structures called centrioles migrate to opposite poles of the cell and produce a projecting array of microtubules called an aster. The chromatids attach to spindle fibers and move toward the equatorial plate of the cell.

- **Metaphase**—Occurs when the pairs of chromatids line up along the equatorial plate and the chromatids separate.

- **Anaphase**—Features the pulling of the chromatids, now chromosome pairs, to opposite sides of the cell by the spindle fibers. At the end of anaphase, an equal separation and distribution of the chromosomes exists on both sides of the cell.

- **Telophase**—Occurs when the chromosomes have completed the migration to opposite poles, the chromatin become visible as the chromosomes disappear, the spindle array is dismantled and the nuclear membrane reforms. Telophase is basically the opposite of prophase.

The process of mitosis is summarized in the following graphic.

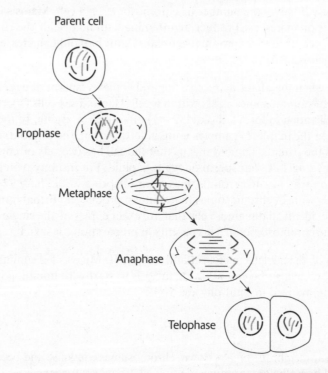

Parent cell

Prophase

Metaphase

Anaphase

Telophase

Two daughter cells

3. **Cytokinesis**—Process where the cytoplasm of the cell divides forming two separate cells. In animal cells, cytokinesis begins with a furrow in the center of the cell where the cell membrane pinches together to form two cells in a process called **cell cleavage.** In plant cells, a cell wall forms from vesicles secreted by the Golgi apparatus in the center. The cell wall grows outward to fuse with the cell membrane which causes the separation forming the two daughter cells. Cell cleavage does not take place in plant cells.

The cell cycle is a continuous process that can be easily visualized in the following graphic.

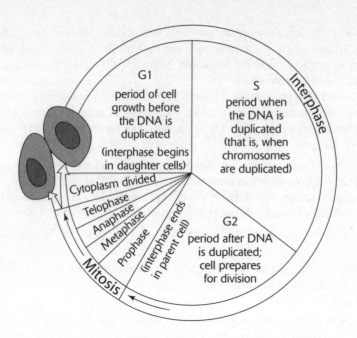

Meiosis

Meiosis is the division of the sex cells in preparation for sexual reproduction. Meiosis is sometimes referred to as the reduction division because it halves the number of chromosomes in a cell. Meiosis is the process where reproductive cells, such as gametes or spores, are produced containing haploid or half the chromosome number of the diploid parent cells. Meiosis occurs in the reproductive organs. Your haploid gametes, either sperm (male) or egg (female) are produced via meiosis.

Sexual reproduction occurs when the offspring receive haploid gametes (sperm or egg) from two parents. Haploid (x) means that only one set of chromosomes exists within a cell. Haploid sex cells (sperm or egg) are mated with haploid sex cells during **fertilization** to form a diploid (2×2) offspring, or **zygote.** In the process of meiosis, the cells must divide so that when the (haploid) gametes unite in fertilization, the (diploid) offspring have the same number of chromosomes as the parents. Diploid means that the cell has two sets of chromosomes. You are diploid and so is your neighbor's dog, but your sperm or egg is haploid. For instance, you have 46 chromosomes. If you mate with another person who has 46 chromosomes, your offspring would have 92 chromosomes! Meiosis produces sperm and egg cells with 23 chromosomes that unite to produce a normal human of 46 chromosomes. Mitosis asexually creates two identical daughter cells that are exact copies of the single parent. Meiosis creates sex cells that contain half the chromosomes of two parents in preparation for sexual reproduction.

Meiosis is a double division of the nucleus: meiosis I and meiosis II. Meiosis I is similar to mitosis in that the chromosomes duplicate before meiosis begins, allowing meiosis to start with homologous chromosomes. The process of meiosis can be summarized in eight phases:

Meiosis I

Prophase I—The nuclear membrane breaks down, chromosomes condense and become visible, and crossing over may occur. Paired homologous chromosomes join at a synapsis forming a tetrad (only in meiosis). A tetrad is the four chromatids from the original chromosome. **Crossing over** is a type of mutation that occurs at this time when parts of one homologous chromosome literally lay on top of or "cross over" and become attached to another chromosome creating a new genome and increasing the species genetic diversity.

Metaphase I—Each homologous pair of chromosomes contains one chromosome from each parent. The pairs of homologous chromosomes, which include two chromatids per pair, four total, migrate to and align along the cell's equator or metaphase plate. The random alignment of the homologous pairs of chromosomes along the equator in preparation for separation also increases the chance for genetic diversity.

Anaphase I—Homologous chromosomes move to opposite sides of the cell. Note: The chromatids do not separate at their centromeres; the chromosome is still made up of two chromatids; in mitosis the chromatids separate.

Telophase I and cytokinesis—Cytoplasm divides and the nuclear membrane reforms around the chromosomes creating two different cells. Both poles contain one chromosome from each pair of homologous chromosomes and remain diploid.

Meiosis II

Prophase II—The spindle fibers form again and attach to the chromosomes.

Metaphase II—The chromosomes migrate to and line up at the equator. Their centromeres attach to the spindle fibers.

Anaphase II—The spindle fibers pull the centromeres apart and the chromatids (now called chromosomes) migrate to opposite poles.

Telophase II—The nuclear membrane reforms around each of the four sets of chromosomes, cytokinesis forms four haploid sex cells.

The net result of meiosis is the creation of four haploid gametes or spores from one diploid parent cell. The haploid gametes (sperm or egg) may now unite in the process of fertilization to form a normal diploid organism. This graphic highlights Meiosis I and II.

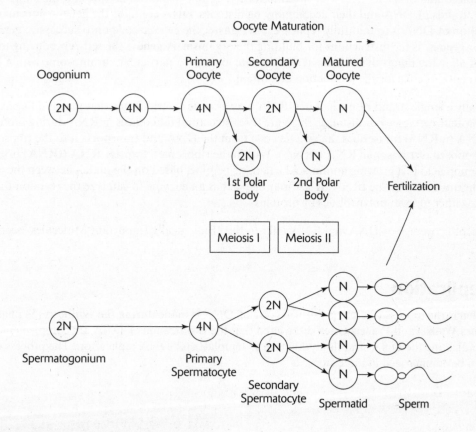

Molecular Basis of Heredity

The inheritance of traits is based on transferring genes that are passed on from parent(s) to offspring(s). Genes are a series of nitrogen bases that are part of the DNA, which is located on chromosomes of an organism. So the inheritance of your traits is based on the molecules that went into your DNA.

Structure and Function of the Nucleic Acids

Deoxyribonucleic acid (DNA) and **ribonucleic acid (RNA)** are the nucleic acids. All of your cells contain nucleic acids, which are polymers of nucleotides. A **nucleotide** is composed of a sugar, one of four nitrogenous bases, and one to three phosphate groups.

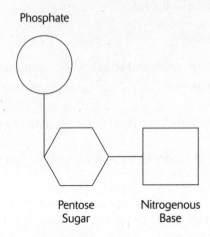

Phosphate

Pentose Sugar

Nitrogenous Base

DNA is a double strand of nucleotides that spiral to form a double helix. Eukaryotic chromosomes are largely made of long strands of DNA and their accompanying histones. DNA contains the genetic information for each cell. The function of DNA is to faithfully replicate and transfer the genetic code onto successive generations. The **genetic code** or **genome** is the instructions for building the organism. A **gene** is the self-reproducing molecular unit of heredity for all living things that is located at a definite locus on a particular chromosome within the DNA molecule and contains code for the production of protein.

RNA is normally a single strand of nucleotides. RNA may assume several forms that match differing functions, especially in protein synthesis. For instance, there are three structural differences in RNA during protein synthesis. Messenger RNA (mRNA) transcribes the genetic code from the DNA and transports it to the ribosomes, which are mostly composed of ribosomal RNA (rRNA). Within the ribosomes, transfer RNA (tRNA) brings the appropriate amino acid to a growing amino acid chain, or peptide, based on the match between the codon of the mRNA and the anticodon of the tRNA. RNA may also act as an enzyme to catalyze the reaction that bonds the amino acids together to form polypeptides or proteins.

For more in-depth coverage of DNA and RNA refer to the "Biologically Important Molecules" section earlier in this chapter.

DNA Replication

DNA replication is the process whereby a faithful copy of DNA is made during the synthesis (*S*) phase of the cell cycle. **James Watson** and **Francis Crick** discovered that the two strands of DNA are complementary and antiparallel, indicating the DNA strands could serve as templates for DNA replication. The process of DNA replication can be summarized in three steps:

1. An enzyme called **DNA helicases** unzips and straightens the DNA molecule by breaking the hydrogen bonds that hold the complementary nitrogen bases (rungs of the ladder) together. Replication forks are areas where the double helix separates forming a *Y*. The replication fork follows the DNA helicases as it unzips the DNA and provides a starting point for DNA polymerase.

2. Another enzyme, **DNA polymerase,** moves along the exposed DNA strands and adds complementary nucleotides to the exposed nitrogen bases according to the purine-to-pyrimidine base pairing rules (A-T, G-C). Interestingly the DNA polymerase always moves in the 3' to 5' direction on the DNA strands, meaning that the DNA polymerase on one strand is moving in the opposite direction of the DNA polymerase operating on the other strand. The DNA polymerase operating in the 5' to 3' direction creates **Okazaki fragments** or discontinuous DNA strands that are then bonded together by the polynucleotide ligase, an enzyme specific to this reaction.

3. **DNA ligase** is an enzyme that catalyzes the attachment of the strands back together to form the double stranded DNA double helix. When finished copying the DNA, the DNA polymerase detaches. The action of DNA polymerase creates two new double helix DNA molecules. The resulting DNA molecules each contain the exact nitrogen base sequence, which is also the same sequence as the parent DNA strand.

Protein Synthesis

Proteins serve many functions within an organism such as providing structure to your cells, working as enzymes to digest your foods, and making fur for your puppy. **Protein synthesis** occurs in two steps: transcription and translation. Transcription and translation make up the **"central dogma"** of biology: DNA → RNA → protein.

Transcription is the process whereby the genetic code contained within the DNA is copied to a messenger RNA or mRNA molecule (DNA → RNA). In eukaryotes, transcription occurs in the nucleus, but occurs in the cytoplasm of prokaryotes. Genes contain the instructions for building a specific protein. The genetic information from the genes is rewritten or transcribed to a messenger RNA (mRNA) molecule during the process of transcription. Unlike during replication, transcription occurs on select parts of the genome rather than its entirety, thus certain genes may be expressed more than others at a particular time based on the needs of the cell. Transcription can be described in four steps:

1. Transcription factors are specialized proteins that bind to a nucleotide promoter. The promoter is a DNA sequence that serves as the starting point location and signals the start of transcription. An enzyme, RNA polymerase, binds to the transcription factors.

2. RNA polymerase unzips the DNA strands which expose the nucleotides on each strand.

3. RNA polymerase matches or "reads" the nitrogen bases or gene sequence as it moves along the DNA strand in a 3' to 5' direction. The RNA polymerase assembles complementary ribonucleotides in a 5' to 3' direction to form a complementary pre-mRNA strand. Recall that in RNA uracil (U) replaces the thymine (T) found in DNA.

4. The RNA polymerase stops translating when it reaches a "stop" signal, signifying the end of a gene in eukaryotes or the end of a gene series in prokaryotes.

Transcription changes the genetic code in DNA into the genetic code in RNA. Like DNA replication, transcription uses DNA nucleotides as a template. However, in transcription the new molecule is a single strand of RNA, not DNA. Examine the following graphic and note the similarities between DNA replication and transcription.

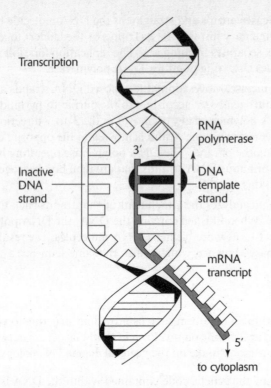

Before the pre-mRNA can leave the nucleus and take the genetic information to the ribosomes for transcribing into the specified protein, the pre-mRNA must be packaged as part of the post-transcriptional processing to become mRNA. A modified guanine (G) molecule forms a cap on the pre-mRNA to prevent its degradation by enzymes. Introns (DNA regions within a gene that do not code for a protein) are removed and the splicing of the remaining exons occurs to simplify the molecule and eliminate noncoding sequences. A poly-adenine "tail" is added to prevent degradation by enzymes and the new mRNA molecule is ready to leave the nucleus through a nuclear pore. The mRNA molecule is specifically organized so that each three nucleotide segments, called a codon, codes for a prescribed amino acid. The **genetic code** consists of $4 \times 4 \times 4$ or 64 possible "triplets" of nucleotide codons that encode for the 20 amino acids. The amino acids are linked together in translation to form the correct protein. Examine the mRNA codons in the following graphic and the amino acids that they encode. Note that the codons UUU and UUC code for the amino acid phenylalanine; and UGA is one of the stop "codons." One codon, AUG, serves two functions: it codes for methionine and also serves as the "start" codon.

Second letter

First letter	U	C	A	G	Third letter
U	UUU, UUC — Phe UUA, UUG — Leu	UCU, UCC, UCA, UCG — Ser	UAU, UAC — Tyr UAA Stop UAG Stop	UGU, UGC — Cys UGA Stop UGG Trp	U C A G
C	CUU, CUC, CUA, CUG — Leu	CCU, CCC, CCA, CCG — Pro	CAU, CAC — His CAA, CAG — Gln	CGU, CGC, CGA, CGG — Arg	U C A G
A	AUU, AUC, AUA — Ile AUG Met	ACU, ACC, ACA, ACG — Thr	AAU, AAC — Asn AAA, AAG — Lys	AGU, AGC — Ser AGA, AGG — Arg	U C A G
G	GUU, GUC, GUA, GUG — Val	GCU, GCC, GCA, GCG — Ala	GAU, GAC — Asp GAA, GAG — Glu	GGU, GGC, GGA, GGG — Gly	U C A G

Translation is the process where the language of the nucleic acids is translated into amino acids (RNA → protein). Translation occurs in the cytoplasm within ribosomes and can be described in seven steps:

1. The mRNA combines with ribosomal RNA (rRNA) and a transfer RNA (tRNA) carrying the amino acid, methionine, which is the start codon, in order to form a ribosome. The mRNA start codon, AUG, attaches to the P site on the ribosome. The anticodon of the tRNA carrying methionine binds to the start codon.
2. The codon in the A site of the ribosome attracts a complementary anticodon of a tRNA. The tRNA brings its specific amino acid and binds to the A site: codon-anticodon. Both the P and A sites are holding tRNA molecules with their specific amino acid.
3. Enzymes help covalently bond the adjacent amino acids together to form a dipeptide. The tRNA in the P site disconnects from its amino acid and detaches from the mRNA and migrates to find, bond, and possibly return with another amino acid to add to the growing peptide chain.
4. The tRNA and mRNA in the A site move into the P site bringing the trailing amino acid (protein) chain. The opening created by the departed mRNA presents a new codon in the A site.
5. Another specific tRNA brings the amino acid called for by the codon and binds with the exposed codon. The arriving amino acid in the A site bonds with the growing amino acid chain.
6. The tRNA in the P site detaches from the mRNA and leaves its amino acid.
7. Steps 2–6 are repeated until reaching one of the stop codons (UAG, UAA, or UGA).

Interestingly, the genetic code is often called the "universal code" because it appears to be almost the same in all organisms! Examine the following graphic, which shows the sequence of events that describes translation.

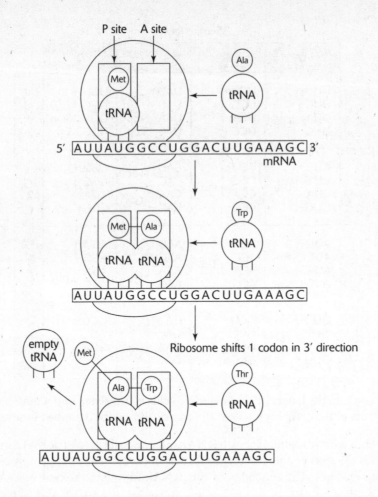

Gene Regulation

Gene regulation is a process whereby the cell determines which genes it will express and when they will be expressed. The control of gene expression may occur at several levels in a cell, although seldom during mitosis. Gene regulation is most noticed in the process of protein synthesis. Certain genes are turned on or off depending upon the needs of the cell. For instance, the gene sequence that controls the formation of structural proteins may be turned on if the cell is about to duplicate. Not surprisingly, both prokaryotes and eukaryotes are able to regulate the expression of their genes.

Prokaryotes, like bacteria, are small but their approximately 2,000 genes provide all of the information necessary to maintain and promote all their life functions. Prokaryote gene regulation in protein synthesis is controlled by an operon. An **operon** is a functional unit that contains: a gene sequence that codes for a protein, its **promoter** site, and the overall controller or **operator.** The operator is positioned to physically control the access to the genes. In most prokaryotes, the *lac* **operon,** which controls the metabolism of lactose, is the most common and best understood.

The function of the *lac* operon is based on the presence of lactose. If lactose is present in the prokaryote cell, lactose binds with the **repressor.** A repressor is a protein that binds to an operator and turns "off" the function of the operon. If no lactose is present, **regulatory genes** produce a repressor that binds with and turns the operator off. Regulatory genes code for proteins that regulate when genes start or stop coding for proteins that determine or affect a function, such as growth. The repressor blocks the RNA polymerase from binding to the promoter site thereby stopping the transcription of the **structural genes** that code for the enzymes that metabolizes lactose. This makes sense because there is no lactose present to metabolize. If lactose is present, the lactose molecules bond with the repressor to change the geometric shape of the repressor, causing the repressor to detach from the operator. Without the repressor, the operator is turned "on" and the operon proceeds with the transcription of genes leading to translation of enzymes leading to the metabolism of lactose.

Most gene regulation in eukaryotes occurs in the nucleus prior to transcription where the RNA polymerase binds to the gene. However, gene regulation often occurs during and after transcription. Like prokaryotes, eukaryotes need to be able to turn their genes "on" and "off" in response to changes in their internal and external environment. Although prokaryotes and eukaryotes both use regulatory proteins to facilitate gene expression, eukaryotes typically have more genes to coordinate, such as you, with roughly 26,000 genes in your genome. To complicate the situation, the genes are located on more than one chromosome. The following describes the most common type of pretranscription gene regulation in eukaryotes.

Eukaryotes use many different regulatory proteins called **transcription factors** to bind with the RNA polymerase to help orient the RNA polymerase on the promoter gene sequence: TATAAT, also called the **TATA box** or **Pribnow box.** Mutations or changes in the TATA box can affect transcription by increasing or decreasing promoter activity. Enhancers and promoters are located hundreds or thousands of nucleotides away from each other. **Enhancers** are sites on the DNA helix that are bound to transcription factors or **activators.** The enhancers cause the DNA to loop so that the activator on the enhancer connects with the promoter. When this happens, transcription proceeds, until these events occur, transcription does not proceed. **Repressors** are proteins that interfere with the binding of activators, thereby preventing transcription. Examine the following graphic to visualize the sequence of events.

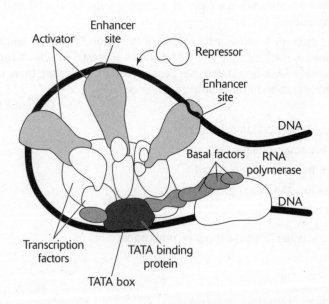

Gene regulation can also be altered after transcription. Before leaving the nucleus, the pre-mRNA is "packaged" so it can move through the nuclear pores and cytoplasm and not be cannibalized. The mRNA is also trimmed of excess baggage. **Introns** "intervening sequences" are long strands of noncoding nucleotides that are spliced out of the mRNA by spliceosomes. The spliceosomes then reattach the exons segments of the mRNA. **Exons** "expressed sequences" are the remaining portions of the mRNA that are translated into proteins. The speed of their activity regulates gene expression.

Mutation and Transposable Elements

A **mutation** is a sudden change in the DNA of an individual. Some mutations are good, some bad, but most have no effect. The following list highlights the various types of mutations:

- **Gene rearrangements**—Large-scale events that change the location of a gene on the chromosome. Gene rearrangements can be problematic because of the new gene regulatory system. Genes can move to new areas as part of a transposon, or moveable gene.
- **Point mutations**—Occur when a single nucleotide is changed.
- **Insertion mutations**—Happen when a section of DNA is inserted into an existing strand of DNA. Large insertions may alter the coding of the gene in extreme ways called a frameshift mutation. Insertion mutations often occur when transposons move locations. **Transposons** are DNA sequences that make up roughly 45 percent of the human genome and can move or transpose themselves to new locations on the genome. Transposons can either replicate and move or delete and move to a new position on a chromosome. In either case, the resulting gene sequence is drastically affected.
- **Deletion mutations**—Occur when sections of DNA are lost. Deletions often occur during meiosis. Deletions are opposite of insertions and both cause frameshift mutations.
- **Duplication mutations**—Happen when genes are duplicated and displayed twice on the same chromosome.
- **Inversion mutations**—Occur when entire gene sections are reversed on the chromosome.
- **Translocation mutations**—Happen when a piece of a chromosome breaks off and reattaches to a nonhomologous chromosome.
- **Frameshift mutation**—Often the result of other types of mutation. The most common frameshift mutations occurs when nucleotides are inserted or deleted. The codon is "read" in sets of three nucleotides or "triplet codon". When the original codon is mutated, the gene is read in the wrong three nucleotide sequence. Consider the frameshift mutation in the following sentence:

  Glen is great.

  Gle nis gre at. = original triplet codon gene sequence

  If 2 deletions occur it becomes: Gle nis rat.

  If an insertion occurs it becomes: Gle nis ara t.

  Glen is a rat is not the same as Glen is great

  Note: my first name is Glen.

The following illustration depicts the different types of mutations:

Types of mutation

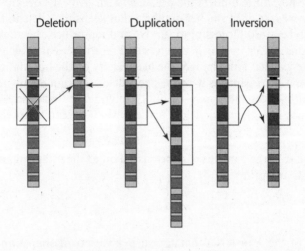

Deletion   Duplication   Inversion

Insertion

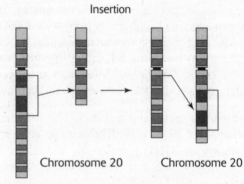

Chromosome 20   Chromosome 20

Chromosome 4   Chromosome 4

Translocation

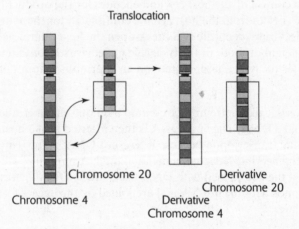

Chromosome 20   Derivative
                     Chromosome 20
Chromosome 4   Derivative
                     Chromosome 4

Mutations increase the **genetic diversity** of a population because they create new alleles. An **allele** is one of the alternate forms of a gene. If the new allele hinders the organism's survival, the organism may not survive to reproduce or reproduce at a slower rate or in smaller numbers that keeps the allele in the population. However, if the new allele helps an organism be more successful to survive and reproduce, the allele becomes multiplied in the population over many generations as that organism survives and reproduces at a faster rate or in larger numbers than competitors without the new allele. This changes the **biodiversity** of the population; some members have the new allele and some do not have it. If organisms with the new allele are dramatically more successful at survival and reproduction, organisms without the allele may die out or migrate. In that case, over time, there are no members of the population that do not have the new allele. This scenario may lead to **speciation** and **evolution** (see Chapter 3).

Interestingly, mutations that occur in the gametes may be passed on to the offspring, but mutations of somatic (body) cells are not transferred to offspring.

Viruses

Viruses are noncellular strands of DNA or RNA that appear in a variety of shapes and are enclosed within a capsid, or protein covering. Some viruses are pathogens, disease causing agents, that are much smaller than prokaryotes ranging in size from 20 nm to 250 nm (1 nanometer [nm] = 0.00000004 in.). Viruses do not grow, metabolize, produce waste products, respond to stimuli, reproduce independently, or worry about maintaining homeostasis. But, viruses do have the ability to enter a cell, either by force or trickery, and replicate themselves using the host cell for parts and nutrition. Are they alive? Most biologists believe viruses are nonliving. Glycoproteins are use to trick a cell into accepting the virus as one of their own.

Viruses have a major impact on the world's health and economy. The influenza virus, a.k.a the flu, killed around 22 million people during the flu epidemic of 1918–1919. RNA viruses are responsible for such diseases as AIDS, (caused by the human immunodeficiency virus [HIV]), influenza, and rabies; DNA viruses cause chickenpox, mononucleosis (mono), and warts. Certain viruses can even cause some types of cancer such a hepatitis B, which can lead to liver cancer. How does a virus infect a cell?

Viruses attach to the membrane of the target host cell and release their nucleic acid into the cytoplasm. The DNA or RNA of the virus assumes control of the host cell and encodes for the production of enzymes that make new viruses. Amino acids and nucleotides from the host cell are confiscated for the synthesis of viral proteins and nucleic acids. In the **lytic** cycle, viruses replicate and break open the host cell releasing new viruses to continue the invasion of new hosts in the neighborhood. In the **lysogenic cycle,** viruses continue to make new viruses in the host cell until triggered to enter the lytic phase whereupon an enormous amount of viruses invade the cellular community.

Interestingly, some RNA viruses, called retroviruses, contain a unique enzyme called reverse transcriptase, which uses RNA as a template to make DNA. The viral DNA is then inserted into a host. The process of reverse transcription is a reversal of normal transcription because RNA, not DNA, is the template. Recently scientists have used this concept in genetic engineering. Selected, individual mRNA molecules are isolated that correspond to a particular gene. The mRNA is then combined with DNA nucleotides, DNA ligases, and DNA polymerase. The nucleotides form hydrogen bonds with the mRNA and are joined by the ligases forming a DNA segment by using RNA, not DNA as the template.

Vaccines are available and effective for some viruses. Vaccines induce the immune system to produce antibodies that specifically attack certain viruses.

Some viruses do have a useful function. Certain viruses, called **bacteriophages,** infect bacteria. Bacteriophages are used in genetic engineering to insert desirable foreign strands of DNA into the DNA of bacteria. The bacteria then produce the desired product coded by the inserted DNA, such as insulin.

Prions and **viroids** may be the next human malady. Although not much is known about either at this time, a prion is a nonliving protein substance with no nucleic acid. Disease-causing prions work by causing an incorrect folding, which denatures the host cell proteins. The folded protein can no longer function. The folding is spread upon contact with adjoining proteins. Viroids are naked strands of RNA that attack plants (so far only plants) and alter their genetic functions thereby ruining the crop.

Molecular Basis for Genetic Disease

Genes are passed from parent(s) to offspring. Normally the process proceeds smoothly and without incident. However, occasionally mutations affect the way that the genes encode for a particular trait. The resulting genetic disease has a molecular basis and consequence.

Sickle cell anemia is a genetic disorder caused by the inheritance of recessive genes that code for abnormal hemoglobin that result in sickle-shape red blood cells rather than the normal disc-shape red blood cells. In certain parts of Africa, sickle-cells are helpful because they provide protection from malaria. Unfortunately, sickle cells also cause poor blood circulation and anemia.

Sickle cell anemia was the first genetic disorder that was discovered. Since then, much has been learned about the molecular basis of the disease. By analyzing the amino acid sequences of normal and sickle-cell hemoglobin, it was discovered that they differ by only one amino acid! Since this discovery, many different types of hemoglobin have been identified.

Hemophilia is a genetic disease cause by the inheritance of a sex-linked recessive gene. Persons with hemophilia do not have normal blood clotting. As a result, even minor injuries can be life threatening.

Factor VIII is the antihemophiliac factor (AHF) that is essential in blood clotting. In humans, AHF is encoded by a particular gene (F8 gene). Mutations of the gene prevent the formation of AHF and produce hemophilia. AHF is a glycoprotein that is normally found bonded to a stable blood complex. Activated by thrombin, the AHF dissociates and begins the coagulation cascade, a series of biochemical reactions that eventually activates more thrombin. Thrombin cleaves fibrinogen into fibrin. Fibrin forms the fibrous network that begins the blood clot. Blocking the formation of AHF prevents blood from clotting.

Cancers are caused by chromosomal mutations that lead to uncontrollable cell growth. More than 100 types of cancers are known and they all have their basis in genetics. Cancers arise from mutations of the genes that control cell growth. Proto-oncogenes encourage cell growth. Tumor-suppressant genes discourage cell growth. Mutation creates overactive proto-oncogenes that may become carcinogenic oncogenes that encode for excessive cell multiplication, which promotes tumor proliferation. Mutated or inactive tumor-suppressant genes fail to inhibit cell growth. Growing tumors receive nutrients via direct diffusion from the bloodstream and then form more direct supply lines.

The harmful effects of genetic mutations impact the physiology of the proteins they encode. Genetic diseases "live downstream" from their genetic cause, which makes them more difficult to diagnose.

Recombinant DNA and Genetic Engineering

Genetic engineering, a.k.a. genetic modification or biotechnology is a laboratory technique resulting in the direct modification of an organism's genome. Genetic engineering introduces heritable genes harvested or produced outside of an organism either directly into the host or into a carrier that is fused with the host cell to produce a product or event. Genetic engineering relies on the universality of the genetic code. For instance, the gene sequence that codes for insulin in humans will also code for insulin in bacteria. How does it work?

New methods of genetic engineering are continually being developed and refined, but the basics are manifested in one of the earliest successful experiments, the production of insulin. The process can be described in five steps:

1. **Restriction enzymes**—Bacterial enzymes that recognize and cut specific sequences of DNA, and identify and cut the needed DNA from an organism.

2. The specific DNA, such as the DNA that codes for insulin, is combined with the DNA of a vector with the help of DNA ligase to form recombinant DNA. **Recombinant DNA** is DNA made from two or more different organisms. **DNA ligase** is an enzyme that glues the ends of the new and existing DNA together. A **vector** is an agent that is used to carry the genes of interest into a host cell. Common vectors are viruses and plasmids. **Plasmids** are circular DNA molecules that can replicate independently of the host bacteria's chromosomes.

3. The recombinant DNA is taken up by or injected into the host cell.

4. The host cells are cultured and grown to produce more copies of the specific gene in a process called **gene cloning.**

5. Cells that successfully received the new genes are producing the desired product, such as insulin. The rest are removed in a process called **screening.**

The following graphic shows the step in the process of genetic engineering and the production of recombinant DNA.

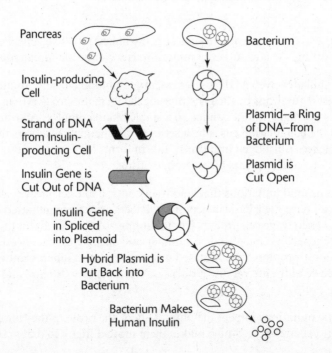

The original intent of genetic engineering was to harness the power of asexually reproducing prokaryotes, like bacteria, to mass produce a desirable product, like insulin. Since then transgenic plants and animals, such as the pigs that have the ability to synthesize human hemoglobin, have been created. Soon humans may have genes within their cells modified to remediate genetic disorders. Currently forensic scientists are able to positively identify individuals connected with a crime scene by multiplying small amounts of DNA found during the investigation.

Genome Mapping of Humans and Other Organisms

The human body contains nearly 26,000 genes. In 2003, the Human Genome Project completed the task of identifying and locating each gene on one of the 23 human chromosome pairs. A **gene** is a particular length of DNA that codes for a particular protein. A **genome** is the sum total of all of the genes in an organism. **Genome mapping** is the locating and assigning of genes to a particular region of a chromosome and determining the distance between genes on a chromosome. There are two types of genome maps: A **gene linkage map** pinpoints the location of a gene in relation to certain marker genes; a **physical genome map** is more precise because it shows the number of nitrogen bases between genes.

Why are genome maps valuable? Genes are spliced from chromosomes to make recombinant DNA that is used in genetic engineering to make a useful product. Knowing the exact location of a prescribed gene allows the researcher to extract the entire gene without cutting it too long or too short. Also the gene sequences for several genetic diseases like cystic fibrosis and Huntington's disease have been located and may be substituted in future genetic medical breakthroughs. Likewise the genome map for plants and animals may continue to produce transgenic organisms that produce a desirable product such as interferon for the treatment of cancer. Currently genome mapping of productive plants and animals continues along with mapping of disease-causing microbes.

Chapter 3

Classical Genetics and Evolution

Classical Genetics

Inheritance is the process in which characteristics (traits) or features are passed from one generation to the next. **Genetics** is the study of how genes transfer the characteristics or traits from parent(s) to offspring. During the 1860s, an Augustinian monk, **Gregor Mendel,** performed simple genetics experiments using a well-known pea plant, *Pisum sativum.* He carefully recorded the data from his experimentation and discovered many principles that are still true today. Mendel opened up the study of the gene and became the "Father of Genetics." **Classical genetics** or **Mendelian genetics** is based on the principles that Mendel discovered. **Molecular genetics** is the study of the mechanisms that describe genetics at the molecular level such as transcription and translation (see Chapter 2).

Although farmers had always experimented with improving their crops and livestock through selective breeding, Mendel was the first to keep accurate records and begin with a solid basis:

1. First he allowed the self pollination of pea plants for several generations to identify true-breeding plants. A **true breeding** organism is one that produces offspring with the same characteristics as the parent, such as yellow seed color. The true breeding pea plants were selected and identified as the **parental generation** or P_1 plants.

2. Next Mendel cross bred P_1 plants with different characteristics, such as purple vs. white flowers. He labeled the offspring of the P_1 generation the **filial generation** or F_1. Mendel discovered that the F_1 generation contained only purple flowers! The white trait was missing.

3. Mendel then mated the F_1 plants and referenced the offspring as the **second filial generation** or F_2. Mendel discovered that the hidden white flower trait reappeared in a few of the plants the F_2 generation. He meticulously counted the traits in each plant and discovered a **3:1 ratio** existed between plants with purple flowers and plants with white flowers. He further checked the results for all seven traits and found that in each case, a 3:1 ratio existed within each trait. For instance a 3:1 ratio existed for tall vs. short plants.

Mendel's experiments yielded several principles of sexual reproduction that still apply today:

- **Haploids**—For each inherited character, each parent contributes one gene (haploid) so the offspring has two copies (diploid) of each gene.

- **Different versions of genes**—The offspring carry two copies of each gene, but different versions of a gene, or alleles, exist. An offspring receives one allele from each parent and therefore may have a different combination of alleles than either parent. **Alleles** are different forms of the same gene that reside at the same locus or location on homologous chromosomes. For instance, an allele may code for yellow seeds while a corresponding allele codes for green seeds. **Homologous chromosomes** are pairs of chromosomes that carry genes for the same traits.

- **Dominant alleles**—Occurs when an organism has two different alleles for a trait and one allele is expressed and masks the effect of the other allele; the masked allele is the **recessive allele.**

- **Mendel's Law of Segregation**—During the meiosis of a diploid organism, the paired alleles separate or segregate and randomly combine during gamete or sex cell formation. Most organisms are **diploid** meaning that they possess a double set of chromosomes. Gametes are **haploid** meaning they contain one set of chromosomes. For instance, human cells are diploid and contain 46 chromosomes. Human sex cells, sperm and egg, are haploid and contain 23 chromosomes. Haploid sex cells from each parent combine during fertilization to form diploid cells.

■ **Mendel's Law of Independent Assortment**—Allele pairs separate from other allele pairs during meiosis. Mendel was experimenting to determine if alleles for different traits were linked together. For instance, do all tall plants produce purple flowers? His data indicated no linkage between alleles for different traits, meaning that the alleles of different traits sorted independently and randomly. In modern genetics, we now know that some linkages do occur (i.e., reside on the same chromosome), such as red hair and freckles. Mendel was very lucky that the traits he chose to study were on separate chromosomes.

Mendelian and Non-Mendelian Inheritance

The value of Mendelian genetics is predicting the results of a particular trait in a mating of two organisms. The probability of a trait can be determined by using a Punnett square to expose all possible allele combinations. How does a Punnett square work?

Punnett squares are an easy and effective way of predicting the probability of expressing an allele or trait in offspring. Consider the following simple mating:

1. The **dominant allele** is signified by a capital letter: P = purple flowers. The **recessive allele** is symbolized by a small case version of the same letter: p = white flowers.

2. Determine the genotype of the parents. The **genotype** is the genetic compliment and shows the alleles present for an individual, such as PP for purple flowers. The genotype may be **homozygous,** meaning that both alleles are identical such as PP or pp. The genotype may also be **heterozygous,** which means that the alleles are different, such as Pp. Interestingly, heterozygous organisms are **carriers** of the recessive trait, but do not express the recessive trait. Carriers of a recessive gene may not know they are carrying a particular trait, such as a genetic disorder caused by a recessive gene (cystic fibrosis).

3. Recall that if the dominant gene is present, the recessive gene is not expressed. In this instance the genotypes PP and Pp produce purple flowers; the genotype pp is the only genotype that produces white flowers. The **phenotype** for an organism is what trait is expressed by the alleles, either purple or white flowers in this example.

4. Construct a Punnett square.

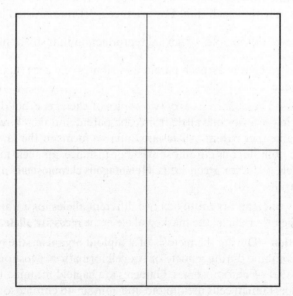

5. Separate the alleles and place the genotype of the female on the top section of the Punnett square and the male genotype along the left side. (Assume that A = tall plants and a = short plants; both parents in this instance are heterozygous for plant height.) To represent the female's contribution to the offspring, place one of her alleles in the two squares directly beneath her allele possibilities. For the male, spread each allele to the right and fill in the two boxes. Each box should have two genes in it; one from each parent.

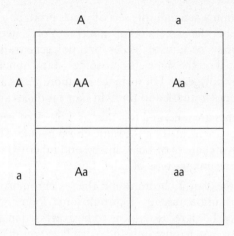

6. Record the possible genotypes for each of the four possible offspring types. In this example the possible genotypes are:

   AA, Aa, aa

7. Next, record the number of potential offspring with each genotype and convert to a percent:

$$AA = 1 \text{ out of } 4 = 25\%$$
$$Aa = 2 \text{ out of } 4 = 50\%$$
$$Aa = 1 \text{ out of } 4 = 25\%$$

What does this information tell you? In this sample cross, the *AA* and *Aa* offspring will be tall. Summed together, the probability of getting a tall plant is 75 percent. The only genotype that expresses a short phenotype is *aa*. The chance of getting a short plant is 25 percent.

In this example, the **genotypic ratio** is 1:2:1, (1 *AA* : 2 *Aa* : 1 *aa*). But the **phenotypic ratio** is 3:1, (3 tall plants : 1 short plant). Punnett squares are helpful in predicting the genotype and phenotype possibilities for an offspring. Punnett square can be used for more complicated matings that involve multiple genes, such as seed color, flower color, and pod color, rather than just one allele. What about inheritance patterns that do not follow the dominant-recessive rule?

Some matings produce offspring that are beyond what Mendel knew and are called **non-Mendelian inheritance.** Some of the more common non-Mendelian inheritance patterns include: incomplete dominance, codominance, multiple alleles, polygenic inheritance, gene linkage, and sex linkage:

Incomplete dominance—Occurs when neither allele is strong enough to dominate the other allele. There is no dominant or recessive allele; both genes are expressed in a blended fashion. The common example of incomplete dominance occurs when a certain red flower crosses with a white flower to produce a pink flower. Neither the red nor the white allele is dominant or recessive, so a blending of the alleles occurs.

Codominance—Similar to incomplete dominance except in codominance both alleles are displayed at the same time creating a third type of phenotype with no blending. In codominance there is no dominant or recessive allele because both alleles are expressed together in the phenotype of the offspring. Human blood types are the most common example of codominance. For instance a person with type AB blood has alleles for both type A and type B. Neither is dominant or recessive, but both are displayed. A roan-colored cow has a mixture of white and red hair giving it a distinctive color.

Multiple alleles—Occur where there are three or more alleles for a given trait. The ABO human blood groups are the best example because there are three alleles that might determine your blood type. Type A and type B blood are characterized by specific carbohydrates on the surface of red blood cells; type O has neither type of carbohydrate. Type A and B are dominant over type O. But type A and B are codominant to each other. As a result, it is possible to have a type A, type B, type AB, and type O blood.

Polygenic inheritance—A situation when multiple sets of genes produce a trait so that the more genes that are inherited for a trait, the greater the expression of that trait. Polygenetic inheritance was a problem for Mendel and more recent geneticists because the genes for a polygene trait may be located on different chromosomes or widely separated on the same chromosome. Many human traits such as height, weight, and hair color are influenced by polygenes. For instance the more genes a person possess for dark hair, the darker the hair; a mixture of genes for dark and for light hair produces an intermediate hair color.

Gene linkage—Occurs when genes are inherited together as a block of genes rather than individual genes. Gene linkage occurs when genes are located on the same chromosome. The closer the genes are located on the chromosome, the greater their chances of being linked and inherited together. Fair skin, red hair, and freckles is a common human gene linkage type of inheritance.

Sex-linked genes—Located on the X or Y chromosome, the sex chromosomes. The genotype of a female is XX and male XY. This is important because the Y chromosome, found only in males, is shorter than the X and therefore carries fewer genes. For a recessive gene to be expressed in a female, it has to be present on both chromosomes. For males, it may require only to be displayed on the single X chromosome. For instance, colorblindness is a sex-linked recessive gene that is present on the X chromosome. The shorter Y chromosome contains no gene for colorblindness. Females (XX) have a lower frequency of colorblindness because they have to receive the recessive gene for colorblindness from both parents. Recall that females inherit an X chromosome from each parent. If males (XY) inherit the recessive gene for colorblindness from their mother, they will be colorblind. Remember that males receive the X chromosome from their mother and Y from their father. The lack of a gene on the Y chromosome means that only one gene is responsible for the expression of that trait.

Probability

Probability in genetics refers to the likelihood of a specific occurrence, such as the genotypic results of a mating. Probabilities can be expressed in words but are also commonly expressed in percentages and fractions. For instance, when a homozygous recessive male and a homozygous dominant female mate, the offspring have a one out of two chance, or a 50 percent chance or half the chance of inheriting the dominant allele.

Determining the probability of a specific allele in a mating is a simple mathematical calculation: multiply the probability of that allele in each parent. For instance assume that you are looking for a trait encoded by gene A. If both parents are heterozygous (Aa) for that trait, then the offspring will have a 1 out of 2 or $\frac{1}{2}$ or 50 percent chance of inheriting the A gene from either parent. Because the offspring have a $\frac{1}{2}$ chance of inheriting the dominant allele from each parent, the event can be expressed in mathematical terms: $\frac{1}{2} \times \frac{1}{2} = \frac{1}{4}$. This indicates that the offspring will have a 1 out of 4 or, $\frac{1}{4}$ or 25 percent chance of inheriting the A allele from a mating of both parents.

What is the probability of the offspring inheriting the heterozygous genotype, Aa, if the parent's genotype is unknown? The Aa genotype can be inherited in two ways: one parent can contribute the dominant allele A and the other parent can contribute the recessive allele, a. Or, the parent who contributed the dominant allele could contribute the recessive allele, a and the parent contributing the recessive allele could contribute the dominant allele, A. Because there are two ways to produce the heterozygous condition, the probability for each occurrence is added. From the previous example, the probability of each parent contributing each combination is $\frac{1}{4}$, $\left(\frac{1}{2} \times \frac{1}{2} = \frac{1}{4} \right)$. In this scenario the probabilities are added so that $\frac{1}{2} + \frac{1}{2} = \frac{1}{4}$. This means that the offspring have a 1 out of 2 or $\frac{1}{2}$ or 50 percent chance of inheriting the heterozygous genotype, Aa.

To confirm your results, work a Punnett square.

Human Genetic Disorders

Many human diseases have a basis in their inherited genome. **Genetic disorders** are the harmful effects on an individual caused by inherited genetic diseases or mutations. Normally genetic disorders are recessive so they are expressed in a small percentage of the population, but are represented by a much larger number of carriers. A **carrier** is a person with a heterozygous genotype for a recessive disorder. The carrier may not know they carry the disorder because they have no outward symptoms because of the presence of the dominant gene. Because they do not show outward symptoms and therefore receive no treatment, carriers may transfer the gene to offspring. Carriers keep a recessive gene in the population. Some of the more common genetic disorders are listed here:

Cystic fibrosis—Cystic fibrosis (CF) is the most common fatal genetic disorder in the United States. CF causes the body to produce a thick mucus that clogs the lungs, and blocks the pancreas from releasing digestive enzymes. CF is a recessive disorder caused by a single gene.

Down syndrome—Mental retardation, learning difficulties, facial feature abnormalities, and poor infant muscle tone are symptoms of Down syndrome. Most cases of Down syndrome are not a result of inheritance. Rather an error in sex cell formation called nondisjunction results in the sperm or egg having an extra chromosome 21. If that sperm or egg is part of the fertilization process, the offspring inherit an extra chromosome.

Hemophilia—Failure of blood to clot. Hemophilia is a recessive, sex-linked disorder that is only carried on the X chromosome. The gene is more likely to be expressed in males because males only have one X chromosome, which they inherit from their mother. If the mother is homozygous for hemophilia, the male offspring have a 100 percent chance of inheriting the disorder. If the mother is a carrier, then the probability of a male offspring inheriting the disorder is 50 percent. The father's condition has no effect on any male offspring, but the female offspring have a 50 percent chance of inheriting the gene for hemophilia from a hemophiliac father.

Huntington's disease—A single abnormal gene located on chromosome 4 causes the gradual deterioration of brain tissue and shortened life expectancy. The gene is dominant, so the offspring only needs one copy of the allele to express the disorder. The probability of receiving the allele from one affected heterozygous parent is $\frac{1}{2}$.

Klinefelter syndrome—Males with Klinefelter syndrome have at least one extra X chromosome caused by nondisjunction during meiosis. Males with Klinefelter syndrome have a XXY genotype rather than an XY genotype, and suffer from infertility.

Sickle cell anemia—Most commonly inherited blood disorder in the United States. Sickle cell anemia is a recessive condition caused by the mutation of the hemoglobin-Beta gene found on chromosome 11. Normal hemoglobin is found in spherical red blood cells and transfers oxygen to the cells. Sickle-shaped red blood cells cause blockages in the circulatory system and are destroyed by their body, creating an anemic condition.

Tay-Sachs disease—Fatal, recessive genetic disease that results in the destruction of the nervous system. Tay-Sachs results from a defect in a gene on chromosome 15 that codes for a specific brain enzyme.

Turner syndrome—Females with Turner syndrome have only one X chromosome, creating an XO genotype rather than the standard XX genotype for human females. Turner syndrome is not inherited but results from nondisjunction during meiosis. Females with this disorder have nonfunctioning ovaries and tend to be shorter than average.

Interaction Between Heredity and Environment

The environment can and does affect the expression of certain genes. Natural environmental influences on the expression of a genotype tend to be an advantage for the organism. In fact, an individual's phenotype is sometimes dependent upon the conditions within the environment.

Natural environmental influences include the camouflage color change of the Arctic fox from red-brown in the summer to white during the winter. The action of the genes that produce the red-brown color during the warm summer months are blocked by the cold temperatures of winter. The blocked genes produce no color so the fur grows with an absence of color, or white. Another common example of the interaction between environment and heredity is displayed by the flowers of the common hydrangea. When planted in acidic soil, the flowers are blue, but they are red or pink when planted in neutral or alkaline soils.

Evolution

Evolution is a theory that explains the gradual change of characteristics within a population over time to better adapt to their environment. Evolution is also described as a change in a population over time. It was first proposed by **Charles Darwin** and was based upon discoveries by Charles Lyell and Thomas Malthus. **Alfred Wallace** proposed a similar theory as Darwin. **Thomas Malthus** described the **"Malthusian Dilemma,"** which states that populations grow exponentially and their food supply grows arithmetically. The Malthusian Dilemma suggests that at some point the struggle for food would cause wars, famine, and pestilence to ravage the human population back to levels supported by the food supply. **Charles Lyell** proposed that the earth is actually much older than anyone at the time thought—somewhere around 4 million years old (4.5 billion would be a closer estimate). Interestingly, Darwin avoided using the term evolution.

Convergent evolution occurs when organisms of different ancestry develop structures that are similar in adaptation to their environment. For instance, the legs of vertebrates and insects are used to perform locomotion but stem from different ancestors. **Divergent evolution** is the process whereby two or more related species become more and more different in response to differing survival strategies in different environments. For instance, the red fox is common in temperate areas and blends in well with the surroundings. The kit fox has adapted to a desert environment with a sandy color and enlarged ears for removal of heat.

Coevolution occurs when two or more species change together, usually in response to a change in the other organism. Some predators and prey; hosts and parasites; and other forms of interaction have led organisms to coevolve. For instance, slow antelopes are consumed by predatory cats leaving faster antelopes to breed the next generation of faster antelopes. In the next generations, slower cats may not be able to capture the faster antelopes, so the slower cats die off leaving only faster cats to breed the next generation… and so on.

Darwin and others believed that evolution is a gradual event that occurs continuously over long periods of time. This theory, called **gradualism,** needed the element of geologic time that was supported by Lyell's research. A more recent theory, punctuated equilibrium, is offered by American biologists, **Stephen Jay Gould** and **Niles Eldredge. Punctuated equilibrium** is the hypothesis that species remain relatively unchanged for long periods of time and then undergo periods of rapid change in response to dramatic changes in the environment.

Evidence

Scientists interpret many forms of direct and indirect evidence to support the theory of evolution:

> **Paleontology**—Fossil records show the increase in organism complexity over time. By using radiometric dating techniques, fossils can be organized into a timeline that shows an orderly pattern of evolution. Fossils also indicate an overall increase in the number of species between modern day and ancient times.

Comparative Anatomy—Darwin noted a distinct similarity in certain features, like forelimbs, even though they served different functions. For instance, birds use their forelimbs for flying; humans for lifting; and dogs for running. Darwin suggested that these structures had a common origin and the modifications were in response to environmental adaptations. **Homologous structures** are features, like forelimbs, that are derived from a common ancestor. The forelimbs of vertebrates such as the alligator, bat, and human contain bones that arose from similar embryologic structures. **Analogous structures** are features that serve a similar function but do not share a common ancestor. For instance the wings of modern birds and bats have a common function but different ancestral beginnings.

Embryology—Darwin was aware of the similarity between the embryonic developmental stages of certain organisms. He reasoned that they came from a common ancestor. Today we know that fish, birds, and humans have a similar appearance in the early embryonic stages. You have gill slits, a two-chambered heart, and a muscular tail in the early stages of your development, the same as a rabbit.

Comparative Biochemistry—One source of evidence for evolution is the similarity in proteins that exist between organisms. The closer the relationship between two or more organisms, the more proteins or amino acids they should have in common. A comparison of amino acids found in hemoglobin shows that humans and gorillas have only one amino acid difference! Humans and mice have 45 differences in amino acids, and humans and frogs have 67, indicating increasing distance from a common ancestor.

Molecular genetics and biochemistry support the similarity in the DNA and RNA composition of organisms. The processes of transcription and translation are also similar in most organisms. Finally, the genetic code is almost universal indicating a strong degree of kinship among organisms. DNA homology has become a more definitive tool in establishing relatedness. Partial or whole DNA strands are compared to determine the amount of similarity. In general, the greater the degree of similarity, the closer the relationship.

Artificial Selection—The domestic breeding of animals for a prescribed purpose has been an ongoing event. Darwin was aware that ranchers tried to breed their best stock to increase the value of their herd. He proposed that the forces of nature also selected for or against certain features and favored those organisms that were most well adapted to survive in a specific environment.

Mechanisms of Evolution

Evolution is measured as a change in populations, not individuals. A **population** is an interbreeding species of individuals. Populations evolve as the gene pool within the population changes. The gene pool changes for five main reasons: natural selection, mutation, genetic drift, gene flow, and nonrandom mating.

Natural selection is the basis of Darwin's theory of evolution. Natural selection occurs when the environment determines which organisms are best suited to survive and reproduce. Reproducing organisms pass their genes on to the next generation. Individuals that are not able to survive and reproduce do not transfer their genes. Natural selection causes an increase or decrease in the frequency of certain alleles in a population over generations.

Five factors underscore the process of natural selection:

- **Genetic variation exists within all species**—In any population, individuals have a slightly different genome. For instance, your genome allows you to look different from your friends—either in height, eye color, or body style. The same is true for the genetic compliment of other organisms—although the difference is often less obvious.

- **More offspring are produced than the environment can support**—At some point, the Malthusian Dilemma will occur when the geometric increase in the population exceeds the arithmetic increase in food supply. When this happens the competition between members of the same species that require the same food source becomes fierce and life-dependent. Some individuals do not receive enough food and die.

- **Environmental changes**—Create challenges for succeeding generations. Changes in the environment create pressure on the individuals to survive. Extreme changes may cause a species to become extinct before they are able to adapt or migrate. For example, in preindustrial revolution England, the peppered moth had a gray and black mottled color that gave them excellent camouflage on the bark of trees. In the late 1800s and early 1900s as soot coated the trees, the gray moths lost their camouflage, and the population of moths became increasingly melanistic becoming black over many generations. Interestingly, with pollution control in the 60s and 70s decreasing soot production, the peppered moth has returned to its mottled phenotype.

- **Extinction**—The process whereby an entire species dies out and its genome is lost.

- **Survival of the fittest**—Slight changes in the environment, such as increasingly cold winters, favor those individuals who are able to keep themselves warm during the cold times either by increasing their fat or fur layer, or moving to another area. Changes in the environment favor certain genetic variations over others allowing that genome to spread in successive generations as the parents survive and successfully reproduce. Individuals most fit for their environment survive, reproduce, and transfer their genes to succeeding generations. Over time, the population will contain the genetic variation(s) selected for by the environment as the less fit die off or fail to reproduce. The surviving individuals will reproduce until the next environmental change, such as increased competition by another species for the same food source, which will increase the environmental pressure and select in favor of those organisms with the best genetic variation to allow survival and successful reproduction and transfer of their genes.

Environmental fitness is the key to understanding natural selection. The phenotype of the individual determines their fitness. Better fitness is translated into more reproductive success. An organism's fitness may be the ability to find food, avoid predation; resistance to disease; or become bigger, stronger, faster, or smarter than the competition. The environment not only includes the physical factors such as temperature and location, but also biotic factors such as parasites and intraspecies competition. The ever-changing environment places the strain on populations to adjust to the new requirements. The environment therefore has an effect on the population structure.

Several types of natural selection affect the structure of a population: directional selection, diversifying selection, and stabilizing selection:

- **Directional selection**—Works when the environment selects one phenotype at the cost of all other phenotypes. Selecting for or against a phenotype also changes the genotype of the population over many generations. Directional selection favors a phenotype because of a specific environmental pressure. For example, directional selection is common when a population recolonizes an area after a major cataclysmic event, such as a volcanic eruption. Presently the most common example of directional selection is the resistance of a growing number of disease causing microbes to antibiotics. The antibiotics purposely select against certain genotypes/phenotypes to destroy the disease-causing germ. However, a microbe that has a genetic variation that allows the microbe to survive will continue to reproduce and change the population over generations. The following graph shows the change in a population due to directional selection.

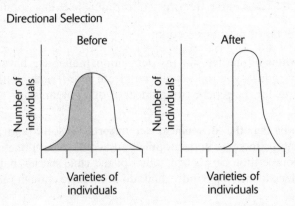

Directional Selection

- **Diversifying selection or disruptive selection**—Signals a changing environment and occurs when the environment favors extreme phenotypes at the expense of the intermediate phenotypes. Diversifying selection tends to increase genetic variability and can lead to two or more different populations. The well-published example of diversifying selection is the case where three different colored moths, black, white, and gray, all inhabited the same area. Through industrial pollution, the black and white moths had better camouflage than the gray morph. Predators gobbled up the gray moths but had difficulty locating the black and white moths. Over generations, the black and white moths predominated in the area with few or no gray moths present. Diversifying selection is the opposite of stabilizing selection. The following graph depicts diversifying selection.

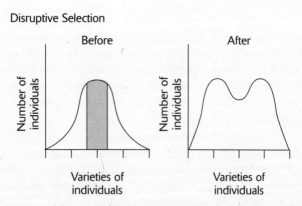

- **Stabilizing selection**—Signals a stable environment and occurs when the environment favors the intermediate phenotype and selects against and eliminates the extreme phenotypes. Stabilizing selection tends to decrease genetic variability and favors maintaining a more homogeneous population. An example of stabilizing selection in humans is the selection against heavy and light babies in favor of the medium weight babies. Stabilizing selection is the opposite of diversifying selection. Refer to the following graph as a reference.

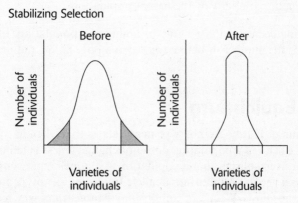

Mutations are a random change in the DNA sequence of a gene which results in a change in the resulting trait. Most mutations are harmless and not noticed, others are more pronounced (see "Mutation and Transposable Elements," in Chapter 2). Mutations are the only source of genetic variation. Other forms of genetic disturbance are a reshuffling of existing genes. Mutations that are advantageous to an individual soon become a part of the population's gene pool, thereby increasing the genetic variability of that population.

Genetic drift is the phenomenon whereby random or chance events change the allele frequency in a population. Genetic drift is most noticeable in small populations where the gene pool is small enough to be greatly affected by loss of the genetic variation. Genetic drift often happens when a splinter group leaves a population and establishes a new population at a geographic location that is reproductively isolated from the parent population. Gradually the two populations change as a result of their normal genetic variation. Genetic drift also occurs when a catastrophic event, such as a volcanic eruption, reduces a population to only a few survivors. The survivors represent a greatly diminished gene pool that differs greatly in genetic variance because of the loss of so many members.

Two types of genetic drift occur when a large population is reduced to a statistically small population: pioneer effect and fragmentation effect:

- **The pioneer effect**—Occurs when a small group breaks away from the larger group to colonize a new territory. Pioneer groups open new territories for future species expansion but also risk extinction. A pioneer group may be a single seed or mating pair that does not contain the genetic variability of the parent population. As a result, pioneer groups may not survive a change in the environment. Interestingly, pioneer groups often have tremendous reproductive success, but their genetic variability remains low and their extinction threat remains high.

- **Fragmentation**—Occurs when a natural or man-made disturbance, such as a damming a stream unselectively divides a population so that it contains less genetic variability that the once larger population. The net result of fragmentation is a small population becomes reproductively separated but still contains the genetic variability of the parent group. Because the fragmented group did not become isolated because of natural selection, the gene pool may contain the same alleles found in the larger group. Like the pioneer groups, fragmented groups that do not contain the genetic variability of the parent group may be an extinction threat because they do not have the genetic variability to survive a change in the environment.

Gene flow or gene migration is the emigration or migration of individuals from their parent population to another established population. New arrivals bring their genome with them and may establish it within the population over generations, thereby increasing genetic diversity. Exiting individuals take their gene pool with them and subtract from the genetic variability of the parent population.

Nonrandom mating or inbreeding decreases the genetic variability in a population. Inbreeding does not change allele frequency but it decreases the number of heterozygotes in a population and increases the number of homozygotes.

Hardy-Weinberg Equilibrium

The **Hardy-Weinberg equilibrium** or Hardy-Weinberg principle states that when in equilibrium with their environment, the frequency of alleles in a population does not change unless acted upon by evolutionary forces. The Hardy-Weinberg equilibrium establishes that a population in a nonchanging environment will demonstrate nonevolving tendencies such as a genetic equilibrium in allele frequency, genotype frequency, and phenotype frequency. The application of the Hardy-Weinberg equilibrium demonstrates why recessive genes are not lost to a population over time and can predict the allele and genotype frequency for each allele. The Hardy-Weinberg equilibrium assumes no genetic drift, gene flow, or mutations but relies on random mating.

The formula that represents Hardy-Weinberg equilibrium is:

$$p^2 + 2pq + q^2 = 1$$

Where

P^2 = the frequency of homozygous individuals with the dominant allele A

$2pq$ = the frequency of heterozygous individuals carrying A and a alleles

q^2 = the frequency of homozygous individuals with recessive allele a

Applying the Hardy-Weinberg equilibrium equation is easy. Assume a fictional population of 1,000 flowers where 700 flowers have the genotype AA = red; 200 are Aa = pink flowers, and 100 are aa = white flowers. To calculate the allele and genotype frequency for each allele, divide the total population into the each genotype as calculated here:

$$AA = \frac{700}{1,000} = 0.7$$

$$Aa = \frac{200}{1,000} = 0.2$$

$$aa = \frac{100}{1,000} = 0.1$$

Once the allele frequency is determined, the prediction of the allele frequency for the F_1 generation is easy:

1. First, determine the total number of alleles in the F_1 generation: 1,000 diploid ($2x$) individuals = $1,000 \times 2 = 2,000$ possible haploid (x) alleles.
2. Determine the probability of each allele: (see allele frequency calculation)

For allele A: $AA = 2$ alleles $\times 700$ individuals $= 1,400$

$Aa = 1$ allele $(A$ only$) \times 200 = \underline{\quad 200}$

Total $= 1,600$

The frequency for the A allele is therefore $\frac{1,600}{2,000} = 0.8$

For the a allele: $aa = 2$ alleles $\times 100$ individuals $= 200$

$Aa = 1$ allele $(a$ only$) \times 200 = \underline{200}$

Total $= 400$

Therefore the frequency of the a allele is $\frac{400}{2,000} = 0.2$

The Hardy-Weinberg equilibrium formula can also predict the F_2 genotype frequencies. Using the information from the F_1 generation, the only possible allele frequencies are $A = 0.8$ and $a = 0.2$. Note that $p + q = 1$; $0.8\ (p) + 0.2\ (q) = 1$.

The probability of an *AA* offspring is $p \times p = p^2$, or $(0.8) \times (0.8) = 64\%$

The probability of an *aa* offspring is $q \times q = q^2$, or $(0.2) \times (0.2) = 4\%$

The probability of an *Aa* offspring is a combination of the *p* and *q* because an allele must come from both parents: *Aa* or *aA* $= 2pq = 2(0.8)(0.2) = 32\%$

Note that the allele frequencies (*p* and *q*) are identical to the allele frequencies in the F_1 generation! Because there are no evolutionary forces (such as natural selection) acting upon the system, the hypothetical situation is in Hardy-Weinberg equilibrium. The allele and gene frequencies will remain identical with no phenotype change. Interestingly, the Hardy-Weinberg equilibrium demonstrates that sexual reproduction does not alter the allele frequencies in a population's gene pool. Finally, the Hardy-Weinberg equilibrium seldom exists in a population because of the evolutionary factors that impact the populations: natural selection, mutation, genetic drift, gene flow, and nonrandom mating. Note that the final four factors do not involve natural selection.

Speciation

A **species** is a population capable of interbreeding to produce viable offspring that maintain a common gene pool. **Speciation** is the creation of a new species by the genetic modification of an existing species by natural selection. Two mechanisms describe speciation: allopatric and sympatric:

- **Allopatric speciation** or **allotropic speciation**—Occurs when a geographic separation such as the formation of a mountain chain divides a species and prevents the two subpopulations from interbreeding. Initially allopatric speciation creates two distinct interbreeding populations from the same species. Once isolated, the two populations separately undergo natural selection, mutation, and genetic drift which contribute to genetic diversity. Eventually the two populations become so genetically diverse that interbreeding between the two groups, if it occurs, does not create viable offspring.

- **Sympatric speciation**—Occurs with species that continue to occupy the same geographic area. Reproductive barriers prevent the interbreeding of a species in sympatric speciation. Two reproductive barriers define sympatric speciation: prezygotic and postzygotic reproductive isolation. Recall that a **zygote** is the organism that is formed at the successful union of sperm and egg.

  - **Prezygotic reproductive isolation**—Any mechanism that prevents intraspecies reproduction prior to fertilization. There are five prezygotic reproductive barriers: territorial, seasonal, behavioral, structural, and genetic. Species that occupy the same territory may not inhabit the same niche, thereby diminishing their reproductive opportunities. Some species have different mating seasons. Environmental pressure such as increased competition for food changes behavior patterns and may alter the biological clock that stimulates the reproductive hormones. Large animals may not be able to successfully breed with much smaller animals of the same species due to size and orientation differences. Interspecies copulation, such as between a dog and a wolf may or may not produce compatible gametes.

  - **Postzygotic reproductive isolation**—Occurs after the zygote is formed. Three barriers exert pressure on the zygote: mortality, infertility, and longevity. A mortality barrier is created when the organism dies before reproducing due to incompatible genes, or inheritance of alleles selected against by the environment. An example of an infertility barrier is the zebroid, the sterile offspring produced by the union of a zebra and a horse. Longevity barriers do not affect the F_1 generation but prevent the successful reproduction in the F_2 generation due to infertility or an environmental incompatibility.

Phylogeny

Phylogeny is the evolutionary history of a species. Evidence that supports the history of a species is found by analyzing fossil records and analyzing radiometric and rock strata data. The phylogeny of the horse is one of the most studied. Horses began as small, dog-sized creatures and pass through many morphs before reaching the variety of sizes that constitute the modern horse.

Biologists create **phylogenetic trees** to show evolutionary relationships among organisms. Clues are also discovered by comparing the anatomy and physiology, contrasting the embryologic development, and comparing the DNA sequences of living organisms. The following model phylogenetic tree simplifies the relationship between the nine major animal phyla.

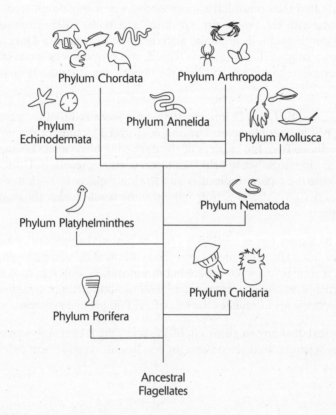

Origin of Species

Scientists estimate based on all the current evidence that the earth was formed approximately 4.5 billion years ago, and the earliest forms of life began around 3.5 billion years ago, give or take a couple of hundred million years. Many hypotheses attempt to explain how life on Earth was formed. Scientists attempt to explain the origin of life in replicable and measurable experimental terms. Several hypotheses provide explanations: Oparin or Primordial Soup model, Miller-Urey model, Bubble model, and the Fox model.

The **Oparin** or **Primordial Soup** model was developed by Oparin and Haldane in the 1920s and hypothesized that the early oceans were filled with a variety of organic molecules that joined together in a series of chemical reactions that were powered by energy from the sun, lightning, and volcanoes. Oparin also theorized that the early atmosphere did not contain an abundance of oxygen.

The **Miller-Urey model** or **Miller-Urey synthesis** combined those gases that were thought to be present in the early atmosphere: water vapor, ammonia, hydrogen, methane, and nitrogen. Miller and Urey subjected this gaseous mixture to a spark to simulate lightning and analyzed the results. They found a mixture of amino acids, fatty acids, and hydrocarbons—the building blocks of life! Recently scientists suspect that the absence of oxygen also precluded the protective ozone layer. The lack of a protective atmospheric layer would likely prevent the existence of stable methane and ammonia gases which were integral to the Miller-Urey model. Scientists have known this for decades. It is now thought that the primordial atmosphere was probably dominated by volcanic gases like CO, SO2, CO2, H2, and H2S along with N2. Follow up experiments to Miller's 1953 work using these conditions (no NH3 and no CH4) showed abiotic synthesis of amino acids and their precursors. Once again, this is how science works, when data and evidence suggest that a model is flawed, you propose a new one based on the best current data, and then conduct experiments to support or reject the hypotheses. If it stands up to decades of scrutiny, it becomes a theory.

The **Bubble model** was formulated by Louis Lerman in 1986, who theorized that the gases that formed the early organic molecules were trapped in ocean bubbles. The bubbles formed by underwater volcanic eruptions would protect the ammonia and methane from the hazards of the damaging ultraviolet (UV) radiation. The bubbles would also keep the reactants close together to help facilitate a chemical reaction. Upon reaching the surface, the bubbles would burst and release the organic molecules into the atmosphere or back into the water where they could continue to react. Energy from solar radiation and lightning would power the reactions once the organic molecules reached the surface.

The **Fox model** was created by Sidney Fox in the 1960s when he powered a mixture of amino acids with UV light and produced dipeptides. His experiments also showed how short chains of amino acids in water form microspheres. A coacervate is similar to a microsphere but is a mosaic of different molecules including amino acids and sugars. Both microspheres and coacervates demonstrate some cellular qualities. In addition he demonstrated that polyphosphoric acid simulates the role of ATP in protein synthesis.

Most scientists remain skeptical that any single origin of life scientific theory fully explains the process. However, it is a common belief among scientists that given the right conditions, certain chemicals do combine to form important biomolecules.

Extinction

Extinction occurs when a species dies out. **Extinction** is the loss of every member of a given species and their genetic complement forever. Extinction is related to natural selection because a species unable to adapt to a new environment will not be able to successfully reproduce as a competitor species. It is thought that the extinction of the dog-bear was brought about by smaller doglike animals that hunted in packs and were better competitors for dwindling food supplies. Fossil evidence confirms more massive extinctions like the Permian or Cretaceous extinctions. The **Permian extinction** or the "Great Dying" occurred about 250 million years ago and was the worst mass extinction. Approximately 96 percent of all marine species and 70 percent of all terrestrial species became extinct in a very short time span. The **Cretaceous (KT) extinction** occurred about 65 million years ago marking the end of the dinosaurs and about half of the known species of other organisms.

Human Evolution

The current thinking is that humans evolved from primates over the course of about 5–6 million years or so. Fossil evidence indicates a progression toward more sophisticated structural and cranial features that increasingly approach modern man. The following timeline illuminates some of the evidence:

4.4–4.2 million years ago: *Ardipithecus ramidus* was discovered by **Tim White** in Ethiopia in 1992 and described in 1994. Cranial bones and molars were dated at 5.8 million years old. The molars indicate that this species may be the first that branched away from the chimpanzees.

4.3–3.9 million years ago: *Australopithecus anamensis* was discovered, but not identified, by a Harvard research team led by B. Patterson on the west side of Lake Turkana in Kenya in 1965. The remains dated around 4 million years ago retained primitive cranial features but also contained more humanlike structural characteristics, such as the humerus bone. The bipedal species was distinctly different from *Ardipithecus ramidus*.

3.5–2.9 million years ago: *Australopithecus afarensis* contains an almost complete skeleton found by **Don Johnson** in 1973 which was dated around 3.2 million years old and named **Lucy.** Adult males were likely in the 5-foot range with shorter females, in comparison to the 2-foot height of *Australopithecus anamensis*. Lucy had pelvis and leg bones increasingly similar to modern day, but a cranial area that remained primitive.

3.0–2.9 million years ago: *Australopithecus africanus* was "discovered" by Raymond Dart in 1925 when a box of bones was handed to him from a cave in South Africa. Further discoveries characterized the primates as slight in build and similar to *Australopithecus afarensis* but featured a larger brain area but still not capable of speech. The teeth and jaw are more similar to modern man than a chimpanzee.

2.4–1.5 million years ago: *Homo habilis* was discovered by Mary and Louis Leakey in Tanzania, West Africa between 1962-1964. *H. habilis*, or "handy-man" is the first to show brain expansion and the ability to make and use tools.

1.8–300,000 years ago: *Homo erectus* was discovered by the Dutch anatomist, Eugene Dubois on the island of Java, Indonesia in 1891. *H. erectus* is the oldest known fossil of the human genus. Homo erectus walked upright (erect), was much larger than Australopithecus, and had facial features that resemble modern humans more than apes.

230,00–30,000 years ago: *Home sapiens neanderthalensis* was discovered by Phillippe-Charles Schmerling in the Engis Caves within Belgium. "Neanderthals" were present at the end of the Ice Age and were cold adapted: short appendages, short (5'5") and muscular frame. Evidence suggests increased tool sophistication and the first to use tools with pointed tips. They buried their dead.

120,000–present: *Homo sapiens* (modern man); includes Cro-magnon, an early modern *Homo sapiens,* which have been renamed "anatomically modern human" (AMH) because of their close relationship to current modern man.

Chapter 4

Diversity of Life: Plants and Animals

Diversity of Life

Currently there are an estimated 1,000,000 species of animals (there are currently more than 1.3 million named species with estimates of 4–6 million) and 300,000 species of plants that inhabit the earth. Life is found everywhere on the planet and abounds in a number of unlikely places. **Taxonomy** is the science of describing, naming, and classifying the vast diversity of living organisms into like-groups. Classifying organisms has been a human endeavor for a long time. In historic times, the classification of living organisms was based on their morphology, or outward appearance. In modern times, taxonomists rely on an analysis of genetic information to establish relatedness.

Why is it important to classify organisms? Aside from the aesthetics of organizing organisms and knowing the degree of kinship among organisms, scientists believe that an understanding of the relationships between various life forms help to maintain the biological diversity on Earth. Maintaining and increasing the biological diversity is important for our well-being both in creature comforts and in the essentials such as clean air and future medicines.

Classification Schemes

In 1735 **Carolus Linnaeus** published *Systema Naturae* which established **binomial nomenclature** as the taxonomic naming system. Binomial nomenclature is the scientific name for any organism which always contains two elements: genus and the "species modifier." The genus is a capitalized noun and the species modifier is an adjective. For humans, the genus is *Homo* and the species modifier is *sapiens. Homo sapiens* is the scientific name for humans written in binomial nomenclature and means "human knowing."

Linnaeus classified all living things as either plant (Plantae) or animal (Animalia). This simple classification system was good enough until the widespread use of microscopes identified microorganisms that did not conveniently fit into either category. In 1969 **Robert Whittake**r proposed five categories or **kingdoms:** Plantae, Animalia, Fungi, Protista, and Monera. Since then, three **domains** have been added to encompass the five kingdoms: Archaea, Bacteria (or Eubacteria), and Eukarya. Archaea and bacteria each compose a single kingdom of prokaryotes. Archaea contains the "extremophiles," those organisms that are able to live in extreme conditions, such as the prokaryotes that live in extremely hot geothermal vents. The Bacteria domain only contains bacteria. Eukarya contains the four eukaryote kingdoms: Protista, Fungi, Animalia, and Plantae. Representative organisms within Eukarya include Protista = algae and protozoa; Fungi = mold, mushrooms, and yeasts; Animalia = sponges, insects, fish, birds, reptiles, mammals, and you; Plantae = ferns, mosses, flowering plants, trees, and grasses.

How does the taxonomic classification system work? Organisms are sorted by degree of similarity beginning with the most general and largest divisions, domain and kingdom. The classification continues into closer and more homogeneous pools until the most specific level, species, is reached. For instance, consider the taxonomic classification of man:

- **Domain:** Eukarya
- **Kingdom:** Animalia
- **Phylum:** Chordate
- **Class:** Mammalia
- **Order:** Primates
- **Family:** Hominidae
- **Genus:** Homo
- **Species:** Sapiens

A closer examination of the human classification reveals the reasoning and similarities that form the taxonomic system. Note how the number of representatives in each level becomes fewer as the categories become more specific:

Domain: Eukarya = All members have a nucleus and cellular organelles. This largest classification includes all eukaryotes in the Protista, Fungi, Animalia, and Plantae kingdoms.

Kingdom: Animalia = All members ingest their food, are multicellular, and do not have a cell wall. This division separates the animals from the protists, fungi, and plants. Kingdom Animalia includes all organisms that you would normally call an animal. Animalia also contains organisms that you may not be familiar with such as the Porifera (sponges), Cnidaria (jellyfish and sea anemones), Platyhelminthes (flat worms), Nematoda (round worms), Mollusca (clams, oysters), Annelida (earthworms and leeches), Arthropoda (spiders, insects), Echinodermata (sand dollars, sea cucumbers), and Chordata (lampreys, reptiles, fish, you).

Phylum: Chordata = All members have a spinal column or backbone (vertebrates). The chordates include all vertebrates such as fish, amphibians, reptiles, birds, mammals, and you.

Class: Mammalia = All members have mammary glands to nurse their young. Mammals include horses, dogs, cats, apes, chimpanzees, lemurs, galagos, tarsiers, and you.

Order: Primates = All members have a high level of intelligence. Primates include lemurs, tarsiers, galagos, apes, chimpanzees, and you.

Family: Hominidae = All members are bipedal, or walk upright. Family includes apes, chimpanzees, and you.

Genus: Homo = Human. Genus includes *Homo habilis, Homo erectus,* and you.

Species: Sapiens = You.

Note how the number of different types of organisms decreases as the classification scheme becomes more specific. Also note that the characteristics of the organisms within the grouping become more similar as the groups become more specific.

Let's classify the common red maple tree, *Acer rubrum,* using the taxonomic classification system in reverse order beginning with the most similar collection of organisms and working to the most general:

- **Species:** Rubrum = red maple
- **Genus:** Acer = all maples
- **Family:** Aceraceae = contain vascular system
- **Order:** Sapindales = produces sap
- **Class:** Angiospermae = flowering
- **Phylum:** Tracheophyta = tissue level of organization
- **Kingdom:** Plantae = contains a cell wall, multicellular, makes own food
- **Domain:** Eukarya = contains a nucleus and cellular organelles

Cladistics and Phylogeny

Cladistics is a method of analyzing the evolutionary relationships between organisms to construct a phylogenetic tree (family tree). Cladistics is based on the idea that organisms should be classified by their evolutionary relationships as determined by their primitive and derived characteristics. Cladistic analysis examines primitive, or ancestral and derived characteristics to create cladograms which display the evolutionary relationships. A **cladogram** is a branching diagram that illustrates the evolutionary relatedness of organisms. A **primitive character** is a feature that all of the organisms under scrutiny possess, such as wings when studying birds. Primitive characters are not as useful in constructing a cladogram as derived characters. **Derived characters** are features that are possessed by some but not all of the members of the group, such as bipedal walking among mammals.

Organisms that are listed closely together on a cladogram share more derived characters than organisms located further away. The closer their location, the closer they are to a common ancestor. Organisms that contain similar derived characters have a greater evolutionary relationship; organisms located further away from each other have a lesser evolutionary relationship. Examine the cladogram shown here. Note that the human and mouse have a closer evolutionary relationship than a human and a frog.

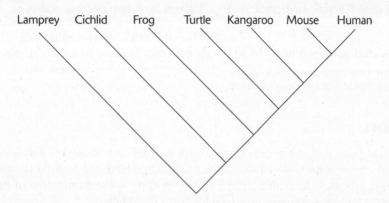

In **evolutionary systematics,** taxonomists allow weighted degrees of importance to certain characters which produces a more subjective analysis of evolutionary relationships than cladistics. Whereas cladistics treats all characters with the same weight, evolutionary or biological systematics emphasizes certain characters. For instance a cladogram may place alligators and sparrows in the same class, but evolutionary systematics would weigh the presence of feathers as a means of flight to place birds in a separate class from reptiles. Evolutionary systematics displays organisms on a phylogenetic tree. A **phylogenetic tree** shows the evolutionary relationships in two ways. The branching order relates group relationships and the length of the branch displays the amount of evolution. The closer organisms are located on a branch, the closer their ancestry. Organisms separated by one or more branches are not as related as organisms on the same branch. The phylogenetic tree describes the diversity of living organisms throughout history. Both cladograms and phylogenetic trees are models that represent an inference about evolutionary history. The abbreviated phylogenetic tree here shows the major branching of different Chordata, or chordates.

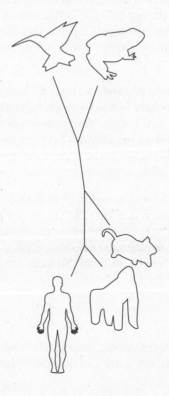

Plants

People sometimes underestimate the value of plants. Aside from generating the oxygen we breathe, the plant world contributes roots, stems, fruits, flowers, and seeds that serve as foodstuff and items of visual and olfactory pleasure for humans. Wood products such as paper and building lumber come from woody plants and plant fibers create cloth and rope. Certain medicines, such as digitalis, are derived from plants. So what is a plant?

Plants are multicellular, eukaryotic, and usually autotrophic organisms. Autotrophic means that they make their own food in a process called photosynthesis. Most plants are green because of the chlorophyll and other pigments they contain which are necessary for photosynthesis to occur. However, some plants, like the giant Rafflesia, are parasites and do not photosynthesize.

Plant Evolution

Looking back 500 million years ago, the oceans teemed with life, but little if any life was found on dry ground. Photosynthetic plant-like organisms, some animals, and protists inhabited the oceans. The photosynthetic green algae are thought to have provided the evolutionary pathway leading to the domination of plants on land. Interestingly, plants are today the dominant terrestrial life form by weight.

The linkage between green algae and land plants is supported by several pieces of evidence. Both land plants and green algae contain the photosynthetic pigments chlorophyll-a and chlorophyll-b. Other forms of algae only contain chlorophyll-a. Both land plants and green algae store their excess glucose as starch. Finally, both green algae and land plants have a cellulose cell wall.

It is thought that green algae inhabiting tidal pools may have developed specialized structures that prevent desiccation. The tidal pools were drenched or dry depending upon the tides thereby providing the opportunity for a genetic variation to adapt to the dry conditions of living on land. Before occupying the land, there were three adaptations that plants required: absorbing nutrients from soil, preventing desiccation, and reproducing in a dry area.

The evolution of plants to a terrestrial habitat required a reproductive adaptation. In water, the sperm cells simply swim or travel in water currents to the egg cells for fertilization. On land these structures were not useful so new adaptations were needed. In response, the plants created sperm enclosed in specialized structures called pollen. **Pollen** is designed to be dispersed in a variety of ways such as wind and animal pollinators rather than via water.

The adaptive jump to absorption of nutrients on land was difficult because green algae do not have or need roots. Scientists hypothesize that green algae may have formed a symbiotic relationship with existing fungi to help absorb nutrients and water. This idea has merit because today the majority of plants have a symbiotic relationship with fungi called mycorrhizae. The **mycorrhizae** relationship between plant roots and fungi form a network of interconnected absorbing tissues that greatly increase the capacity of modern day plants to absorb water and nutrients. Water is required by all cells for all biochemical reactions.

Leaving an aquatic environment created major desiccation challenges for plants. The earliest plants created a waxy covering called a cuticle that prevented water loss. The cuticle sealed the plant except for tiny structures called guard cells and stomata that allow the flow of the waste gas oxygen out and the required gas carbon dioxide into the plant. The guard cells are semicircular cells that expand by osmotic pressure and when paired together create an opening called a stomata between them. Stomata are usually found on the underside of leaves and allow the free flow of gases.

Major Plant Divisions

The plant kingdom is divided into two types of plants: nonvascular and vascular. **Nonvascular** plants are simple and do not have specialized tissues to transport water and nutrients. Nonvascular plants (bryophytes) do not contain true roots, stems, or leaves. Bryophytes do not produce seeds or flowers and seldom grow more than an inch in height. Mosses, hornworts, and liverworts are the only major groups of nonvascular plants.

Vascular plants are more complex than nonvascular plants. Vascular plants (tracheophytes) are characterized by specialized structures that transfer water and nutrients throughout the plant. Specialized **xylem** cells conduct water and minerals from the roots to the other plant parts. The xylem cells are stacked upon each other like joined water pipes and add structural support for the plant. Xylem tissue contains two types of specialized cells. Tracheids are thick-walled cells that form long thin tubes. The **tracheid** cells lose their cellular contents upon maturity leaving a cell wall surrounding an empty cell. The transfer of fluids occurs easily through the remaining empty area. Vessels are another specialized cell component of xylem. **Vessels** are larger tubes than tracheids and are usually featured in angiosperms (flowering plants). Both tracheids and vessels are perforated at the ends and have pores that allow the translocation of water and minerals from one tube into another.

Phloem cells transport food, usually photosynthetic sugars, from the leaves to the remainder of the plant. Phloem tissue is made of sieve tubes and companion cells. **Sieve tubes** are the porous conducting cells. Sieve tubes lack cellular organelles and only contain a cell wall, cell membrane, and cytoplasm. Each sieve tube is porous, allowing nutrients to pass freely between cells. **Companion cells** are located next to the sieve tubes and carry out cellular respiration and other metabolic functions for the sieve tubes. The graphic here shows the relationship between sieve tubes and companion cells.

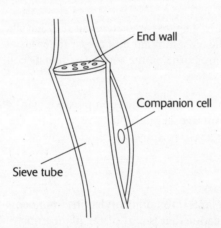

Xylem and phloem cells are located in the vascular bundle. The **vascular bundle** includes supportive and protective tissues in addition to the conducting tissues. Phloem is usually found closer to the exterior of stems and roots as well as the bottom side of leaves. Why are aphids normally found on the underside of leaves? That is the closest distance to the sugars that are transported by the phloem. Xylem is typically found near the center of roots and stems and on the topside of leaves. Interestingly the leaf vein contains the vascular bundle which terminates at the end of the leaf. The model of a vascular bundle including xylem and phloem tissue is featured here.

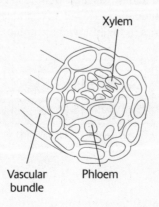

There are three main types of vascular plants or **tracheophytes:**

- Protected seeds = angiosperms: flowering plants
- Naked seeds = gymnosperms: pine trees
- Seedless = ferns

Angiosperms are the most developed and complex tracheophytes. They reproduce by using flowers that contain the sex cells and supporting organs. The seeds of angiosperms are enclosed by a female tissue called an endosperm that provides nourishment. The **endosperm** often develops into the fruit of the plant. So the angiosperm seed is often found inside of the fruit. Angiosperms represent more than 250,000 species of flowering plants including hardwood trees, grasses, crops, and roses.

Gymnosperms are mostly woody trees with seeds that are not protected by an endosperm, and are considered "naked". Gymnosperms produce seeds without the benefit of flowers. The four divisions of gymnosperms are:

- Cycadophyta = cycads
- Ginkgophyta = gingko
- Gnetophhyta = gnetae
- Coniferophyta = conifers

Most people have never heard of cycads, gingkos, or gnetae, but they have heard of pine trees. The **coniferophyta** or **conifers** are cone-bearers and are the most familiar and most numerous of the gymnosperms. Conifers are distinguished by the naked seeds that are borne on the surface of female cone scales. Typical conifers include pine, giant redwood, spruce, and cedar trees.

Seedless tracheophytes are represented by the ferns (division pteridophyta). Ferns produce spores via meiosis and store them on the underside of leaves during the sporophyte generation. The spores germinate in moist ground forming haploid plants that fertilize egg cells forming a diploid zygote.

Monocots and Dicots

Taxonomists also separate flowering plants into monocotyledons (monocots) and dicotyledons (dicots). A **cotyledon** or seed leaf is a leaf-like structure that is part of the plant embryo. The process of seed germination requires energy that is stored within the seed provided by the cotyledon or endosperm. Cotyledons function to transfer nutrients to the embryo. Plants with two or more cotyledons are called **dicotyledons** (dicots); a single cotyledon within a seed is called a **monocotyledon** (monocot). Monocots include about 25 percent of the flowering plants and are characterized as having leaves with parallel veins, fibrous roots, flower petals in multiples of 3, and a random vascular bundle arrangement. Grasses, asparagus, corn, rice, wheat, orchids, lilies, irises, agave, aloe vera, and palm are common examples of monocots. Dicots are evolutionarily younger older than monocots and are characterized by branched or networked leaves, vascular bundle in rings, taproot, and flower petals in multiples of 4 or 5. Common examples of dicots include: most flowers, vegetables, rag weed, peanuts, clover, and oak trees. Examine the features of monocots and dicots in the following graphics.

One cotyledon   Usually parallel   Usually in multiples of three   Scattered

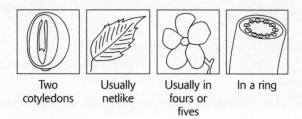

| Two cotyledons | Usually netlike | Usually in fours or fives | In a ring |

Anatomy

Plants have two organs systems: shoots and roots. Shoots include everything above ground such as stems, buds, leaves, and flowers. Roots contain everything below ground such as roots, rhizomes, and tubers. Typical plants contain the structures found in the following model.

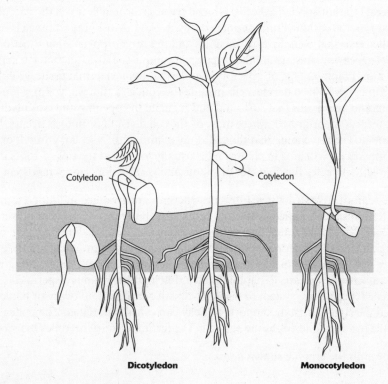

Shoots contain the following main structures:

Flower = the reproductive structure of angiosperms

Flower stalk = structure that supports the flower

Internode = the stem between two nodes

Lateral shoot or branch = a branching of the stem

Leaf = the major photosynthetic part of the plant

Node = the part of a stem where leaves, branches, or aerial roots may begin

Petiole = attaches the leaf to the stalk

Stem = the main support for the plant

Terminal bud = the bud located at the apex of the stem that contain meristematic, or growing, cells

Vascular bundle (not shown) contains xylem and phloem cells

Roots contain the following main structures:

Lateral root = horizontal roots that develop from the primary or tap rot

Root = the structure that absorbs water and nutrients from the surroundings and anchors the plant; may grow above or below ground

Root cap = protective tissues at the growing end of roots that protects the meristem or growing area of the root

Root hairs = tiny thread-like membrane projections that greatly increase the absorption capacity of the root

Primary or tap root = the main root that supports the plant, grows vertically and may store plant food; typically found in dicots (monocots have a fibrous root system)

Vascular bundle (not shown in model) = consists of xylem and phloem cells surrounded by cortex, made of ground tissue

Plants are made of several types of specialized cells. **Ground tissue** is located between the vascular and dermal tissues and is responsible for storing the carbohydrates produced by the plant. Most ground tissue is made of **parenchyma** cells which are thin-walled cells that contain large vacuoles and many chloroplasts that function in photosynthesis and nutrient storage. **Sclerenchyma** cells are another type of ground tissue that functions to support and strengthen. **Epidermal** cells are the most common type of cells found in dermal tissue. Dermal tissue covers the outside of plants that do not have bark. Other specialized dermal cells include the cuticle, a thin waxy, water-repellent layer of cells that covers the epidermis and **guard cells** that surround and regulate the opening and closing of the stomata. **Meristematic tissue** is the location of growth where most of the cell division or mitosis occurs. Meristematic tissue is composed of undifferentiated cells meaning that the cells may mature into vascular, ground, or dermal tissue. The **apical meristem** is the primary growth area in plants and is usually located at the tips of roots and stems. Lateral growth or secondary growth increases the diameter of plants and is caused by lateral meristem tissue.

The **flowers** contain the reproductive structures. Flowers structures are arranged in four concentric rings. Sepals occupy the outer whorl. **Sepals** are modified leaves that protect the bud (and subsequent flower) from damage. Sepals fold back to uncover the flower petals. The petals are often very colorful and may take on a variety of shapes and designs. **Petals** are designed to attract pollinators and make humans happy. Located inside the petals for easy access by pollinators are one or more stamens, the male reproductive structures. The **stamen** consists of a thread-like filament topped by an **anther** which produces haploid pollen. Each pollen grain is a sperm cell. The inner most part of the flower is the female reproductive system or **pistil.** The pistil consists of an ovary or haploid egg cell that produces a thin stalk, called the **style.** The style supports a sticky cap called the **stigma.** The pollen sticks to the stigma, sends a pollen tube to the ovary, and fertilizes the egg cell. The fertilized ovary becomes the seed.

Examine the model flower in the graphic shown here.

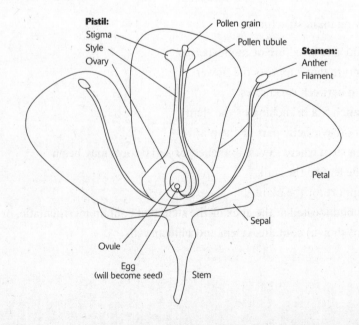

Although flowers receive the most attention, the foundation for a plant is the root system. Roots anchor the plant and absorb and transport water and nutrients to the rest of the plant. The structure of a root is designed for maximum absorption and transport. The vascular bundle containing xylem and phloem cells is surrounded by a single layer of **endodermis** cells and **pericycle** that function as a filter. The **cortex** surrounds the endodermis and vascular bundle and is made of thin-walled and loosely packed parenchyma cells. The parenchyma cells protect the vascular bundle and permit the movement of water and nutrients. A single layer of **epidermal** cells cover the root except for the root cap. The epidermis protects the root and maximizes absorption by creating root hairs. **Root hairs** are thread-like projections of the cell membrane that increase the surface area available for absorption. The **root cap** is made of thick-walled cells, usually dead, that form the leading edge of the root and functions as protection while pushing through the soil for continued growth.

The root structure can be divided into three sections. Behind the root cap, the **apical meristem** serves as the primary growth location. The apical meristem performs mitosis and produces cells that grow to form the **area of elongation.** In the area of elongation, cells grow and differentiate. As the cells complete their differentiation and mature, they form the **area of maturation** of the root. Refer to the following graphic for a generalized model of a typical root.

Stems support the plant, orient the leaves and flowers for maximum advantage, transport water and nutrients, and offer some photosynthetic sites. Some specialized stems also store food (potato) and water (cactus) for the plant. There are two types of stems: woody and nonwoody.

Nonwoody stems or **herbaceous** stems are characterized as soft, flexible, and green. Herbaceous plants are not well protected and usually die off after the first hard frost or freeze. Herbaceous stems are mostly made of meristematic tissue. The vascular bundles are surrounded by the cortex, composed of parenchyma cells, or ground tissue. In monocots, such as corn, the vascular bundle are scattered in the ground tissue. In dicots, such as most flowers, the vascular bundle is arranged in a ring around the stem. **Pith** is the ground tissue inside of the vascular bundle ring. View the graphic here that shows a cross section of a monocot stem and note the scattered vascular bundles.

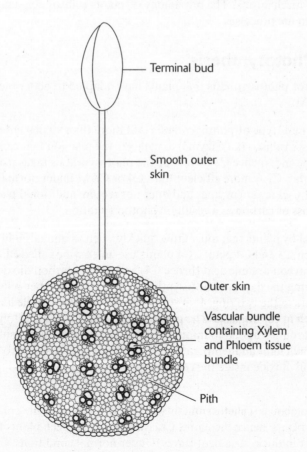

Terminal bud

Smooth outer skin

Outer skin

Vascular bundle containing Xylem and Phloem tissue bundle

Pith

Woody stems are strong because of the secondary tissue that is added as nonphotosynthetic support and protection. The secondary tissue is created by **the vascular cambium,** a thin layer of lateral meristematic cells located between the xylem and phloem. The vascular cambium creates secondary xylem on the inner side of the stem and secondary phloem on the outer side of the stem, thereby increasing the overall diameter of the stem. Layers of xylem become the major component of wood and form annual rings. The phloem cylinders combined with tough cork tissue to become the bark of the woody stem. The cork tissue is produced by the cork cambium located around the phloem. Mature woody stems are covered by many layers of wood and a thick bark to protect the plant. The heartwood is the central tissue of the stem where nonfunctional xylem provides support for the plant. The sapwood located around the heartwood contains active xylem cells.

Leaves are the primary site for photosynthesis and their organization is designed to maximize the capture and processing of solar radiation. In the larger sense, leaves contain photosynthetic mesophyll ground cells surrounded by epidermis with a central vascular system that connects the leaf to the branch via petiole. A water-retaining **cuticle** surrounds the leaf to prevent desiccation and adds a protective skin. The mesophyll is divided into a palisade and a spongy layer. The **palisade layer** is beneath the upper epidermis and is packed with chloroplasts that perform most of the photosynthesis for the plant. The vertical alignment of the columnar shaped palisade cells offers solar exposure to the maximum number of photosynthetic cells. The **spongy layer** is beneath the palisade layer and is composed of loosely packed parenchyma cells that allow the transfer of gases into (carbon dioxide) and/or out of (oxygen) the palisade layer. Below the spongy layer on the bottom side of the leaves are semicircular **guard cells** that create openings called stomata when osmotic pressure causes them to swell. Carbon dioxide gas needed for photosynthesis and the waste product of photosynthesis, oxygen gas, readily diffuse into/out of the **stomata.** The stomata are also the site of **transpiration**, the process where excess water is removed from the leaf.

Plant Physiology

How are plants able to absorb water and minerals, transfer and store food, respond to photoperiods, and photosynthesize via different mechanisms? The physiology of plants is intriguing and explains how the plant structures function to perform life processes.

C3, C4, and CAM Photosynthesis

There are three mechanisms for photosynthesis that plants have adapted to better meet their environmental restrictions: C3, C4, and CAM.

C3 photosynthesis is the "normal" type of photosynthesis that more than 90 percent of existing plant species employ. C3 photosynthesis uses rubisco (an enzyme) to catalyze the reaction that captures and binds atmospheric oxygen with a 3 carbon compound, (hence C3). Most of the photosynthesis takes place in the leaf and the stomata are open during the day. C3 is more efficient than C4 or CAM under normal temperature, moisture, and lighting conditions because it uses fewer enzymes and does not require additional plant structures. One drawback to C3 photosynthesis is the loss of carbon as a result of photorespiration.

C4 photosynthesis is employed by plants that must grow quickly, such as annuals and some crops like corn. There are several differences between C3 and C4 plants. C4 plants use an enzyme called PEP carboxylase to bind carbon dioxide forming a 4-carbon organic acid (hence C4) and deliver carbon dioxide directly to rubisco. Like C3, the stomata are open during the day, but photosynthesis occurs within inner cells, called **Kranz anatomy.** Kranz (wreath) anatomy refers to the two rings that surround the vascular bundle like a wreath. The inner ring bundle of sheath tissues is rich in chloroplasts. The purpose of Kranz anatomy is to provide a site where carbon dioxide can be concentrated around rubisco to minimize photorespiration. As a result, C4 plants photosynthesize faster than C3 plants under high light and temperature conditions. Water loss is also minimized because the PEP Carboxylase brings the carbon dioxide inside the cell faster allowing the stomata to remain closed to prevent transpiration.

CAM (Crassulacean Acid Metabolism) **photosynthesis** was first discovered in the crassulaceans, such as cacti, orchids, jade, and kalanchoe plants, hence the name. Crassulaceans are green plants that thrive in dry and cold areas because they store water in thick, succulent leaves. Under normal conditions, CAM plants convert carbon dioxide gas into an organic acid which is stored at night. The organic acid is converted back into carbon dioxide gas during the day and delivered to rubisco for photosynthesis. CAM plants are more water efficient than C3 or C4 plants for several reasons: They only open their stomata at night when evaporation is at a minimum. CAM plants can also "CAM-idle" meaning that they can keep their stomata closed day and night during extremely dry spells. Although they cannot CAM-idle forever, the oxygen created during photosynthesis is transferred for use in cellular respiration and the carbon dioxide given off by cellular respiration is a raw material in photosynthesis—making a closed loop.

Plant Hormones

Hormones are biochemical substances that are produced in one part of the plant and transported to another part of the plant where the hormones produce their effect. Plant cells produce hormones that cause physiological changes that regulate the growth, development, and function of the plant. **Tropisms** are involuntary responses whereby plants grow or turn in response to an environmental stimulus, such as a plant hormone. A phototropism is the bending of a plant toward or away from light; geotropisms are the bending of a plant toward or away from gravity. Stems tend to be positively phototropic because they bend to the light and negatively geotropic because they grow opposite of gravitational effects; roots display the opposite tropisms. One of the most interesting tropisms is the thigmotropisms (touch). An example of a thigmotropism is the collapsing of young mimosa plant's leaves when touched. There are five common plant hormones:

- Auxins are the most familiar type of plant hormone. **Auxins** are chemicals produced in the apical meristem that affect several areas of a plant. The most common auxin is indole acetic acid (IAA).

  How do auxins work? Let's examine a phototropic response to auxins. Auxins make the cell walls more acidic causing them to elongate. Auxins are denatured by light causing their concentration to be greater on the dark side of a stem. Elongation of the stem cells on the dark side of the plant causes the stem to bend toward the light thereby increasing its photosynthetic capacity.

  Auxins also inhibit bud production in stems in a process called apical dominance. Apical dominance keeps the pyramidal shape of the plant allowing greater photosynthetic surface. Pruning the apical meristem removes the auxin-producing area which allows the buds to grow, creating a more bushy plant. The graphic here shows the affect of auxins on cell elongation.

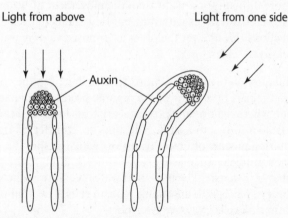

- **Abscisic acid** helps maintain winter dormancy in plants. Abscisic acid is produced in mature leaves and prevents the germinating and growth of seeds and developing leaves during the winter. It also helps form the layer of abscission between the leaf stalk and the stem, allowing the leaf to fall off during autumn without harming the plant. It also triggers closure of stomata in response to water stress.

- **Ethylene gas** is produced by most plants to help with the ripening process and the dropping of fruit and leaves from trees. Commercially ethylene is added to speed up the ripening of certain crops that are harvested before they fully ripen, such as bananas and tomatoes. Ethylene also helps to loosen hard-to-pick fruit like blackberries and blueberries, allowing them to be harvested in mass by a picking machine.

- **Gibberellins** are growth-regulating hormones that are produced in developing shoots and seeds. Gibberellins stimulate fruit development, seed germination, and rapid growth through stem elongation. Commercially gibberellins are used to enlarge certain seedless fruit such as Thompson seedless grapes, apples, and mandarin oranges.

- **Cytokinins** are growth-regulating hormones produced in the root tips that stimulate mitosis in cells to promote growth in roots and stems. Cytokinins also slow the aging process in plants and are commercially sprayed on vegetables and cut flowers to keep them fresh.

Photoperiods

Photoperiodism is the growth and flowering response of plants to the length of the nights in the day-night cycle. Light sensitive chemicals in the leaves respond to changes in the amount of darkness and trigger the growth and flowering response as a seasonal effect. Commercially the seasons can be manipulated by adjusting the amount of darkness in a greenhouse. Short-day plants, like poinsettias are given extra darkness to force them to bloom in time for Christmas. Long-day plants, like irises, are given extra light to produce blooms in early spring. The growth and flowering of day-neutral plants is independent of the day-night cycle.

Water and Nutrient Uptake and Translocation

Plants must obtain water from their environment. Water is initially drawn into the root hairs by osmosis. The solute concentration is greater inside the cell, which draws water into the roots hairs creating a root pressure. The root pressure moves the water into the xylem in an unending column from the roots to the leaves. Water molecules stick to each other because of hydrogen bonding in a phenomenon called cohesion. However, water molecules stick to the walls of the xylem by adhesion. Water molecules are drawn through the empty xylem tissue (remember mature xylem has no cellular organelles) by cohesive forces that pull the water column upward when water in the leaves is lost by transpiration or used in photosynthesis. As water evaporates via transpiration it creates a siphoning effect on the remaining water in the xylem. On the underside of most leaves, two kidney-shaped guard cells surround an opening called a stomata. As photosynthesis occurs, sugars and ions such as K^+, Cl^-, and H^+ are transported into the guard cells followed by the osmosis of water. As the water pressure increases the guard cells swell and create the stomata opening. The opening of the stomata is regulated by photosynthesis at just the right time to allow carbon dioxide to enter and oxygen to leave the plant.

The movement of nutrients is more difficult for a plant than the movement of water. First, unlike xylem cells, phloem cells still have cytoplasm which interferes with nutrient flow; phloem cells must handle a variety of compounds that move in all directions throughout the plant as opposed to only water. Further, nutrients do not diffuse through membranes as easily as water.

Although food is mostly manufactured in the leaves, it must be distributed to the entire plant. Source cells, like photosynthetic leaf cells, refer to the part of a plant where organic products are made for use by other parts of the plant. A "sink" is the location where the organic products are translocated. **Translocation** is the process where organic compounds are moved from a source to a sink. Nutrients are transferred from the source cells into the phloem tissue by the energy requiring process of active transport which pushes the nutrients through a cell membrane against a concentration gradient. Increasing sugar concentration in the phloem causes water from the xylem to be drawn into sieve tubes by osmosis. The increased water pressure in the sieve tubes pushes the nutrient-water solution through sieve plates into adjoining phloem cells. The final part of translocation occurs when the nutrients are pushed into sink cells by active transport.

Plant Reproduction

Reproduction in plants is essential for the continuation of the species. The reproductive cycle in plants contains a haploid and a diploid stage. This **alternation of generations** includes the haploid gametophyte, or gamete-producing stage, and the diploid sporophyte or spore-producing stage. The cycle includes both a gametophyte and sporophyte stage. Gametophytes produce haploid sperm and eggs (gametes). Eggs are produced in specialized structures called an archegonium and sperm are created in an antheridium while spores are produced in a sporangium. The diploid sporophyte generation makes haploid spores through meiosis. The haploid gametophyte generation makes the gametes that unite in fertilization to become the diploid zygote. The model for alternation of generations is depicted in the following graphic.

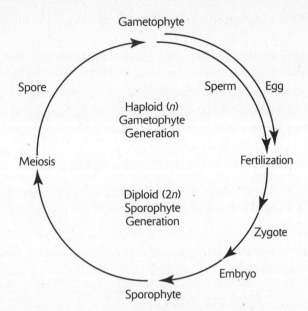

Reproduction in nonvascular plants and in seedless vascular plants is similar and commonly characterized by the life cycle of a fern plant. The generalized cycle can be summarized in three steps:

1. The barely recognizable haploid gametophyte generation produces haploid eggs in the archegonium and haploid sperms in the antheridium.

2. Sperm and egg unite in the process of fertilization to form a diploid sporophyte zygote. This is the first step into the sporophyte generation.

3. The zygote performs mitosis and grows. The mature diploid sporophyte undergoes meiosis to create haploid spores. The haploid spores fall onto favorable growing conditions and grow into male and female gametophytes. This is the first step into the gametophyte generation.

The cycle continues. Follow the haploid and diploid generations in the graphic shown here.

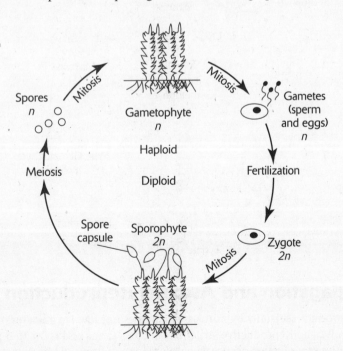

Reproduction in gymnosperms shows a dominant diploid sporophyte generation, like a pine tree. The life cycle of a pine tree can be summarized in five steps:

1. A diploid zygote forms when a haploid sperm fertilizes a haploid egg. The diploid zygote begins the sporophyte generation.

2. The zygote develops into a dormant embryo, which along with the surrounding tissue forms a seed. When mature, the seeds are dispersed usually by birds or wind and hopefully land in favorable growing conditions.

3. The embryos undergo mitosis and grow into the familiar sporophyte, such as a pine tree.

4. The pine tree produces both male and female cones, which perform meiosis to produce spores. The spores mature into gametophytes which perform mitosis to produce the haploid sperm and eggs. This is the beginning of the gametophyte generation.

5. Pollination occurs and the sperm fertilizes the egg to form a diploid zygote.

Reproduction in an angiosperm also displays the dominant sporophyte generation, the flowering plant. The life cycle of a typical angiosperm is unusual because of a double fertilization event. Angiosperm reproduction can be summarized in four steps:

1. Fertilization creates a diploid zygote. The zygote and surrounding tissues of the ovule develop into a seed. This begins the sporophyte generation.

2. The seed undergoes mitosis and grows into the mature diploid sporophyte, such as a flowering plant. Adult sporophytes undergo meiosis to produce haploid spores.

3. The spores mature into gametophytes. The female gametophytes, or eggs, grow inside of the ovules; the male gametophytes, or pollen, are formed in the anther of the stamen.

4. Each pollen grain contains two sperm cells. One sperm fertilizes the egg to form a diploid zygote; the other sperm cell performs a double fertilization by combining with two haploid cells creating a triploid ($3x$) cell. The triploid cell develops into the endosperm that provides nourishment for the embryo.

Examine the life cycle of an angiosperm in the graphic shown here.

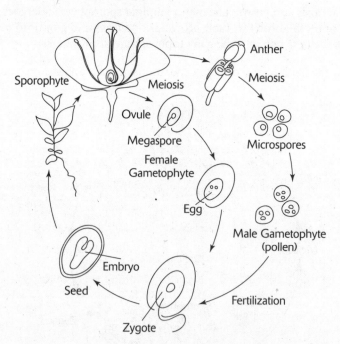

Vegetative Propagation and Asexual Reproduction in Plants

Some plants are able to reproduce asexually by mitosis which does not involve gametes or fertilization. Asexual reproduction by plants involves nonreproductive structures such as stems and roots that produce identical clones as the parent plant. **Vegetative reproduction** occurs when plants use nonreproductive parts to create offspring. Vegetative reproduction has several advantages. It is faster than sexual reproduction and the offspring receive a genome that has proven successful in that environment. A single plant can colonize an entire territory over a relatively brief period. The disadvantage of vegetative propagation is the lack of genetic diversity that allows members of the species to survive a changing environment. Commercially, vegetative reproduction, or propagation, is common in growing potatoes and irises. There are five main ways that plants vegetatively reproduce:

1. Runners or stolon are horizontal above ground stems that grow their own roots then develop a new plant, such as strawberries, airplane plants, and Bermuda grass.

2. Rhizomes are underground runners that develop their own roots and develop another plant, such as irises, ferns, and sugar cane.

3. Corms are very short, thick, underground storage stems that are similar to bulbs but with thin, scaly leaves such as gladiolus and crocus.

4. Bulbs are short underground storage stems that grow into new monocot plants, such as onions, amaryllis, and tulips.

5. Tubers are fleshy underground storage stems which develop new plants after a dormant season, such as potatoes and caladiums.

Germination, Growth, and Differentiation

Seeds contain plant embryos that are able to remain dormant until the arrival of favorable growing conditions, such as adequate soil moisture levels and appropriate temperatures. Seeds sprout or **germinate** when water and oxygen penetrate the seed coat and cause the tissues to swell, bursting the seed coat and allowing the young plant to grow. The emergence of the root is the first sign of growth.

Plants grow by adding new cells onto the tips of their growing regions not by elongating cells to excessive lengths. For instance, items nailed to a tree like a birdhouse or fence do not increase in distance from ground level as the tree grows. The **meristematic region,** or meristem, is the area of a plant that undergoes rapid cell division, or mitosis, to create new undifferentiated cells for growth. The **apical meristem** is the growth region of plants that is found in the tips of roots and stems. Apical meristems are areas of undifferentiated cells that produce the primary growth in plants. Primary growth adds to the length of a plant, not the width. The new undifferentiated cells mature and **differentiate** to become the primary tissues, such as vascular, dermal, or ground tissues that become the plant's leaves, stems, and roots.

Secondary growth is stimulated by the end of the primary growth. Secondary growth is caused by **lateral meristem** areas that increase the amount of vascular tissue in a plant to compensate for the increased need of water and nutrients that extend beyond the capacity of the primary tissue. As a result, secondary growth adds to the width of a plant and is most apparent in woody plants. Secondary growth produces secondary tissues in two meristem regions, the cork cambium and the vascular cambium. The cork cambium forms under the epidermis within the bark. The cork cambium produces cork cells that surround and protects the vascular cambium. The vascular cambium produces the vascular tissues and is located beneath the bark. As an example, woody stems develop annual rings which are formed when the vascular cambium adds a layer of secondary xylem tissue. The cork cambium and secondary phloem constitute the bark. The simplified graphic here shows the location of the secondary growth areas.

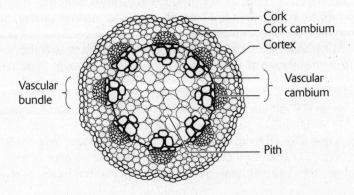

Cork
Cork cambium
Cortex
Vascular bundle
Vascular cambium
Pith

Animals

The kingdom Animalia contains an assortment of organisms such as your dog, horse, and you; but also contains creatures that do not resemble "animals." The initial classification of animals separates invertebrates (no backbone) like a mosquito from vertebrates (backbone), like you. **Invertebrates,** like sponges, worms, and insects, do not have an internal backbone. Arthropods, mollusks, and crustaceans are also considered invertebrates because they have an exoskeleton but no backbone. But amphibians, reptiles, birds, and mammals are **vertebrates** because they have a backbone. Interestingly, there are more invertebrate than vertebrate phyla. What does such a diverse mixture of creatures as are found in the animal kingdom have in common? Animals share several features:

- **Heterotrophic**—Cells do not contain cell walls or chloroplasts so they cannot make their own food.
- **Mobility**—Muscle cells and other specialized structures allow animals at some stage of their life cycle the freedom of movement.
- **Multicellular**—Composed of more than one cell that form specialized tissues and organs, except for sponges; small cell size remains relatively constant throughout the animal kingdom; the size of your skin cells is the same size as the cells in a bird's stomach or the cells in the lungs of a lizard.
- **Sexual reproduction and diploidy**—Almost all animals reproduce sexually with haploid gametes contributed by a male and female which produce a diploid offspring.
- **Embryology**—Except for sponges and chidarians, the zygotes of all animals begin as a blastula or hollow ball of cells and go through gastrulation, which forms the three primary germ layers: ectoderm, endoderm, or mesoderm that produce the tissues and organs.
- **Symmetrical anatomy**—Most animals exhibit some form of symmetry in their body styles: radial symmetry occurs when the body is circular-shaped with body parts arranged around a center point, such as a sand dollar; and bilateral symmetry occurs when the body can be divided into two identical or mirror-image halves, like you.

Animal Evolution

Scientists think that during the Precambrian period (approximately 2 billion years ago), prokaryotes (cyanobacteria) on primitive Earth photosynthesized and added significant amounts of oxygen into the atmosphere. Increased oxygen in the atmosphere allowed the formation of ozone (O_3) in the upper atmosphere. Ozone made the earth a more acceptable place to live by filtering the harmful ultraviolet (UV) rays from the sun. How were the first eukaryote cells formed?

Although scientific skepticism surrounds evolution and how the first eukaryotes began, scientists have developed the **endosymbiotic theory.** Endosymbiosis states that bacteria were engulfed and formed a mutualistic relationship with larger cells. The bacteria performed certain biochemical reactions for the cell, such as aerobic respiration, and the cell provided protection and nutrients to the engulfed bacteria. It is thought that the engulfed cells became the mitochondria and reproduced within the cell. A significant amount of evidence supports the endosymbiotic theory. Mitochondria cannot be made by a cell unless parent mitochondria are part of the cell. Mitochondria have their own genome contained within a circular DNA structure that is separate from the double helix DNA of most cells. So cells do not code for the production of mitochondria—only the existing mitochondria can perform their reproduction. Mitochondria have ribosomes for making protein that resemble bacterial ribosomes more than eukaryote ribosomes. Streptomycin blocks protein synthesis in bacteria and mitochondria but not in eukaryote cells. Mitochondria are enclosed by a double membrane as if the host cell placed its own membrane around the existing membrane of the invading bacteria. It is thought that these cells became the first animal cells.

During the Paleozoic Era about 600 million years ago multicellular marine animals appeared in abundance. At some point, estimated at 530 to 600 million years ago, marine animals developed protective exoskeletons and more complex body systems that allowed them to survive on land. Movement onto the land quickly followed the "Cambrian Explosion" between 533 and 525 million years ago, when the number of animal phyla proliferated in a very short period of geologic time to an estimated 100 different phyla. Interestingly, most of these phyla became extinct during the P-T or Permian extinction that started the Mesozoic Era or the K-T or Cretaceous-Tertiary extinction at the end of the Mesozoic Era. The varied anatomy that evolved during the Cambrian explosion formed the arthropods (insects), echinoderms (starfish), mollusks (clams), and chordates (worm-like animals that evolved into the vertebrates).

Vertebrates evolved from the protochordates into fishes, amphibians, reptiles, birds, and mammals. However, the K-T mass extinction created an environmental change that did not allow reptiles like the dinosaurs to survive and reproduce, thereby ending the age of the reptiles. The Cenozoic Era began about 65 million years ago and is called the age of mammals because the mammals that survived the K-T extinction radiatively adapted to fill niches that were once held by dinosaurs and other extinct organisms. Fossil traces of the earliest primates are dated about 35 millions years old and modern humans are thought to have appeared around 40,000 years ago.

Animal Phyla

The 10 major phyla of the animal kingdom are listed next in order of simplest to most complex:

- **Porifera**—Sponges do not look like the common image of an animal and do not have a typical radial or bilateral symmetry. Sponges have specialized cells, but are the only animal that does not have tissue-level organization.
- **Cnidaria**—Cnidarians are mostly marine animals that exhibit tissue-level organization. Every member of this phylum possesses nematocysts or stinging cells that are used for defense and prey capture. They are composed of two cell layers and lack a complete digestive system and have no respiratory, circulatory, or excretory system. Hydra, jellyfish, anemones, and corals are typical examples.
- **Platyhelminthes**—Flatworms have paper-thin, ribbon-like body structure that exhibits bilateral symmetry. Platyhelminthes is the first phylum to exhibit cephalization (head) which is a mass of nerve cells; and the third germ layer, mesoderm, which gives rise to their muscular, digestive, and reproductive system. Flatworms are both free-living in water or soil and are parasites living inside off their hosts. Examples include planaria, tapeworms, and the Chinese liver fluke.
- **Nematoda**—Roundworms are sexually reproducing thread-like worms with bilateral symmetry and a nervous system but no circulatory system. Nematodes are everywhere, including the soil, where they eat bacteria and detritus. Almost every living organism has been parasitized by a nematode. Parasitic nematodes include hookworms, pinworms, trichinosis, the popular intestinal worms, and *C.elegans*.
- **Annelida**—Annelids are bilaterally symmetrical segmented worms that have tissue and organ-level organization. Although no respiratory system is required, annelids have a closed circulatory system, a nervous system with a ventral nerve cord, and a sexual reproductive system. Annelids are both aquatic and terrestrial and include the common earthworm and leeches.
- **Mollusca**—Adults are bilaterally symmetrical with bodies divided into three parts: head, foot, and visceral hump. They have a true coelom or body cavity that includes internal organs (visceral hump). Most have a soft body while some are covered with a hard calcium exoskeleton. Mollusks have a radula, a sharp tongue-like structure that is used for scraping algae and other food from surfaces. Members of mollusca include snails, clams, squid, oysters, and octopus.
- **Arthropoda**—Arthropods are the most plentiful phylum thanks to the insects. Almost 70 percent of all named animal species are insects. Arthropods have an external skeleton (exoskeleton) that sheds during molting or growing. Arthropods have an open circulatory system, compound eyes, jointed appendages, and some have wings. Common examples of arthropoda include insects, crabs, bees, spiders, grasshoppers, mosquitoes, lobsters, and millipedes.
- **Echinodermata**—All echinoderms are marine animals with an endoskeleton. Young exist as free-swimming bilaterally symmetrical larvae and become radially symmetrical as adults. Many species can regenerate a lost body part. Examples include sea stars, brittle stars, sand dollars, sea cucumbers, and sea urchins.
- **Invertebrate chordates**—Invertebrate chordates are all marine animals that are bilaterally symmetrical. At some point in their growth, they have a hollow dorsal nerve tube, a dorsal cartilaginous rod called a notochord, and gill slits. Some invertebrate chordates are fish-like while others look like flukes or are attached like plants. Although not very common, examples include sea squirts, acorn worms, and amphioxus.

- **Chordata**—The chordates possess a bony or cartilaginous endoskeleton that protects internal organs and provides shape and structure, a backbone that surrounds and protects the spinal cord, and a skull that surrounds and protects the brain. Chordates also have a complete digestive system, closed circulatory system, ventral heart, and a tail at some point in their development. Chordates include fish, amphibians, reptiles, birds, and mammals.

Vertebrates are a subphylum of the chordates. The following six classes of animals are vertebrates:

- **Chondrichthyes**—Chondrichthyes are fish with a cartilaginous skeleton and placoid scales that make the skin feel rough. They breathe through gill slits and can lay eggs or give live birth. Common examples include sharks, rays, and sawfishes.
- **Osteichthyes**—Osteichthyes is the largest class of vertebrates. It includes bony fish with a swim bladder, two-chambered heart, paired pectoral and pelvic fins, and dorsal, anal and caudal fins. Bony fish have a lateral line of sensory organs called neuormasts that detect vibrations and help the fish find food as well as avoid becoming food. Common examples include salmon, piranha, catfish, perch, trout, and anchovies.
- **Amphibians**—Amphibians are considered close evolutionary descendants of fish. Like fish they lay eggs without shells in water and are cold-blooded (ectothermic) animals. Unlike fish they have pulmonary veins, a three-chambered heart, and come with four limbs and four toes on each webbed foot. Even though they do possess lungs, respiration is mostly through the skin which requires that their skin remains wet. Common examples include frogs, toads, and salamanders.
- **Reptiles**—Reptiles are considered evolutionary descendants of amphibians with better land adaptations. Like amphibians, they are ectothermic, have a bony skeleton, separate sexes, and most lay eggs. Unlike amphibians, reptiles have dry epidermal scales, paired limbs with five toes, have a three-chambered heart, and respire through lungs. Lizards, snakes, and turtles are common examples.
- **Aves**—Birds are considered evolutionary descendants of reptiles with four major differences: feathers (although recent findings indicate that certain dinosaurs may have been covered in feathers) are modifications of the epidermis that provide insulation, protection, and enable flight; bills are toothless mandibles that function instead of teeth; furcula is the "wishbone" that prevents the collapse of the chest cavity during flight; and endothermic (warm-blooded) with a four-chambered heart and hollow bones. Robins, buzzards, eagles, turkeys, ducks, sparrows, cardinals, pheasants, and your pet canary are common examples.
- **Mammalia**—Mammals are diversified to occupy an array of niches. There are three features that only mammals possess: hair, mammary glands, and three inner ear bones. Mammalian characteristics also include four-chambered heart, large cerebral cortex, internal fertilization, and live birth. Humans, cows, whales, apes, and dogs are common examples.

Life Functions

Life functions are tasks that an organism must perform to remain alive and fulfill their life cycle. Life functions include: digestion, circulation, respiration, excretion, nervous control, contractile systems and support (muscular and skeletal system), integument, immunity, reproduction, and the endocrine system.

Digestive System

Animals are heterotrophic organisms that do not make their own food but receive it from other sources. In most cases, the food most be broken down from a variety of large organic molecules into smaller forms that can be used by the cells. **Digestion** is the process of converting food into nutrients that are usable by the cells. Herbivores, like horses, are animals that survive by only eating plants; carnivores, like leopards, eat herbivores; omnivores, like bears and you, eat everything.

The food ingestion and digestion techniques of animals are interesting. Sponges filter small particles of food that happen to pass through pores in the sponge. The sponges are the only animals that digest their food inside of their cells. Although this technique sounds easy, it limits the size of the food source to only those substances that can pass through their membrane and fit into the cell. Most animals digest their food within a digestive cavity where sigestive enzymes help break down food that can be much larger than can cross the limited size of the permeable cell membrane holes, so the food enters via energy-requiring mechanisms of the consumer.

Cnidarians and platyhelminthes have an extended gastrovascular cavity with no anal opening that performs digestion. No cell specialization is needed because every cell is exposed to the digestion process.

Annelids and arthropods are somewhat similar because they both have a one-way gut with a mouth and anus. Ingested materials are stored in a crop, an expandable portion of the esophagus, before their physical grinding and chemical digestion in the gizzard. The digested food is then absorbed across the intestinal epithelium.

Oysters and other bivalve mollusks filter water and feed on the nutrients that are trapped in a layer of mucus on their gills. Parasitic worms attach to their hosts and suck the nutrients out of their blood. Echinoderms thrust a portion of their stomach out of their mouth where digestive juices liquefy the food which is then ingested.

Fish use a digestive system that is similar to digestion in all vertebrates. Food is ingested via a mouth and passes through the esophagus into the stomach. Their liver (gall bladder) secretes bile and their pancreas secretes pancreatic juices into the small intestine. Digested food is absorbed through the inner lining of the intestines and undigested food exits the body through the anus. Note the similarities between the digestive system of a fish and yours.

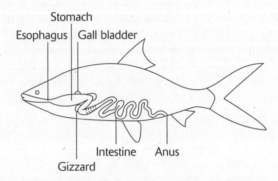

Birds (Aves) are similar to fish except birds have an expandable crop to hold large meals and two-chambered stomach. In the first chamber stomach acids chemically break down the food. In the second chamber, or gizzard, the contents are physically digested into smaller pieces. Undigested food exits through the cloaca. Interestingly, the cloaca is a common collecting chamber that serves the digestive, excretory, and reproductive systems.

Complicated digestive patterns occur in omnivores because of the variety of foods that their digestive system must simplify. The human digestive system is the best example of an extensive digestive system because humans have the most varied food sources of any organism on Earth. Human digestion occurs in specialized structures that create a unique environment to digest the variety of foods that you are known to eat. The main structures include the mouth, esophagus, stomach, and small and large intestine. Other specialized organs, like the liver, gall bladder, and pancreas add digestive chemicals that help digestion:

- Your **mouth** mechanically digests food by the chewing action of the teeth and tongue (mastication), and chemically digests food by the mixing of saliva. Three pairs of salivary glands produce saliva which contains amylases. **Amylases** are enzymes specific to the breakdown of carbohydrates into monosaccharides or simple sugars. The tongue pushes the masticated bolus of food toward the pharynx, which triggers a swallowing response.

- The **esophagus** receives the food from the mouth and transfers it to the stomach. The thick-walled esophagus is a muscular organ that moves the food toward the stomach in rhythmic muscular contractions in a process called **peristalsis.** Peristalsis causes the smooth muscles to contract behind the food pushing the bolus into the stomach. Interestingly, reverse peristalsis (vomiting) is something that most people try to avoid. No new digestion takes places in the esophagus. The 5- to 10-second trip to the stomach allows the digestion that began in the mouth to continue, however.

- The **cardiac sphincter** is a circular muscle with the esophageal wall that surrounds the opening to the stomach. The sphincter is designed to prevent the acid reflux from the stomach from backwashing into the esophagus. Failure of the sphincter to close properly allows acid-soaked foods to regurgitate and irritate the lining of the esophagus. This irritation of the lining is a process commonly called heartburn, or acid indigestion, or it may cause the more serious GERD (gastroesophageal reflux disease).

The kidney-shaped **stomach** is an expandable muscular organ that churns the bolus of food and adds gastric juices to form chyme. Gastric juices are a combination of hydrochloric acid and the digestive enzyme pepsin. The hydrochloric acid denatures the three-dimensional protein structures into protein chains that are then cut into smaller pieces by the pepsin. Specialized parietal cells in the stomach lining secrete hydrochloric acid which converts pepsinogen into pepsin. Chief cells located in the stomach lining secrete pepsinogen, the nondigestive form of pepsin. Note that pepsin only works in an acidic environment. (The stomach has an approximate pH of 1.5.)

Why doesn't the hydrochloric acid dissolve the lining of the stomach? Sometimes it does, forming ulcers. The stomach lining prevents ulcers by secreting a protective mucus covering. Stomach peristalsis churns the mixture between two to six hours before releasing it through the pyloric sphincter into the small intestine.

- The **small intestine** in an adult is somewhere around 20 feet long, and lies in a coiled position in the abdomen. The small intestine is the organ where most of the food digestion and absorption occurs. The small intestine receives the chyme and submits it to a completely different chemical environment. The first part of the small intestine, called the duodenum, secretes digestive enzymes and receives pancreatic juice from the pancreas, and bile from the liver (gall bladder). The pancreatic juice is made of bicarbonate and enzymes. The bicarbonate neutralizes the acid (from the stomach) chyme and creates a more alkaline or basic environment. The digestion of proteins began in the stomach and continues in the small intestine with two major enzymes, trypsin and chymotrypsin. Bile breaks up large fat globules so that the pancreatic enzymes called lipases can finish the job. Another common enzyme is amylase, the same one found in saliva, which digests starch into maltose; however, the major source of amylase is in pancreatic juice. Pancreatic juice contains a plethora of other enzymes, like the ribonucleases RNAase and DNAase, that actively digest other macromolecules.

Absorption of foods mostly occurs in the jejunum, the next section of the small intestine. Villi and the microscopic microvilli are epithelial projections within the small intestine that increase the absorptive surface area of the small intestine. Nutrients diffuse into the capillaries while amino acids and sugars are actively transported into the capillaries within the villi where they are carried to the liver for metabolism or whisked away to other parts of the body. Fatty acids and glycerol, the digested products of lipids, are absorbed by lymphatic tissue called lacteals in the villi and also eventually enter the circulatory system. The final absorption of digested foods occurs in the ileum, the last segment of the small intestine. The remaining indigestible food is passed onto the larger intestine.

- The **large intestine** or **colon** is designed to absorb water and minerals. Balancing the water content of the body via reabsorption in the large intestine requires coordination with the nervous system. Material moving through the small intestine too quickly produces diarrhea, or watery feces; conversely, moving materials through too slowly causes constipation, or dry feces. Both phenomena can be instigated by illness.

Although no human digestion takes place in the large intestine, a colony of bacteria synthesize several useful compounds, like vitamin K and several of the B vitamins. The resident microbes also help by compacting the undigested and unabsorbed mixture into feces. Interestingly, a strong regimen of antibiotics may wipe out or minimize this colony of microbes and create other problems for the host. Feces mostly consists of indigestible foods, like cellulose, bile pigments, and a host of bacteria. The feces is stored in the rectum, the final segment of the large intestine until stimulated by peristalsis to move through anal sphincters and out the anus.

Examine the structures that contribute to the digestion of your foods in the following graphic.

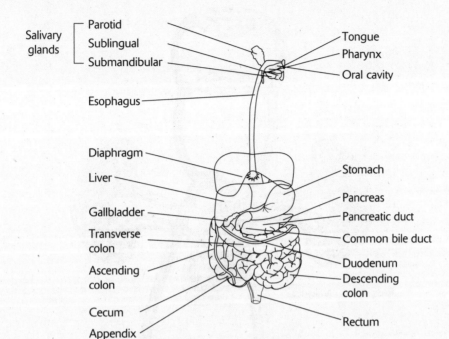

Circulatory System

The circulatory system functions to transport food and oxygen to all cells and remove their wastes, like carbon dioxide. The circulatory system also carries hormones, provides white blood cells, delivers heat, constricts blood vessels to conserve heat, and works in conjunction with other systems like the nervous system to help maintain homeostasis.

Unicellular organisms, sponges, cnidarians, and flatworms do not need a circulatory system because their cells are in contact with their environment. More complex organisms require a mechanism whereby even their interior cells have the benefit of exchange with their environment.

Invertebrates may have an **open circulatory system** where the blood bathes the organs without the benefit of an organized flow using blood vessels, or a more efficient **closed circulatory system** where the blood is delivered to the cells via blood vessels. Mollusks, except for squid and octopuses, have an open system powered by a three-chambered heart. Insects have an open system with a series of tubular, muscular pumps located along the dorsal side that pushes the blood in both directions and onto the organs before recycling to the pumps.

In general, fish have a higher rate of metabolism than invertebrates and require a closed system with a more efficient blood pump. The fish heart is a **chamber-pump heart** that pushes deoxygenated blood in one direction through four chambers arranged in series to the gill for oxygenation. The fish heart is a recognizable advancement in efficiency because it pumps fully oxygenated blood through a single loop of vessels to all cells.

Amphibians are the first phylum to exhibit a **double circulation system,** like yours. A double circulation system includes the extra pulmonary circulation that delivers oxygen-rich blood from the lungs to the heart and removes wastes. So amphibians are the first to have a pulmonary circulatory system that separates the circulation to the lungs from the general body circulation. A double circulatory system also creates a higher blood flow in the remainder of the body. The blood passes through the heart after returning from the lungs to get a boost through the body rather than trying to make it around the body and lungs (or gills in fish) with only one heartbeat. The amphibian heart is somewhat inefficient because it does not have a septum that divides oxygenated from nonoxygenated blood. So the blood that delivers oxygen to the cells may have deoxygenated blood mixed in with it. The graphic here shows the double circulatory system.

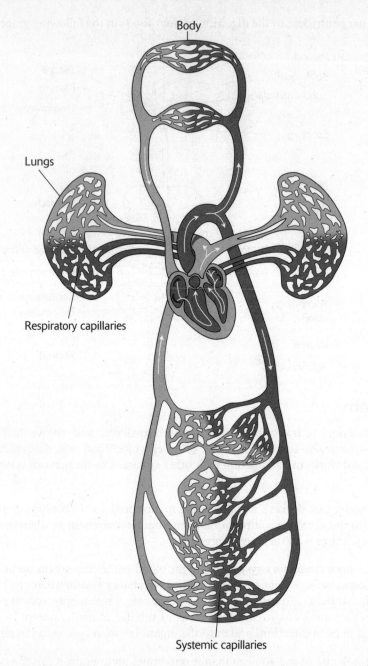

Reptiles have a **mostly completed septum** that allows a more efficient transfer of oxygen than amphibians. Crocodiles and birds have a **full septum** that completely divides the ventricle, or pumping section of the heart, creating a four-chambered heart that provides a more efficient transfer of oxygenated blood.

The mammalian circulatory system is a masterpiece of fluid flow. The variety of substances that are transferred and the interconnections with the endocrine, exocrine, and nervous systems make the mammalian circulatory system extraordinary.

Heart Circulation

The circulation of blood is dependent upon the correct functioning of the heart. The cardiac cycle is one complete heartbeat and is composed of two separate phenomena: systole and diastole.

Diastole is the resting phase of the cardiac cycle where all four chambers are relaxed and filling with blood. In humans, the diastolic function lasts about 0.4 seconds and includes two actions. The deoxygenated blood returning from the body collects in the vena cava and enters the right atrium of the heart; simultaneously, oxygenated blood returns from the lungs via the pulmonary system and enters the left atrium. The atrioventricular valves (AV) open, allowing the blood to drain from the atria into the ventricles. The AV between the right atrium and right ventricle is the tricuspid valve while the left atrium and left ventricle are separated by the mitral valve.

Systole contains two separate events and also lasts 0.4 seconds. The first action takes about 0.1 second and is a slight contraction of the atria to drain any remaining blood into the ventricles. The sinoatrial node (SA) or pacemaker creates an electrical impulse causing both atria to contract in unison. During the next 0.3 seconds, the electrical signal from the pacemaker is received by the atrioventricular node (AV) located between the right atrium and right ventricle. The AV node is so dense that the contraction message is delayed by 0.1 seconds so that the ventricles do not contract at the same time as the atria. The AV node amplifies the impulses and relays them through specialized cardiac muscle cells called Purkinje fibers to the muscular ventricles. The ventricles contract from the bottom up and push the blood through one-way semilunar valves into the arteries. The right ventricle sends blood through the pulmonary valve into the lungs, the stronger left ventricle forces blood through the aortic valve throughout the body. Ventricular contractions close the AV valves to prevent the backflow of blood into the atria.

Your blood pressure is the force of your blood against the walls of your blood vessels. Blood pressure is created when the left ventricle contracts and pushes a pulse of blood into the body via the aorta. Normal blood pressure is $^{120}/_{80}$ mm Hg; the 120 is the systolic pressure and the 80 is the diastolic pressure.

Ventricles contract about 70 times per minute which is the pulse or pulse rate. Interestingly, the "lub-dub" sound that is characteristic of a healthy human heart is caused by the contraction of the ventricles. The *lub* is the sound of the AV valves closing; the *dub* is the sound of the semilunar valves closing. Doctors listen for a swishing or leaking sound instead of the lub-dub, which indicates a possible valve defect. Heart murmurs are when blood squirts back through one of the valves. Follow the blood flow through the heart in the following diagram.

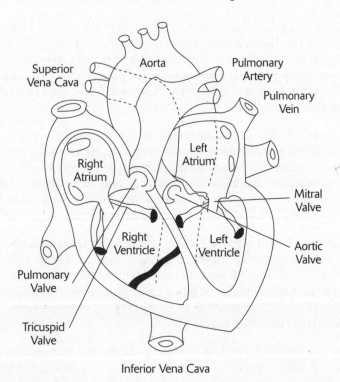

Circulation of Blood in the Body

The human circulatory system is a double circulatory system that separates the pulmonary flow to the lungs from the systemic flow to the rest of your body. The right side of the heart (right atrium and right ventricle) pumps blood through the pulmonary loop whiles the left side (left atrium and left ventricle) pumps blood through the systemic loop.

The **systemic system** is powered by the contraction of the left ventricle which pushes a volume of blood (normally around 70 mL or 2.4 ounces) into a stretching aorta. The aorta is the largest artery and immediately branches to deliver oxygenated blood to the heart (via coronary arteries), head, and upper body. Blockage of the blood flow to the brain causes a stroke while blockage to the heart is called a heart attack. The descending loop of the aorta behind the heart branches to supply blood to the middle and lower body. The arteries branch into smaller (arterioles) and smaller vessels until the smallest microscopic capillaries are only wide enough to allow one red blood cell to pass through them at a time. To compensate for the lack of vessel size, there are numerous capillaries that form capillary beds. Capillaries maintain the total amount of blood flow by increasing the numbers of vessels while decreasing the size of each vessel. Decreasing the size of the vessel serves a critical need. The movement of nutrients, water, waste, and other substances happens more efficiently when the red blood cells are moving slowly (low blood pressure) and are in contact with the blood vessel lining. All of these conditions facilitate exchange of nutrients and wastes, which is why capillaries are often called the functional blood vessels.

Once through the capillary beds, most of the oxygen and nutrients have been removed from the blood, wastes have been added, and the systolic pressure is much lower. The deoxygenated blood is routed into larger (venules) and larger veins until the blood in the lower body is collected in the inferior vena cava and the blood draining from the upper body pools in the superior vena cava. The movement of the blood is assisted by muscles and body movement to compensate for the depleted systolic pressure. Both vena cavae deliver their blood to the right atrium.

The **pulmonary system** begins when the waste-laden, deoxygenated blood enters the right atrium from the vena cavae and is delivered through the tricuspid valve into the right ventricle. The right ventricle contracts and sends the blood via pulmonary arteries to the right and left lungs. Capillary beds within the lungs exchange the carbon dioxide waste for oxygen, which is why you breathe out carbon dioxide and inhale oxygen. The pulmonary veins carry the oxygenated blood to the left atrium.

Human Blood

Blood is the transport medium for the circulatory system. Blood appears in many forms in the animal kingdom, but still performs the same basic functions and contains similar elements. Human blood is 55 percent water with dissolved minerals, proteins, nutrients, and waste. The remaining 45 percent consists of mostly red blood cells, a few white blood cells, and even fewer platelets. The straw colored liquid component of blood is called plasma. Serum is plasma without the clotting proteins. A "normal" human holds about 5 liters or a little more than 5 quarts of blood on a good day.

Red blood cells (RBCs) are small cells that are made by stem cells in the marrow of large bones and are called erythrocytes. RBCs function to transport oxygen and carbon dioxide. Hemoglobin is the red pigment in blood that forms loose bonds with oxygen and carbon dioxide. Interestingly, carbon monoxide forms a strong bond with red blood cells and in great enough quantities can lead to carbon monoxide poisoning and death. The element iron is the centerpiece of the hemoglobin molecule. Iron-deficiency anemia is a lack of iron in the body which causes a lack of hemoglobin which limits the amount of gases that can be transported.

Antigens are glycoproteins that are attached to the surface of RBCs and serve as immunity stimulators. The ABO blood group system refers to the antigens that trigger an immune response. People with type A blood have the A antigen on their RBCs; type B blood has the B antigen; type AB blood has both the A and B antigen; type O blood has neither antigen. Because of the danger of blood clotting, antigens must match before a blood transfusion. People with type AB blood can receive blood from all other blood types (universal recipient); type O blood can donate to all other blood types (universal donor).

White blood cells (WBCs) are called leukocytes and function to defend the body against diseases and invaders. There are five different types of WBCs that work together. Basophils help protect the body against diseases and help fight infections. They also function to release histamines that dilate blood vessels so that other WBCs can move between cells and blood vessels to fight infections. Mast cells primarily function to ward off parasites and are not the principle agent against bacterias or viruses. Do you want to go that deep under WBCs? This inflammatory mechanism is part of the immune system. Neutrophils, the most abundant WBC, and monocytes function as phagocytes to engulf and destroy microbes. Eosinophils are specialized phagocytes that attack parasitic worms. Finally, lymphocytes produce antibodies that are specific to particular invaders.

Platelets are thrombocytes that start the blood clotting process. The platelets stick to the damaged blood vessel walls and trigger a series of biochemical reactions that eventually creates fibrin, which forms a mesh over the wound that traps other blood cells thus forming a blood clot.

Interestingly, RBCs, WBCs, and platelets are made by stem cells in red bone marrow.

Lymphatic System and Immunity

The **lymphatic system** is an extension of the circulatory system and function to fight invaders, infections, and return fluids to the blood supply. The functional parts of the lymphatic system are the lymphatic vessels and lymph nodes.

The pressure of blood often forces some liquids through the capillary walls and into the intercellular spaces around the neighboring cells. These fluids are called **lymph,** connective tissue fluid, and are picked up by the one-way lymphatic vessels and eventually delivered back into the bloodstream. The lymph passes through lymph nodes (which are small bean-shaped structures) while moving through the lymphatic vessels. The **lymph nodes** are located throughout the body but clumps of lymph nodes can be felt in the neck, armpits, and groin. Lymph nodes function to filter dead bacteria, viruses, and other harmful substances from the lymph. Specialized WBCs, called lymphocytes accumulate in the lymph nodes and signal the destruction of unwelcome substances. Lymph nodes often swell at the first sign of an infection as more WBCs are added to the lymph nodes. The location of the major lymph node areas are depicted here.

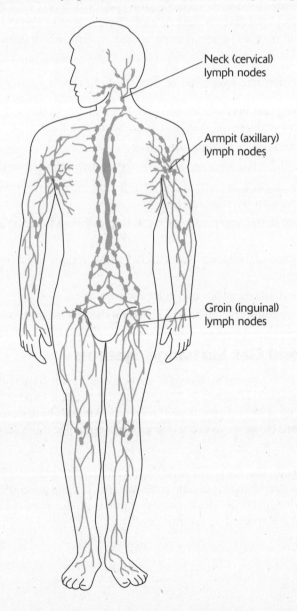

Neck (cervical) lymph nodes

Armpit (axillary) lymph nodes

Groin (inguinal) lymph nodes

The immune system is activated by the presence of foreign antigens. An **antigen** is a protein or glycoprotein molecule attached to the exposed surface of a cell; an **antibody** is a blood plasma protein that binds with the receptor site on the antigen and destroys the invading cell. There are two types of immune response: cell-mediated immunity and antibody-mediated immunity. B-lymphocytes (B cells) and T-lymphocytes (T cells) are stored in the lymph nodes. Both B and T cells are stimulated to function by the presence of a foreign antigen.

B cells secrete antibodies starting the antibody-mediated immune response. The **antibody-mediated immunity** occurs in two steps:

1. B cells bind at receptor sites with the antigen and produce more B cells: plasma cells and memory B cells.
2. Plasma cells secrete antibodies as a first response. The antibodies are released into the bloodstream and flow to the site where they bind to the surface of an invading substance. The coating of antibodies may be enough to prevent an infection. If not, the antibodies serve as a marker that alerts other immune system defensive mechanisms. The second response occurs when the memory cells create new plasma cells and memory B cells as needed. Memory cells "remember" the antigen of an infection for swift reaction to another similar infection. This secondary response provides long lasting immunity to that specific antigen and is the principle behind vaccination.

Cell-mediated immunity occurs when T cells respond to foreign antigens. There are two types of T cells: helper T cells and cytotoxic T cells. Through a double identification system, helper T cells bind with the invader and produce interleukins which prompt the development of more T cells, B cells, and cytotoxic T cells. Cytotoxic T cells bind with the invader and releases perforin, a specialized protein, which drills a hole in the infected cells' membrane causing cell death.

Immunity or prevention is also increased by a series of other techniques:

- **Skin** is a protective covering that prevents foreign invaders and allows the body to be cleaned; sebaceous skin glands secrete oils and acidic sweat to inhibit microbe reproduction.
- **White blood cells** function to engulf foreign substances.
- **Sweat, saliva,** and **tears** contain lysozyme, an enzyme that destroys the cell walls of most bacteria.
- **Mucus membranes** secrete mucus that traps microbes and lines the organ systems that connect to the environment such as the respiratory and digestive.
- **Nose hairs** and **cilia** located in the respiratory channels trap airborne invaders and hold them until engulfed by mucus or expelled.
- **Complement proteins** circulate in the bloodstream and alter the antigen of an invader for easier identification by neutrophils or macrophages.
- **Stomach acid** kills almost all the microbes that enter the stomach.
- **Interferon** is produced by cells infected by a virus signaling the defense systems of neighboring cells.

Animal Respiration and Gas Exchange Systems

Respiration can be simplified as the gaseous exchange of carbon dioxide for oxygen in animals. Oxygen is needed for cellular aerobic respiration to provide energy to power cellular functions. In return, cellular aerobic respiration releases carbon dioxide, which must be removed from the system. Animals have developed numerous creative ways to accomplish this function. However, in every case gaseous exchange must occur across a moist surface, such as a gill, lung, or wet skin.

For unicellular and simple animals, like the porifera (sponges) and cnidarians (jellyfish), respiration is easy because all cells are in direct contact with the aquatic environment. The diffusion of gases occurs across the cell membrane as needed by the individual cells. More complex animals do not have the luxury of cellular service, so the gases must be captured and transported to and from each cell.

Mollusks have two main methods of respiration. Gills are common in most aquatic mollusks. Oxygen is absorbed directly and easily from the watery environment. A primitive "lung" provides gaseous exchange in terrestrial mollusks. Terrestrial mollusks, like snails, struggle to keep the respiratory surfaces wet to allow diffusion. To help prevent water loss, mollusks are most active at night, occupy the underside or shady side of leaves, or limit activities to times when it is raining or high humidity.

Arthropods signify an evolutionary advantage because most have valves that prevent water loss as air is exchanged in spiracles. Spiracles are openings in the body that connect the environment to many tracheae. **Tracheae** are hollow tubes that are linked together in series to form a network that runs lengthwise in the organism. The tracheae branch to form smaller tubules called tracheoles that are interspersed and reach individual cells or cell clusters to distribute air to the body structures. Examine the structure and location of the spiracles and tracheae in the following model.

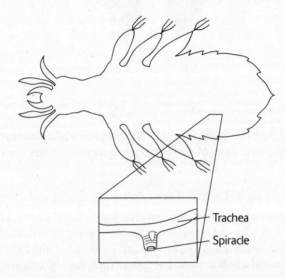

Annelids and echinoderms respire directly through their skin. Although some echinoderms have gills, most rely on skin as the medium of transfer. Echinoderms also have a slight advantage because they have fingerlike projects of epidermis that increase the surface area available for gaseous exchange.

Fishes have expanded the use of gills. When a fish gulps (watch your pet goldfish sometime) they are not feeding, but sending a current of water past their gills. The gills are made of rows of gill filaments which are fingerlike projections that increase the surface area available for gaseous exchange. Fish have also developed a **counter-current exchange** to improve the efficiency of oxygen absorption. As the water flows in one direction across the gill filaments, the blood flows in the opposite direction within the gills. This counter-current increases the availability of hemoglobin for every oxygen molecule, thereby increasing the overall efficiency of the gaseous exchange.

Amphibians mark the breakthrough to **lungs.** Although amphibians are able to respire through their skin, they also have lungs. Amphibian lungs are sac-like structures that contain folded inner membranes to increase their surface area. Most reptiles are not able to respire very well through their skin (*Note:* Some aquatic turtles and snakes obtain 20 to 30 percent of their oxygen dermally), so their lungs contain more folded tissue to provide even greater surface area. In addition, reptiles have thoracic muscles that assist with the process of breathing, making the process more dynamic.

Birds add another level of efficiency by forcing air in one direction through their lungs, in much the same way that fish push water in one direction of their gills. Birds contain nine air sacs that hold the oxygenated air from the environment until needed by the lungs. This level of organization keeps fresh oxygenated air passing through the lungs and provides the efficiency necessary for flight. The model here shows the location of the air sacs in relation to the lungs.

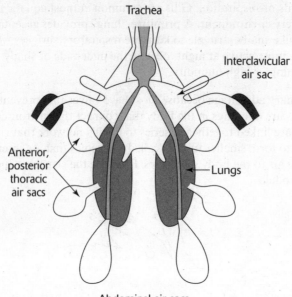

Trachea

Interclavicular air sac

Anterior, posterior thoracic air sacs

Lungs

Abdominal air sacs

Human respiration integrates the respiratory system with the nervous and circulatory systems to exchange carbon dioxide for oxygen. The most important parts of the human respiratory system are the nose, pharynx and larynx, trachea, and lungs:

- The **nose** is more than a pretty facial feature. The nose warms, filters, and moistens the inhaled air.

- The muscular tube called **pharynx** or throat is connected to the nasal cavity. The pharynx serves as a dual passageway for air and food. A flap-like structure called the epiglottis covers the esophagus to keep air out of the stomach and flips over to cover the larynx to keep food out of the lungs. The larynx is also known as the voice box because your vocal cords are located there. Your vocal cords are paired flap-like tissues that vibrate and make sounds, songs, or words when you exhale.

- The **trachea** is the windpipe that maintains its shape thanks to rings of cartilage that provide rigidity and keep the pipe open. The trachea extends into the chest cavity and branches into a right and left bronchus, which branches to form smaller vessels called bronchioles that branch into extremely small alveoli. The trachea and bronchial tree secrete mucus that traps foreign particles that make it past the lining of the nasal cavity. The mucus is then moved by cilia (and/or coughing) up the tubes and down into the stomach via the esophagus where the foreign particles are destroyed by your stomach acid.

- Your **lungs** contain approximately 300 million alveoli. Alveoli are tiny air sacs that form the terminal and functional end of the "bronchial tree." Each alveolus is surrounded by a capillary bed that exchanges carbon dioxide for oxygen. The following diagram shows the important structures associated with the human respiratory system.

Breathing is the act of inhaling atmospheric air and exhaling body air. Breathing is regulated by the amount of carbon dioxide in the blood. A high carbon dioxide concentration leads to an increase in breathing rate. When you inhale, your rib muscles and diaphragm contract thereby increasing the volume of your chest cavity. Air moves in because of the lower air pressure and moves out when your rib muscles and diaphragm relax.

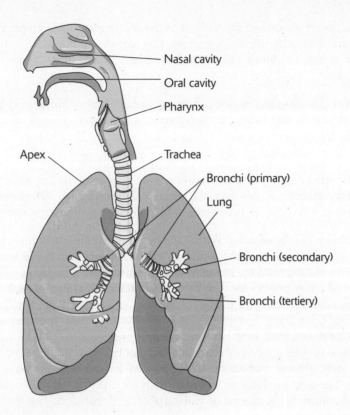

Nasal cavity
Oral cavity
Pharynx
Apex
Trachea
Bronchi (primary)
Lung
Bronchi (secondary)
Bronchi (tertiery)

Animal Excretion and Excretory System

Excretion is the filtering, collecting, and removal of metabolic wastes from the animal body. In more complex animals, the excretory system also maintains osmotic and pH balance by receiving signals from the nervous and endocrine systems to regulate the absorption or excretion of excess water, salts, and carbon dioxide.

In simpler animals, wastes leave the cell by passing through the cell membrane and then exit into the environment. In more complicated animals wastes are picked up by the circulatory system and transported to filtering, collecting, and removal structures. In large concentrations, wastes are poisonous and must be removed before critical levels are reached. The most important waste is ammonia, a nitrogen containing compound (NH_3). Fish, unicellular organisms, and aquatic invertebrates dilute ammonia with water and then excrete the ammonia directly into their environment. For instance, the platyhelminthes flatworms, like the planaria, have flame cells that are specialized excretory cells that direct water and metabolic wastes into excretory canals. The excretory canals join together to form excretory tubules that conduct the waste out of the body through pores. But terrestrial organisms conserve water by first diluting the ammonia with water and then converting the ammonia into the less toxic form, urea, $(NH_2)_2CO$. The water is reabsorbed in the kidneys and large intestine of humans.

Mollusks are the first animals to have an efficient waste collecting system. Mollusks and annelids have a structure called a coelom for collecting bodily fluids that contain waste. Within the coelom, cilia create currents that pull the wastes into specialized structures called **nephridia,** which recover nutrients and useful substances like sugars and water for return to the body. The remaining waste is excreted through a pore in the mantle. Nephridia are common in simpler organisms.

Terrestrial arthropods, like insects, have **Malpighian tubules** which are fingerlike projection of the gut that are washed with blood. Water and waste in the blood move into the Malpighian tubules where water, valuable ions, and other useful substances are reabsorbed. The remaining waste is moved into the intestines and exit through the anus. Terrestrial arthropods excrete their nitroenpous waste in the form of uric acid.

Birds have an efficient, and, more important, lightweight excretory system. Birds simply convert ammonia and other nitrogen waste into uric acid, a harmless white paste. The harmless white paste is then deposited on your favorite chair, car, window, or hat, whichever and whenever the bird selects. Birds do not have a bladder to store their liquid wastes.

The human excretory system contains three major functional organs: lungs, skin, and kidneys. Your lungs in combination with the circulatory system excrete carbon dioxide and a small amount of water. Your skin removes excess water as perspiration along with some metabolic waste substances. Your kidneys are responsible for cleaning your blood.

The **kidneys** are paired, (fist-sized organs in humans) that are the primary excretory structure of most vertebrates. In general, the kidneys filter metabolic wastes from the blood and excrete them into the urinary tract as urine. Urine is mostly water and urea, uric acid, and creatinine which are nitrogen-based waste products.

The functional unit of the kidney is the **nephron.** Within the nephron, specific structures perform three functions: filtration, secretion and reabsorption, and urine formation. Filtration occurs in the Bowman's capsule, a cup-shaped structure that receives plasma from the glomerulus, a capillary bed. The glomerulus acts as a filter as the blood pressure from the renal artery powers the flow of blood in the capillaries and pushes blood plasma into Bowman's capsule, creating a fluid called filtrate. The filtrate contains amino acids, urea, water, salts, and glucose. Red blood cells, proteins, and other large substances that are too large to pass through the membrane remain in the blood system. The filtrate passes from Bowman's capsule into the proximal tubules where reabsorption and secretion begin. The proximal tubules are convoluted coils surrounded by a capillary bed that reabsorbs water and useful substances like salts, glucose, and amino acids by active transport. Additional waste is secreted into the filtrate from the blood. The loop of Henle or Henle's loop is an easily recognized structure that links the proximal and distal tubules and continues the process of reabsorption and secretion. The remaining waste materials are not needed by the body and move from the distal tubule into the collecting ducts as the first step in urine formation. The urine is collected in larger ducts that finally join to form the ureters. The ureters contain smooth muscles that rhythmically contract to deliver the urine to the urinary bladder. When the urinary bladder fills to near capacity, specialized nervous system stretch receptors signal for muscular contractions in the urinary bladder and an opening of a muscular sphincter. The contractions force the urine into the urethra, the final stop before exiting the body. Humans produce vasopressin, also called antidiuretic hormone (ADH) in the posterior lobe of the pituitary gland which regulates urine production by controlling the rate of water absorption by the tubules. The simplified model here shows the major functional units of the nephron. A key point to remember is that although urine is a filtrate of blood, renal blood flow does not equal urine flow.

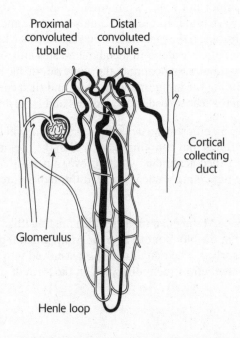

Proximal convoluted tubule

Distal convoluted tubule

Cortical collecting duct

Glomerulus

Henle loop

Animal Nervous Control, Coordination, and Sensory Systems

Nervous coordination allows an animal to rapidly respond to an internal or external stimulus. Nerve receptors are usually located in the sense organs, including your skin. In general the nervous system in all animals has four basic functions: nervous receptors receive internal or external stimuli, their message is transmitted to a nerve processing center, the data are analyzed and an action decision is made, and the processing center sends the appropriate response to glands or muscles for action. The stimulation of nerve receptors invariably produces a reaction in a gland or muscle.

Unicellular animals and sponges do not have or need a nervous system. However, cnidarians, like the hydra, possess a **"nerve network"** throughout their body. Echinoderms are more advanced because they have the **firstnerves,** which are clusters of neurons acting as a team. Cephalization and centralization are features of the platyhelminthes. **Cephalization** is the beginnings of a head area where the nerves are concentrated in a central processing and coordinating location. **Centralization** is the establishment of a central nervous system (CNS), which includes the brain and vertebrae, and is coordinated with a peripheral nervous system (PNS) that innervates the rest of the body. Cephalization and centralization are characteristics of increased animal complexity.

The human body contains many sensory receptors that are specific to a particular sensation. There are six main types of sensory receptors located in appropriate locations within your body.

- **Thermoreceptors**—Sense temperature changes and are located everywhere in your skin.
- **Baroreceptors**—Respond to the stretching of tissue, such as the stretching of the urinary bladder to signal muscle contractions to relieve the situation.
- **Mechanoreceptors**—Also located throughout your skin and are concentrated in your fingertips and face because they detect pressure and changes in tension.
- **Pain receptors**—Often work with other receptors in a reflex action to avoid further injury and are also located primarily throughout your skin.
- **Chemoreceptors**—Found in your nose and on your tongue because they enhance flavor, but mostly they distinguish between food and something you shouldn't eat.
- **Photoreceptors**—Light-sensitive receptors that are almost always found in the cephalic (head) region, such as in your eyes, and no place else.

The human nervous system is composed of specialized nerve cells called neurons. **Neurons** are the functional unit of the nervous system because they conduct electrical signals to: each other, glands, organs, the central processing unit, and muscles. Sensory neurons send electrical impulses from the various sensory receptors to the interneurons in the central nervous system (CNS). The interneurons summarize the sensory input and relay the appropriate response to the necessary body part via motor neurons.

Neurons have the same basic anatomy and physiology although they may take a variety of forms. Typical neurons contain dendrites, cell body, and axons; some neurons are wrapped by a myelin sheath, which has nodes of Ranvier. The dendrites are the "antennae" or receiving end of the neuron. Dendrites receive a signal and relay it to the cell body. The cell body contains a nucleus that determines the next action. The message may have no effect, or it may be forwarded to the next neuron via the axon. The axon is the long part of the neuron that terminates at axon terminals where the nervous signal may be sent to the dendrite of the next neuron. Schwann cells are protective cells that surround and electrically insulate the axons. Schwann cells link together to form a myelin sheath. The presence of a myelin sheath is an advantage because it allows the electrical signal to bypass the normal cellular transmission channels. The signal jumps between nodes which separate the myelin sheath segments. The nodes are called nodes of Ranvier. Jumping between the nodes of Ranvier increases the speed of the electrical signal by 30× because the signal does not have to pass through each of the nerve cell's channels. The anatomy of a typical neuron is pictured here.

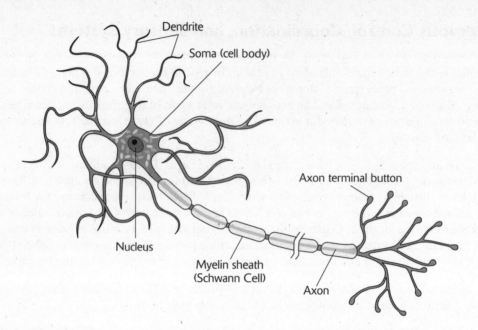

The transmission of an electrical impulse or nerve impulse is fascinating! An electrical impulse is the electrochemical signal that neurons send to each other, to organs, and to muscles. An electrical impulse is also known as a wave of depolarization because of the electrical charge that moves through the neuron. In an inactive neuron, sodium ions are actively transported out of the cell creating a positive charge outside of the cell and a negative charge in the cytoplasm inside the cell. The charge difference across the membrane is called the **resting potential** and is measured at –70 millivolts. The membrane remains in this stage until the dendrite receives a nerve impulse. The nerve impulse opens specialized protein channels in the cell membrane that allows sodium ions to rush back into the cell. The movement of the sodium ions into the cell changes the polarity, or depolarizes the cell. If the depolarization is greater than –50 millivolts, the threshold potential, it signals neighboring channels to open allowing more sodium ions to enter the cell. This wave of depolarization continues from dendrite through the cell body to the axon. As fast as sodium channels opened, they close and potassium channels open allowing potassium ions to rush out of the cell, thus restoring resting potential (repolarization). After the wave of depolarization, or nerve impulse passes, the cell pumps potassium ions in and sodium ions out of the cell, to reestablish ion concentrations. The repolarization of the cell membrane happens quickly so that another wave of depolarization may be instantaneously transferred. The electrical impulse, nerve impulse, wave of depolarization, and action potential all describe the same phenomenon: the change in the electrical charge across the membrane that occurs in approximately $\frac{1}{1000}$ of a second. It is the movement of sodium and potassium ions that establishes the resting potential, action potential (depolarization), and then the resting potential (repolarization).

What happens when the wave of depolarization reaches the end of the axon? How does it depolarize the adjoining neuron? The gap between neurons is called a synapse. The nerve impulse activates specialized structures in the axon terminals called **synaptic vesicles** to release chemical neurotransmitters, like acetylcholine, into the synapse between neurons. The neurotransmitter binds to a specific receptor on the post-synaptic cell causing opening of sodium channels and depolarization of the post-synaptic cell. Additional chemicals may be released by the axon terminals to neutralize the neurotransmitters and prepare the synapse for the next wave of depolarization. The graphic here demonstrates the action at a synapse.

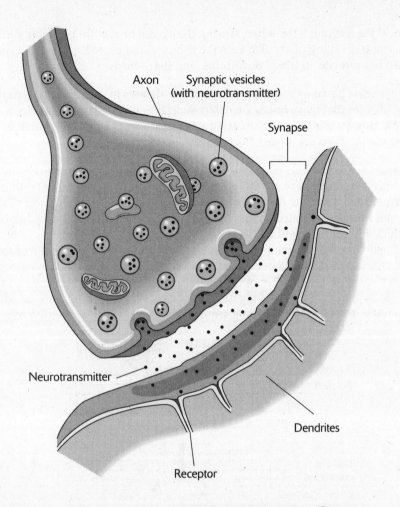

Contractile Systems, Movement, and the Muscular System

Movement or locomotion separates animals from plants. Animals have developed numerous methods of locomotion including sliding on slime, crawling, burrowing, swimming, walking, running, and the most unique, flying. The variation in types of locomotion has allowed animals to occupy a variety of niches. The common feature in all forms of locomotion is a contractile system or muscular system.

Cnidarians like the hydra are mostly sessile, but they can and do move by loosening the grip of their basal disks and tumbling to a new location. Locomotion among mollusks is quite varied. Most herbivore mollusks have a muscular "foot" that allows them to glide to another plant or dig into the sand, but carnivorous mollusks often move in water by a type of jet propulsion when water is squirted through their siphon. However Cephalopod mollusks like squid are very strong swimmers using a combination of fin movements and water jet propulasion.

Annelids, like earthworms, crawl and tunnel by anchoring their setae, specialized "feet," in the rear segment, and then contracting muscles in front of the anchored segment. The muscle contraction causes the segments ahead of the anchored segments to stretch and elongate, thereby increasing their length. Setae in the front segments then anchor into the surface and release the anchored setae in the rear segments. The circular muscles in the rear segments contract, which pulls the rear segment forward. Some annelids do not have setae and undulate their body to move by contracting their muscles which retracts the body, and relaxing the muscles which expands the body.

The movement of starfish exemplifies the movement in echinoderms. Starfish have a radial symmetry marked by five "arms" that extend from the center. Each arm contains hundreds of tube feet that are connected to a water reservoir called ampulla. When the ampullae force water into the tube feet by muscular contraction, the tube feet expand outward. Tiny suckers located on the ends of the tube feet grab onto the surface when the tube feet are at maximum extension. Muscular contraction pushes water out of the tube feet into the ampullae and the tube feet shorten, thereby pulling the starfish in that direction.

Fish have fins that propel them through the water. Waving the caudal or rear fin back and forth pushes the fish forward. Dorsal or fins located on top of the fish keep the fish trim and prevent rolling. The pectoral (side) fins and pelvic (underneath) fins provide lift, drag, downturns, and sharp turns.

The human muscular system is based on muscular contraction. Muscles move bones, tighten tissue, and move organs by contracting. Muscles that move bones are called skeletal muscles. Skeletal muscles work antagonistically in pairs. A flexor muscle causes a joint to bend; an extensor muscle causes a joint to straighten. Muscles are attached to bones by tendons, which are made of dense strips of connective tissue.

A single muscle is composed of thousands of muscle cells called muscle fibers. Sarcomeres are the contracting structure of a muscle fiber. Sarcomeres are composed of thick proteins called myosin and thin protein filaments called actin that are arranged in a parallel fashion within the cell. The parallel orientation of the myosin and actin filaments gives some muscles a striated appearance. A strong protein filament called the Z line runs perpendicular to the thick and thin filament and is attached to the actin (thin) filaments to maintain their orientation and define the length of a single sarcomere. Muscle contraction is described in the **sliding filament model.** The model shows that muscle contraction occurs when a nerve impulse reaches the sarcomeres stimulating the myosin and actin fibers to slide past each other. As the actin fibers draw toward the center of the sarcomere, they drag the attached Z lines along with them. Moving the Z lines closer together contracts the sarcomere and thereby contracts the muscle. Examine the following sequence that shows the contraction of a sarcomere.

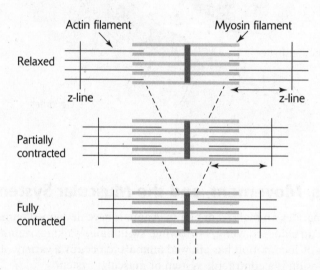

There are three types of muscles and are easily identified by their striations. **Cardiac muscles** are involuntary striated muscles that contract the heart. Cardiac muscle cells are dense and interconnected so that the nerve impulses stimulate the cells to contract in unison for a normal heartbeat. Intercalated disks are double membrane structures in cardiac muscle that synchronize the contraction. **Smooth muscles** are not striated and are usually involuntary. They line the digestive tract, respiratory tract, blood vessels, and urinary bladder. Smooth muscles are not capable of a long contraction like skeletal muscles. However, smooth muscles do provide a slow smooth contraction that moves substances, such as food through the digestive system. **Skeletal muscles** are multinucleated, long, slender cells that move bones. The typical example of skeletal bones is the opposing pair of bones in the arm. The bicep is a flexor muscle that pulls the forearm toward the upper arm by bending the elbow joint. The tricep is the flexor that pulls the lower arm away from the upper arm and straightens the elbow.

Skeletal and Support Systems

Skeletal and support system function to maintain body shape, provide protection for internal organs, and provide a surface for muscle attachment and movement. The animal kingdom has evolved interesting support and skeletal systems.

Yes, sponges do have a skeleton, but not like yours. Sponge skeletons are made of **spicules** which are needlelike structures made of silica, calcium carbonate, or spongin. The spicules are added in a geometric pattern to increase the surface area of a sponge without adding a weight burden.

Cnidarians and annelids exhibit a **hydrostatic skeleton** that supports each segment by the force of the fluids in that segment. There are no bones or hard structures in a hydrostatic skeleton, just the pressure of fluid in a closed system. The hydrostatic skeleton is not strong enough to support a terrestrial upright body style.

An exoskeleton is a characteristic of arthropods, like insects, but some mollusks also have exoskeletons. An **exoskeleton** is a hard, nonliving external structure that develops from the ectoderm and provides overall protection and support. Muscles are attached to the inside of the exoskeleton to provide a wide range of movement. As the organism grows, it outgrows its shell or exoskeleton. In the process of molting, the organism loses its shell and grows another larger one. The time spent without a shell during molting is when these animals are the most vulnerable.

Vertebrate **endoskeletons** are usually made of cartilage-bone combinations, like yours, or just cartilage, as in sharks. An endoskeleton is a feature of echinoderms. Echinoderms develop **ossicles** or calcium-rich, hard individual plates that fuse together to form the endoskeleton.

All fishes have an endoskeleton made of either cartilage or bone and cartilage. Their brain is fully encased in a protective covering called the **cranium** or **skull** and the spinal cord is protected by a vertebral column. Amphibians, except for salamanders and caecilians, have a similar endoskeleton except that all but nine vertebrae have been fused together for greater support.

Reptiles have a strong bony skeleton. Snakes exhibit an interesting reptilian body structure. Snakes have several hundred vertebrae each attached to a pair of ribs. They also have no supporting bones (pectoral girdle) for the forelimbs. This skeletal combination gives snakes their unique style of movement.

Birds have a lightweight endoskeleton designed for flight. Bird bones tend to be hollow, thin, and fused in several spaces making the bird skeleton more rigid than reptiles.

The human skeleton contains 206 bones, the same number as a giraffe. The human skeleton is divided into the axial and appendicular skeletons. The **axial skeleton** includes the skull, backbone, sternum, and ribcage and serves to protect the sensitive organs. The **appendicular skeleton** provides support for the body and includes the appendices such as your arms, shoulders, legs, and pelvis. The pelvic girdle and legs are oriented vertically in humans to support an upright stance. The graphic here shows the axial skeleton and also designates some of the more common bones in the human skeleton.

Human bones begin to form when the fetus is six weeks old and continue to grow until maturity, around 18 years of age for females and 21 for males. Bones are living tissues that require a blood supply so they are surrounded by a **periosteum,** a fibrous sheet of connective tissue and blood vessels. Inside of the periosteum **osteocytes** secrete flexible collagen fibers that are embedded into nonflexible calcium compounds, notably calcium carbonate. The collagen allows the bones to bend a little and the calcium keeps the bones rigid. The osteocytes create the matrix which forms the compact bone or hard part the bone. In compact bone, new bone cells are added around Haversian canals, which are hollow channels that contain blood vessels and run the length of the bone.

One of the problems with an exoskeleton or shell is the lack of bending allowed by the organism. An endoskeleton that consisted of a single bone would not be any better. Fortunately, we have joints that connect bones and allow greater types of movement. Bone to bone articulation requires ligaments which are tough, flexible, and contain connective tissue that holds the bones in alignment and orientation. The tips of bones are covered with cartilage to minimize friction in high-use areas, such as fingers. High pressure areas, such as your pelvic girdle, have specialized cells that secrete synovial fluid to lubricate the joints to further minimize the degradation caused by friction. Tendons connect bones to muscles.

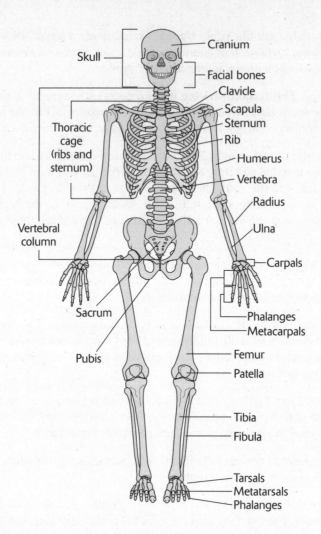

Integumentary System

Your **skin** is your largest organ and makes up about 12 to 15 percent of your total body weight. Your skin covers your body and is continuous with, but different from the lining of the mouth, anus, urethra, and vagina. Skin offers protection from injury, helps regulate body temperature, prevents water loss, provides sensory reception, synthesizes important biochemicals, absorbs useful substances, and serves as the first line of defense against infections. The two primary layers of skin are the epidermis and dermis.

The **epidermis** is the outer layer of skin that interacts with the environment. The epidermis is made of several layers of epithelial cells "keratmocytes" that contain keratin, a protein that makes your skin waterproof and tough. The epidermal cells on the skin surface are constantly abused by the environment and must be replaced on a regular basis. Basal cells within the inner layer produce new skin cells that migrate to the surface and become the layer of dead skin cells that surround your body and eventually wear off. Melanocytes are specialized cells in the inner epidermal layer that produce the pigment melanin. Melanin protects the skin by absorbing UV light which stimulates the production of more melanin. That is why people who spend a lot of time in the sun are darker than others. Nails, hair, scales, horns, and claws originate in the epidermis and also consist of keration. Hair is mostly dead cells that contain varying amounts of keratin. Nails are modified epidermal cells that contain a lot of keratin giving them their hardness.

The **dermis** is the layer of connective tissue beneath the epidermis. The dermis is called the functional layer of skin because it contains elastic fibers, nerve endings, capillaries, and sensory receptors. The dermis also anchors hair follicles and contains the muscles that contract and pull the hair shafts upright to help insulate the body. Conversely, when temperature receptors in the skin signal increased heat, the hypothalamus sends a message to dilate skin blood vessels and a message to sweat-producing skin glands to release more water to evaporate the heat from the body. Hair follicles are also lined with cells that produce the protein that forms your hair. They also contain sebaceous glands that add a thin layer of oil to your hair. When plugged and infected the sebaceous glands form a pimple.

Subcutaneous tissue is a layer of connective tissue that connects the skin to underlying organs and located directly beneath the dermis. Subcutaneous tissue also acts like an insulator from temperature changes and shock, and stores energy compounds. Subcutaneous tissue is mostly fat and is found in varying levels throughout your body, such as the pads of your feet and the pads of your buttocks. The graphic here shows the location of each skin structure.

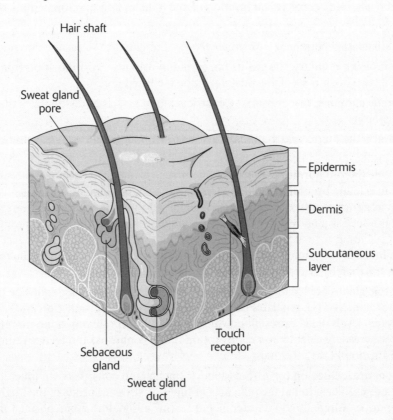

Endocrine and Exocrine System

Endocrine and exocrine systems are similar in that they both secrete a product that alters functions within the organism. Their difference lies in their mode of delivery. **Endocrine glands** (endocrine = to secrete within) are called ductless glands because they produce hormones that are secreted into the extracellular fluid and may affect neighboring cells or are secreted into the bloodstream to broadly affect structures anywhere in the body. **Exocrine glands** (exocrine = to secrete out) are considered ducted glands because they secrete their products via ducts into the digestive tract (e.g., pancreas, salivary glands) or onto the body surface (e.g., sweat, lacrimal glands).

The human endocrine system produces several types of hormones that may be secreted into the interstitial fluid and affect neighboring cells or emptied into the bloodstream where they affect a broader range of cells. Peptide hormones or amino acid-based hormones are water soluble hormones that are made from one or more amino acids. Steroid hormones are fat soluble hormones made from cholesterol.

There are ten major endocrine glands:

1. The **hypothalamus** is located in the brain and is referred to as the receiving-processing center because it receives sensory input from the nervous system and chemical information from blood hormones then releases hormones to the pituitary gland for requisite action.

2. The **pituitary gland** is a small gland composed of two main lobes, anterior and posterior, that is located beneath and next to the hypothalamus at the base of the human brain. The hypothalamus releases hormones into the blood network between the hypothalamus and the anterior lobe of pituitary gland. The anterior pituitary reacts to these chemical stimuli to secrete the six hormones that are listed here:

- **ACTH (adrenocorticotropic hormone)**—Stimulates the release of steroid hormones from the adrenal cortex.
- **FSH (follicle stimulating hormone)**—Targets the testes and ovaries, stimulates the development of follicles which contain egg cells, and regulates the development of the male and female gametes.
- **GH (growth hormone, somatotropin)**—Stimulates protein and bone synthesis as well as the growth of muscles.
- **LH (luteinizing or lactogenic hormone)**—Acts on the testes and ovaries to stimulate secretion of sex hormones and ovulation; completes maturation of the follicles and development of the corpus luteum.
- **Prolactin**—Stimulates milk production in mammary glands.
- **TSH (thyroid stimulating hormone)**—Activates the thyroid gland to release the thyroid hormones.

The posterior lobe of the pituitary releases its hormones in response to stimulation from neurons from the hypothalamus. The two hormones of the posterior lobe are listed here:

- **ADH (antidiuretic hormone, vasopressin)**—Constricts blood vessels and stimulates the reabsorption of water in the nephrons.
- **Oxytocin**—Targets the uterus and mammary glands to stimulate milk secretion and uterine contractions.

3. The **thyroid gland** is located just below the larynx (Adam's apple) in the front and base of the neck, atop the trachea. The peptide thyroid hormones are thyroxin and calcitonin. Thyroxin regulates the metabolic rate of the body. Thyroxin is made by adding iodide to the amino acid, tyrosine. If iodine is missing from the diet, a condition known as goiter results, creating a greatly enlarged thyroid gland. An undersecretion of thyroxin produces cretinism which is a body dwarfism with possible mental retardation; oversecretion results in Graves' disease. Calcitonin regulates the level of calcium in the blood. In a negative feedback loop, high levels of calcium in the blood stimulate the production of calcitonin which causes the rapid uptake of calcium by the bones thereby lowering the blood calcium levels.

4. The four **parathyroid glands** are located on the posterior side of the thyroid gland. The parathyroid hormone, parathormone (PTH), regulates calcium metabolism. PTH production and secretion is stimulated by low blood calcium levels. PTH raises blood calcium levels by stimulating bones to release calcium ions into the blood, by increasing calcium ion reabsorption in the nephrons, and by activating vitamin D which helps calcium absorption in the intestines.

5. Both **adrenal glands** are located on top of the kidneys. Each gland consists of an inner adrenal medulla and an outer adrenal cortex. The adrenal medulla acts in times of stress to produce the "fight or flight" hormones, epinephrine (adrenalin), and norepinephrine (noradrenalin). Epinephrine functions to increases heart rate, blood pressure, blood glucose levels, and the blood supply to the muscles. Norepinephrine increases the effects of epinephrine.

The adrenal cortex secretes the corticosteroids, a family of steroids that provide a slower more long-term response to stress than the adrenal medulla hormones. The two main adrenal cortex hormones are mineralcorticoids, such as aldosterone, and glucocorticoids, such as cortisol and cortisone. Aldosterone helps regulate blood pressure by stimulating the reabsorption of minerals and water from the filtrate so that needed ions, like sodium, are not discharged in the urine. Aldosterone also stimulates the kidneys to release potassium ions into the urine. The reabsorption of sodium ions and water and the release of potassium ions increase the blood volume and therefore the blood pressure. Cortisol stimulates an increase in the blood glucose levels to make more energy available to the body during stressful situations. Cortisol also aids in fat, carbohydrate, and protein metabolism. High levels of cortisol also minimize the immune system. Interestingly, man-made, copy-cat drugs such as prednisone are used as anti-inflammatory drugs.

6. The **pancreas** is located posterior to your stomach. The pancreas is an endocrine and an exocrine gland. The endocrine part of the pancreas consists of specialized cell clusters called the **islets of Langerhans.** The two hormones that are made by the islets of Langerhans work antagonistically: insulin and glucagon. Insulin lowers blood sugar by stimulating the uptake of glucose and synthesis of glycogen in the liver. Glucagon increases blood glucose levels by stimulating the liver to release glucose (stored as glycogen). Diabetes mellitus is a medical condition where insufficient insulin causes the removal of glucose from the blood. The glucose and water are absorbed by the nephrons and are excreted as urine. Diabetics are characterized by glucose in their urine, heavy urination, and excessive thirst.

7. The **pineal gland** is a pea-sized gland located in the midbrain. The pineal gland secretes melatonin, a hormone that is thought to help establish daily biorhythms, such as day-night cycles and perhaps mating behaviors. The pineal gland may also cause seasonal affective disorder syndrome (SAD) as a response to darkness.

8. **Ovaries** and **testes** secrete hormones that regulate reproduction. The testes secrete testosterone and the ovaries secrete estrogens and progesterone. These hormones stimulate the development of secondary sex characteristics such as hair growth, breast size, and muscle development. They also assist the development of gametes and influence mating behavior.

9. The **thymus gland** is located in the neck and influences the development of T-lymphocytes, a component of the immune system, by secreting the hormone thymosins.

10. The **kidneys** produce erythropoietin which functions in the production of red blood cells. Various tissues secrete prostaglandins which are chemical messengers that affect contraction and relaxation of smooth muscle, the dilation and constriction of blood vessels, control of blood pressure, and modulation of inflammation.

The location of the major endocrine glands is displayed in the following graphic.

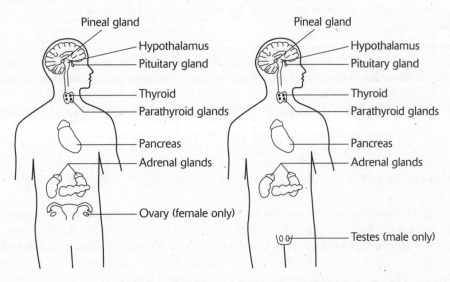

Exocrine glands are glands that discharge secretions secrete their products through ducts to the body surfaces. There are numerous exocrine glands; the most common are listed here:

- **Bulbourethral glands** or Cowper's glands—Located at the base of the penis and function during sexual arousal to produce a clear pre-ejaculate fluid that neutralizes the acidic urethra and clears away any foreign debris. This gland is homologous to Bartholin's glands in females.

- **Bartholin's glands**—Located below and on both sides of the vagina. When sexually aroused, these glands secrete a vaginal lubricant.

- The **pancreas**—An exocrine and an endocrine gland. The exocrine pancreas secretes pancreatic juice into the small intestine. The digestive enzymes contained in pancreatic juice breakdown fats, proteins, and carbohydrates in the chyme.

- The **prostate gland**—Produces a slightly basic fluid that is milky white in appearance that becomes part of semen. The alkaline pH of the semen neutralizes the acid pH of the vaginal tract, thereby increasing survival chances for sperm.

- The **pyloric glands**—Found in the lining of the stomach, the pyloric glands secrete gastrin, which aids in digestion. Enteroendocrine cells located near the base of the gastric glands also secrete gastrin into the blood.

- **Sebaceous glands**—Microscopic skin glands that secrete sebum to lubricate the fur and hair of mammals. Human sebaceous glands are mostly concentrated where hair normally grows, such as on top of your head.

Reproduction and Development

Successful reproduction is essential for the continuation of a species. In sexual reproduction, the reproductive system functions to produce viable reproductive cells, called gametes. The male gamete unites with the female gamete in a process called **fertilization,** which forms a zygote. The female reproductive organs provide a protective and nourishing environment for the fertilized egg cell. The developing embryo passes through a series of developmental stages to become a fetus and then an offspring. Animals have developed some unique reproductive styles.

The porifera, sponges, can reproduce both asexually and sexually. Asexual reproduction occurs in three ways: budding—when buds form on the sponge and then break off to become new sponges; fragmentation—when a piece of sponges breaks off or is torn off and grows to become a new sponge; and gemmule formation, where sponges avoid harsh conditions by forming gemmules or cell clusters encased in a protective coat. The gemmules release the cells to grow into a new sponge when conditions improve.

Sponges are hermaphroditic, meaning they contain both male and female parts. Sexual reproduction in sponges occurs when a cloud of sperm cells from a neighboring sponge are received into the interior of a sponge where they are passed onto the egg cells. The fertilized egg develops into a free-swimming larva that leaves the sponge and eventually attaches to an object and grows into a mature sponge. Interestingly, the release of the gametes is coordinated so that the sperm and eggs do not mature at the same time to avoid self-fertilization.

Mollusks have an interesting reproductive profile. Although most species of mollusks are distinctly male or female, some slugs and snails are hermaphroditic. Also, sea slugs and oysters can repeatedly change sexes. External fertilization is the norm for aquatic mollusks, but internal fertilization is frequent in terrestrial mollusks. Most mollusks lay eggs that hatch to become free-swimming larvae called trochophores. Most snails hatch from eggs and resemble tiny adults, because they mature past the larval stage while in the egg.

Members of the platyhelminthes phylum are hermaphroditic. During sexual reproduction, two flatworms align and exchange sperm simultaneously fertilizing each other. Their asexual form of reproduction occurs by fragmentation or binary fission. Binary fission occurs when one cell divides to form two identical daughter cells.

Amphibian reproduction is varied. Frogs and toads employ **external fertilization** where the male releases a cloud of sperm onto freshly laid eggs. Salamanders are less vulnerable because the male deposits packets of sperm that are scooped up by the female and deposited into her cloaca thereby accomplishing internal fertilization. Caecilians use internal fertilization like mammals, birds, and reptiles. Most amphibians are not good parents. They lay their eggs in water and then abandon them.

Reptiles are different from amphibians because their eggs are fertilized within the female in a process called **internal fertilization.** Reptiles may be oviparous, meaning that the young hatch from eggs, or ovoviviparous, which means the embryos develop inside eggs that are retained in the mother's body or remain as eggs within the female until shortly before hatching.

Although all mammalian reproduction is through internal fertilization, mammalian reproduction has three variations. The monotremes, like the duck-billed platypus, are the simplest of the mammals and are represented by only one order, monotremata. Monotremes are the only mammal that reproduces by laying eggs. The eggs are leathery-like reptilian eggs and like birds, the mother incubates the eggs.

Marsupials, such as kangaroos, wombats, and opossums birth their offspring within days of fertilization. The fledglings are not completely developed except for their front limbs which they use to climb into the mother's pouch where they access the nourishment provided by mammary glands.

Placental mammals, like you, develop within the mother. The **placenta** is a specialized organ that allows the diffusion of nutrients, water, oxygen, and wastes between mother and offspring. Placental animals have an ecological advantage because their offspring are often ready for the world trials within hours, such as horses. Human offspring require extended care compared to other placental animals.

The human reproductive system is likely the one that you are the most familiar with. Internal fertilization is accomplished by male and female counterparts. The resulting zygote develops over the next nine months or so and then bursts into the world as a beautiful baby.

Male Reproductive System and Gametogenesis

The male reproductive system is designed to produce sperm in the male reproductive organs, the **testes.** The testes are paired, egg-shaped organs that are located between the legs in a pouch called the scrotum. Sperm production is stimulated by two hormones secreted by the anterior pituitary gland, follicle-stimulating hormone (FSH) and luteinizing hormone (LH). LH stimulates the production of testosterone while FSH and testosterone stimulate sperm production in the seminiferous tubules. The seminiferous tubules are where spermatogonia undergo meiosis to become haploid sperm cells. The sperm cells mature in the epididymis where they gain mobility. Sperm cells are transferred into the vas deferens where they migrate to receive the secretions from the prostate gland, seminal vesicles, and Cowper's gland (bulbourethral gland) to create semen. Semen provides lubrication and a medium for the sperm that neutralizes the acidic conditions of the urethra and vagina. Examine the following graphic, which shows the anatomy of the male reproductive system.

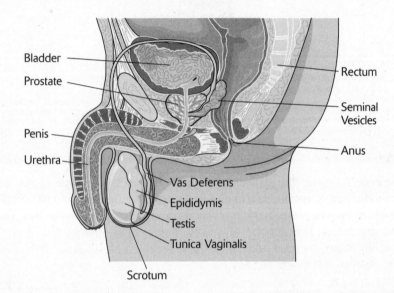

Female Reproductive System

The female reproductive system prepares an egg for possible fertilization approximately every 28 days. Interestingly, a female is born with all of the eggs that she will present for fertilization during her reproductive time span. For most females, only 300 to 400 of the roughly 2 million egg cells will mature to become an **ovum.**

Follicle cells located in the ovaries secrete the hormone estrogen, as well as protect and nourish the ovum. The right and left ovaries alternate releasing an ovum into the **fallopian tubes** or oviduct in a process called ovulation. Fallopian tubes are the passageway that the ovum takes to the uterus. Once ovulation occurs, the ovum is moved in a three- to four-day journey by cilia and the rhythmic contractions of the smooth muscle in the fallopian tubes to the uterus. What remains of the egg follicle develops into the corpus luteum, a specialized tissue that secretes progesterone while continuing to secrete estrogen. The hormone progesterone stimulates the buildup of the uterine lining in preparation for a possible pregnancy. If the ovum is not fertilized within 48 hours, the ovum and corpus luteum degenerate.

For fertilization to be successful sperm are delivered through the vagina to an egg. The vagina is a muscular organ that connects to the cervix, which marks the entrance to the uterus. The fertilized egg or zygote attaches to the uterine lining for nourishment and protection. The development of the offspring occurs in the uterus, normally a hollow, muscular organ about the size of an orange. The endometrium, or uterine lining, is a network of blood vessels that nourishes the growing fetus. A healthy mother provides adequate nourishment to promote rapid growth through the embryotic stage. The embryo becomes a fetus after about nine weeks when body structures begin to form. Try to locate the structure of the female reproductive system on the graphic shown here and follow the pathway of the egg cells.

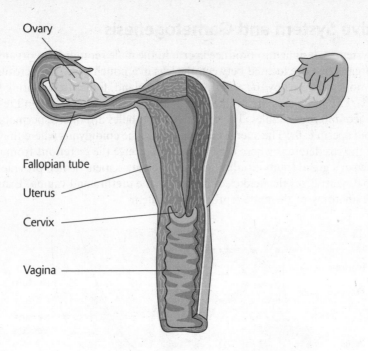

Ovary

Fallopian tube

Uterus

Cervix

Vagina

Gametogenesis

Gametogenesis is the process of making the gametes or sex cells. In males, gametogenesis is called **spermatogenesis** because it involves the production of sperm. Spermatogenesis occurs in the seminiferous tubules within the testes when an oversized diploid cell undergoes meiosis I, producing two secondary spermatocytes. The two cells resulting from meiosis I then undergo meiosis II to become four haploid cells called spermatids. The resulting cells mature in the epididymis part of the testes and grow a tail to become the male gamete, spermatozoa, or sperm. The gametogenesis of sperm is called spermatogenesis.

In females, gametogenesis is called **oogenesis** and takes place in the female gonads, the paired ovaries. Oogenesis begins with the unequal dividing of the cytoplasm of a primary oocyte, an immature egg cell, following meiosis I. Large numbers of primary oocytes are present in the ovaries at birth. The cell receiving an abnormally large amount of cytoplasm following cytokinesis, called the secondary oocyte, will become the egg cell. The smaller cell, called the first polar body, will eventually die. The secondary oocyte is released from a mature follicle during ovulation. After ovulation, the ovum migrates to the fallopian tube for possible fertilization. Interestingly, after fertilization the oocyte completes meiosis II and for a second time, the cytoplasm is again divided unequally. The larger cell develops into the zygote, while the two additional smaller cells, called the second polar bodies, die. The abnormal amount of cytoplasm serves as the reservoir of nutrients for the embryo. Examine the process of oogenesis in the following graphic.

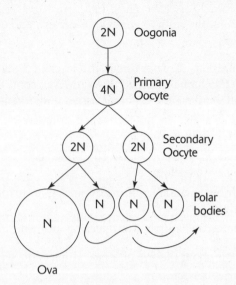

Ova

Fertilization, Embryogenesis, Growth, and Differentiation

Fertilization occurs when sperm unite with egg. Fertilization normally occurs in the first section of the fallopian tubes. When 1 of the 200 million sperm penetrates the clear zone around the egg, the egg releases substances that prevent a second sperm penetration. The resulting zygote begins developing via the mitotic cleaving of new cells as it travels toward the uterus. Upon arrival in the uterus, the zygote attaches to the endometrium and begins the growth and development phase. By the time the zygote reaches the uterus, it has formed into a hollow ball of cells called a blastocyst.

The growth and development of a human offspring can be described in trimesters. However, during the first two weeks after fertilization, amazing things happen:

Day 1: One cell becomes two cells = first cleavage.

Day 2: Two cells become four cells = second cleavage.

Days 3–4: The existing 32 cells form into a solid ball of cells called a morula.

Day 5: The morula develops into a hollow fluid filled blastocyst = blastula stage.

Days 6–7: The blastocyst attaches to the endometrium (implantation) and begins secreting human chorionic gonatotropin (HCG). HCG stimulates estrogen and progesterone to prevent menstrual flow, and can cause morning sickness. Pregnancy tests detect the presence of HCG.

Days 8–14: Gastrula forms, and the young embryo has three germ layers: endoderm gives rise to the linings of the digestive tract and internal organs; mesoderm creates the heart, muscles, and bones; ectoderm produces the skin and nervous system.

During the first month after fertilization, the embryo grows considerably and develops unique features that are held in common with other vertebrates:

- **Gastrulation or cellular reorganization**—Creates three germ layers: ectoderm, endoderm, and mesoderm. All of the cells of the resulting gastrula have the same DNA, however, some of the cells are beginning to be activated by certain genes to differentiate into different tissues and organs.
- **Notochord**—Forms from the mesoderm. The notochord is a primitive backbone that is also found in mature amphioxus and lancelets, both very simple animals.
- **Coelom**—Forms from the mesoderm. The coelom is a fluid-filled cavity that separates the gut from the body wall. Insects and mollusks also have a coelom.
- **Amniotic sac**—The tough and transparent layer of membranes that surround and protect the developing embryo and contain amniotic fluid.
- **Gill pouches**—Yes, you had them as an embryo. They develop into your middle ear.

At the end of one month, the embryo is about the size of a pea with a defined head, rudimentary facial features, and tiny buds that will grow into arms and legs.

At the end of the first trimester, the fetus has developed structures that are clearly human in nature. The first trimester is characterized as a time of differentiation as the embryo develops anatomical structures including organs. The listing that follows is sequential within the first trimester:

1. The umbilical cord attaches the placenta and the fetus. The placenta nourishes the embryo, but the maternal and embryonic blood does not mix. The umbilical cord contains two arteries and one vein.
2. All organs found in an adults are present, but still under development.
3. Arms, legs, and feet are present with movable fingers and toes.
4. Male or female anatomy is confirmed.
5. The zygote appears human.
6. The head is large and out of proportion to the rest of the body.
7. Bone begins to replace cartilage.

The second trimester is characterized as a period of rapid growth as described in the sequential listing that follows. The placenta is a more efficient structure and takes over as the medium that nourishes the fetus as the corpus luteum degenerates. The placenta begins secreting progesterone. The end of the second trimester shows areas of rapid growth:

1. The skeleton begins to take shape, including facial features and tooth formation; both eyes are open.
2. The heartbeat is present and can be heard through the mother's abdominal wall.
3. Movement increases; the fetus rotates into the "fetal position."
4. The mother's midsection becomes noticeably expanded.
5. A layer of fine hair appears.

The third trimester marks the completion of the fetus and preparation for birth in the sequence of events that follows:

1. All bones finish hardening except for the head.
2. All organ systems complete development, with the lungs being the final organs to finish maturing.
3. Movement slows as uterine space becomes confining.
4. Muscle mass increases.
5. The fetus is ready to become a child.

Childbirth

Childbirth is regulated by hormones and can be described as the interaction of hormones with the female anatomy. Childbirth can be summarized in five steps:

1. The placenta increase secretion of estrogen which riggers the release of oxytocin by the pituitary gland. Oxytocin stimulates smooth muscle receptors in the uterine lining to rhythmically contract. Oxytocin also stimulates the placenta to release prostaglandins, which increase the uterine contractions beginning a process known as labor.

2. Labor achieves the opening of the cervix large enough for the baby's head to pass through (about 4 in or 10 cm). The baby moves headfirst as the cervix incrementally expands the opening—typically this is the longest part of labor.

3. The movement of the baby toward the cervix breaks the amniotic sac and the fluid flows out of the vagina. Contractions move the baby headfirst through the cervix and out of the vagina and into the world.

4. The umbilical cord is cut and an attendant will make the baby cry to create the first inspiration, which precedes the first cry. The placenta and remainder of the umbilical cord are passed out of the mother within an hour. The site of attachment of the umbilical cord becomes the "belly button" for the newborn.

5. All organ systems are operational.

Note the structures and location of the fetus in the following graphic.

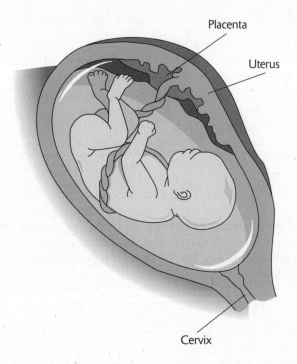

Placenta

Uterus

Cervix

Parthenogenesis

Parthenogenesis is virgin birth. This form of asexual reproduction occurs when the female produces eggs, but the eggs grow and develop without fertilization. The offspring become a clone of the mother. Parthenogenesis is common in several types of insects, some fish, and a few frogs and lizards, but unlikely in mammals. The most common display of parthenogenesis occurs when the queen honeybee deposits unfertilized eggs that hatch and mature into male worker bees, or drones.

Metamorphosis

Metamorphosis is a biological process in which an animal makes drastic body style changes as they mature. Metamorphosis is a characteristic of insects. Almost all insects perform a complete metamorphosis. In a **complete metamorphosis,** the animal matures through four stages: egg, larva, pupa, and adult. A typical example that demonstrates complete metamorphosis is the butterfly. The adult butterfly deposits eggs which hatch to become a larva. Larvae are caterpillars and are often mistaken for worms, but cannot be mistaken for butterflies. The larvae spend every minute eating to gain enough stored energy to pass into the pupa stage. When enough energy is stored away, the larva surrounds itself with a protective cover called a chrysalis, thereby entering the pupa stage. Within the chrysalis, the larva develops into the adult butterfly. When mature, the butterfly emerges from the chrysalis and begins life as a winged creature. Interestingly, most insect larvae do not feed on the same food sources that are consumed by the adult, which may help eliminate competition for food as shown here.

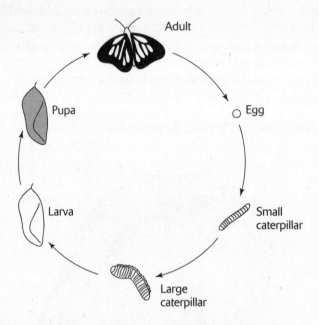

Incomplete metamorphosis is a shortened and less dramatic form of metamorphosis. Animals that mature via incomplete metamorphosis grow through three stages: egg, nymph (sometimes called larva, or naiad), and adult. The eggs hatch into a juvenile form that resembles a wingless adult. The nymphs usually molt several times as they grow into the adult stage. Animals in the nymph stage bear some resemblance to the adult form, as opposed to the larval stage of complete metamorphosis. The life cycle of a dragonfly is a common example of incomplete metamorphosis as seen in the following graphic.

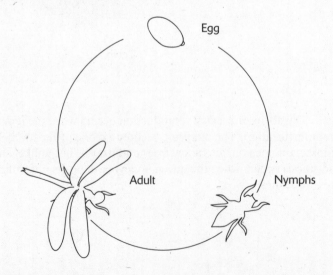

Aging or Senescence

Aging is defined as the gradual deterioration of physiological functions with age. In biology, the process of aging is called **senescence.** Cellular senescence is the failure or limited ability of cells to divide. Organismal senescence is the aging of the organism. After a period of nearly perfect cellular renewal up to around 35 years of age, the characteristics of organismal senescence begin to appear, such as increased homeostatic imbalance, risk of disease, and declining ability to respond to stress or sensory input. Currently, organismal senesce is irreversible and leads to death.

Although there are many theories that attempt to explain the aging process, none are without scientific skepticism. There are several commonalities among the theories however. Many researchers agree that genetics favor survival up to and through the reproductive years. After the reproductive years, one theory states that pleiotropic genes begin degrading the body, while another theory suggests that genes that were active during the reproductive years diminish their effect in later years. Another theory states that genes do not have a direct effect on aging. This theory shares some of the ideas of prior thinking in that molecular disorder accumulates in cells after the reproductive season because the need to maintain functional integrity is no longer required. Combined theories also suggest that limited resources are better spent on organisms prior to their reproductive span than afterward. Summarizing several theories, genes may determine the longevity of an organism, but they do not directly program the aging process.

Gene loss as a source of aging presents four mechanisms by which the aging process may occur:

- **Gene repression**—The "turning off" of genes whose function is needed to maintain health. Some genes maybe "switched off" by nutritional deficiencies, or environmental factors such as pollution, pesticides, alcohol consumption, or smoking.
- **Accretion defects**—The accumulation of waste materials such as lipofuscin and bilirubin reduce the functionality of the organs.
- **Depletional defects**—The loss of functioning parts, such as muscle mass or heart and brain cells.

Some of the latest research conducted on older sport competitors highlights the old adage, "use it or lose it." Senior citizens who are still competing in sports do not show the muscle, brain, or heart atrophy of their more sedentary counterparts. In a recent study, the muscles of active elderly people contained almost as many functioning mitochondria (powerhouse of the cell) as is found in much younger people, but considerably more than sedentary older people. In recent studies older lab rats given exercise were able to regrows muscle cells indicating that their bodies could now build and repair tissues more effectively. Interestingly, one of the champion Ironman triathletes is 71 years old and one of America's best marathon runners (26.2 miles) is older than 45 years old.

Cellular senescence in humans and other mammals has been linked to the shortening of the telomeres with each cell cycle. Telomeres are regions of repetitive DNA that are located at the ends of a chromosome that protect the chromosome from deterioration. The length of the telomeres has been described as the "molecular clock." The graphic here shows the location of the telomeres on the DNA double helix.

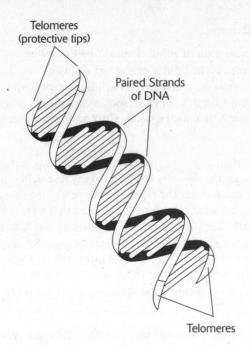

Telomeres
(protective tips)

Paired Strands
of DNA

Telomeres

Animal Behavior

Behavior is an action that is the directed response of an organism to an environmental stimulus. Although simple organisms like bacteria and paramecium exhibit behavior, the animal kingdom demonstrates the most elaborate and extensive forms of behavior. The behavioral tendencies of an animal reflect the evolutionary fitness of that species. Natural selection favors behavioral patterns that increase the likelihood of successful reproduction.

Innate and Learned Behaviors

Konrad Lorenz and Niko Tinbergen are among the first animal behavioral specialists. Through their experiments, they defined innate behavior. **Innate** behaviors are also called instinctive behavior, or instinct. Innate behaviors are genetically programmed behaviors that are coded for in the genes and do not have to be learned, such as nest building in birds. Innate behaviors are considered an inborn trait because in a given situation, every member of that species responds in the same way, such as when a newborn kangaroo instinctively searches for the protection and nourishment provided by the mother's pouch. In order for innate behaviors to occur, they must be triggered by an environmental stimulus.

Learned behaviors are life lessons that are learned and remembered through experience. There are five types of learned behavior:

- **Associative learning** occurs when a specific behavior receives a reward or punishment, such as a pat on the head for passing the Praxis II: Biology exam. **Classical conditioning** is a particular type of associative learning where an abstract stimulus creates an association with a reward or punishment. Classical conditioning was demonstrated by Ivan Pavlov in his now famous experiment where he rang a bell when feeding his dogs. Before long, the dogs began to salivate at the sound of the bell before the food was presented to them. Operant learning is another type of associative learning that is more common in nature. **Operant learning** is the "trial and error" type of learning because the animal learns to behave in a particular way because of prior experiences. The classic operant conditioning experiment was conducted by B. F. Skinner, who placed lab rats in a special box that had a lever that released food when pushed. Sooner or later one of the rats would hit the lever and food would appear. Over time, the rats learned to hit the lever whenever they were hungry.

- **Habituation** is considered the easiest type of learning. Habituation is the decreasing response to a repeated stimulus that has no effect. In essence, the animal learns to ignore the stimulus. Parents who fail to follow through with their disciplinary procedures soon find that their threats of discipline have no effect on the offending child.

- **Imitation** is the direct copying of a model behavior that has demonstrated success. Imitating an organism that is successful at a task, such as hunting for food, is also a survival strategy.

- **Imprinting** is a different type of learning because it draws from both innate and learned behaviors. Konrad Lorenz produced the classic experiment when he divided an equal number of fertilized goose eggs into two separate piles. The control group remained with the mother and the experimental group was incubated in a separate location. Upon hatching, the control goslings found their mother and began following her everywhere and imitating her actions. The experimental group found Dr. Lorenz and followed him everywhere!

- **Reasoning** is the capacity to assimilate previous learning in order to behave correctly in a new situation. Reasoning requires the correct remembrance of a situation and the ability to extract and transfer the behavior to a new situation. Reasoning has not been exhibited by any animal grouping below the primates, as any pet owner knows when animals are tethered. They inevitably wrap themselves around a pole or tree.

Social behavior among animals is the most varied type of behavior and involves the interaction of individuals and populations. Social behaviors minimize intraspecie conflicts, reduce training time, increases survival, coordinate activities, and simplify courtship. There are eight types of social behavior:

- **Agonistic behavior** is a type of aggression that is often called "play fighting" where neither opponent is injured. Opponents perform a ritualistic display prior to conflict which determines the winner and therefore eliminates the need for violence and the risk of injury. Ritualistic behaviors vary with the species but are most recognizable in the "dancing" of a prairie chicken or the barking and growling of your pet dog. Interestingly, the losing opponent also has a ritual of defeat that may be a "turn tail" and run, or the lowering of stance. Agnostic behavior is exhibited in hierarchical dominance and territoriality social behaviors.

- **Altruism** or altruistic behavior occurs when a member or members of a community sacrifice themselves for the benefit of the group. Mammalian mothers display altruistic behavior toward their offspring. Have you tried getting between a mother bear and her cub? Don't.

- **Communication** is varied in the animal kingdom. A nimals signal messages to other animals for a variety of reasons. Effective communication strategies increase survival, minimize fights, and maximize courtship. The swift movement of a deer signals the entire herd to run, the dominant display of the rooster keeps the rest of the male chickens in line, and the constant croaking of a spring peeper alerts all females within the sound of his voice that he is available and ready for a springtime courtship. Communication strategies are species-specific and must be communicated in a way that is correctly received and understood by the other party. Examples of communication strategies include body or body part movement, voice tone and level, posture or posturing, facial expressions, color or change of color, and scent.

- **Courtship** is a ritualized behavior that brings members of the opposite sex together for continuation of the species. Correctly communicating courtship intentions prevents being consumed by a hungry and unknowing partner or being slapped by an unsuspecting female. The correct use of mating signals is the first step toward courtship. Courtship behaviors generally include what the male of the species will perform: peacock or wild turkey "displaying" to capture the favors of a female; swimming in front of and around the female as in most fish; birds singing; the croaking of frogs; and the proper introduction by humans. The ritualistic head nodding seen in the Adelie penguin is a mating signal.

- **Defensive** behaviors may be summarized by group and individual behaviors. Group defensive behaviors are common when bees attack an intruder, or when humans band together to protect life, liberty, and the pursuit of happiness. Individual defensive behaviors are usually either submissive or dominant. When threatened, musk oxen form a defensive perimeter around injured or weaker members.

- **Dominance, dominance hierarchy,** or **pecking order** is named after a social interaction popularized by chickens. The rank of an individual within a population confers the right to act condescendingly toward all beneath you in the dominance hierarchy while receiving the same treatment from those above you. In chickens the top hen literally pecks all other hens; the lowest ranking hen is pecked by all other hens. Dominance is often established based on survival adaptations such as strongest, biggest, or fastest. Establishment of the hierarchy creates problems as individuals try to move up the chain, but overall establishes peace and a niche for all. Dominant individuals, male and female, in most animal populations reproduce with greater frequency and have higher rates of offspring survival than subordinate members, which improve the survival adaptations of all resulting offspring.

- **Migration** is the regular movement of a population from one area to another area. Mass movements are usually the result of a movement towards a better food supply, often based on climatic conditions, such as the dry season on the African grasslands.

- **Territorial behavior,** or **territoriality,** is signified when an individual or population reserves a particular location for their exclusive usage. Most often the claiming party will mark their territory with aggressive acts, or scents from glands or urine. Territory is usually reserved for mating, food, or nesting purposes. A pride of lions will aggressively maintain their territory and leave scent signs.

Species interaction behaviors are actions that have evolved over time between members of different species that occupy the same habitat at the same time. The four types of species interaction (commensalism, mutualism, parasitism, and predator-prey) are discussed in detail in Chapter 5.

Taxes are how an organism responds to a stimulus, by either moving toward or away from the stimulus. As an example, the phenomenon whereby *E. coli* bacteria will alter their locomotion to congregate at a blood drop is an example of a chemotaxis. Interestingly, the bacterium *Magnetospirillum magnetotacticum* contains a particle of magnetite that always orients the bacterium to the North Pole. This magnetotaxis helps the bottom-dwelling bacteria to swim downward to return to its niche in the sediment.

Chapter 5

Ecology

Ecology is the study of how organisms interact with other organisms and with their physical environment. Ecology is the study of how organisms live, react, and fit into their environment. Ecologists are particularly interested in understanding the ecology of populations as a way of understanding the balance of nature and knowing trends that may affect humans.

Populations

A **population** consists of all of the individuals of a single species found in a given habitat at one time. A population of ducks would be all of the ducks that live together on the same pond or the total number of ants belonging to the same colony. Their habitat is the location where a particular population lives. The habitat for the ducks in the previous example is their pond. Adding two or more populations together in the same habitat creates a community. The ducks, fish, water spiders, and aquatic plants form a community that lives in the same pond habitat. An ecosystem or ecological system is a community of organisms and the biotic and abiotic factors that affect them. Biotic factors are living organisms; abiotic are nonliving factors.

Intraspecific Competition

Intraspecific competition occurs when members of the same species are competing for the same result, usually a food source or mating opportunities. Everything is great as long as there is plenty of food and available mates. But what happens when the supplies become limited?

Let's create a food shortage. There is no longer enough for everyone in the population to have enough food to survive. In some cases the dominant organism excludes all subordinates. When this happens, the subordinates must either die-off, depose the dominant organism and become dominant, migrate, or feed at odd times when the dominant organism is predisposed. Indeed, some organisms do die of starvation while others move away and may begin the process of speciation (see Chapter 3). Territorial battles are common with herding animals and some herds do break apart to become a separate population. When starvation is a real threat to life, those organisms that are best equipped to live in an area (perhaps biggest, strongest, fastest, smartest, prettiest) survive and reproduce at a faster rate than those who may not have these advantageous adaptations. In other words, organisms that are better equipped to get food survive, the others have to invent another strategy or die. This is the basis behind natural selection (see Chapter 3).

Density Factors

Population density is how many individuals live in a given area at the same time. For instance, in a recent survey it was found that the population density for humans in the United States was about 30 individuals for every square kilometer (0.38 square miles). At the same time in Japan, the population density was 330 individuals per square kilometer—making Japan almost 10 times as crowded as the United States. Population density has several biotic and abiotic affects on the population as well as the community and ecosystem, such as competition for food, reproductive rate, and transmission of diseases or abundance of predators. To better understand the effects of population density, it is important to know the dispersion of the population.

Dispersion Patterns

Knowing the population density for a given population provides useful information. However, it does not indicate how the population is dispersed or located within the ecosystem. Does the population live close together in a pond or are they free roaming like individual male bison? There are three population dispersion classifications: clustered, even, and random:

- **Clustered dispersion** occurs when all members of the population live in a confined area. Herding animals such as wildebeest live close together in a tight group or cluster.

- An **even dispersion** is the regular or ordered placement of individuals. An exactly even dispersion often occurs by the deliberate actions of man, such as the planting of a row of fruit trees. Male frogs are relatively evenly spaced around a pond at evening mating time to maximize their opportunity for a mate and geese flying in formation are evenly spaced. An even dispersion is the opposite of a random dispersion.

- **Random dispersion** is a chance event. There is no set pattern or regular spacing in random dispersion. Domesticated cows grazing in a field are randomly dispersed and trees in a temperate deciduous forest are often intermixed in a random dispersion.

Population Growth

Populations are stable, declining, or growing. Populations grow when more individuals are added to the population, either by birth or immigration, than leave the population, whether by death of emigration. Predicting the growth of a population is tricky because there are several uncontrolled variables. Uncontrolled population growth variables include events such as: are the birth and mortality rates seasonal or random? What about the rate of emigration vs. immigration? Is there a never-ending food supply, and are their active predators? Population growth can be estimated with two models: Exponential Growth model and the Logistic model.

The **Exponential Growth** model is based on the assumptions that the conditions for growth are ideal including minimal predation and unlimited resources. The resulting growth is exponential after a few generations. Graphically, exponential growth forms the classic *J* curve indicating a slow start but a rapid acceleration as shown here in the graph.

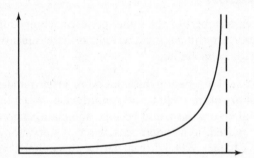

Populations in nature do not grow exponentially for very long. The population *J* curve inevitably bends and may flatten out or take a nose dive in the other direction. Biotic and abiotic factors such as increased predation and dwindling food supplies are limiting factors that combine to define the carrying capacity for an ecosystem. The **carrying capacity** is the maximum stable population size that an environment can sustain over time. The limiting factors that define the carrying capacity for an area can be further classified as density-dependent and density-independent.

Density-dependent limiting factors are those factors that reduce the population proportionate with the density of the population. As the population increases, the effect of the density-dependent factors also increases. For instance, increasing the population places a greater strain on the amount of food available per individual. There are two main density-dependent factors: competition and predation. Competition for limited resources, like water, increases as the population increases. Predation rates increase as the population increases because there are more targets of opportunity for the predators.

Density-independent limiting factors operate to reduce the rate of population growth regardless of the population size or dispersal. There are three types of density-independent limiting factors: weather and climate, natural disasters, and human interaction. Changes in weather or climate patterns affect the growth of populations without regard to the size, density, or dispersal of the individuals. For instance, an early autumn or late spring freeze can devastate the insect population. Volcanic eruptions, wildfires, and hurricanes are natural disasters that can eliminate a population within the perimeter of the event. Perhaps the largest limiting factor is human intervention. Although usually unintentional, clear cutting a forest, urban sprawl, and overfishing can wreak havoc on the native populations.

The **Logistic** model is more realistic than the exponential growth model because it takes into account both density-dependent and independent limiting factors. The logistic model assumes that a population will continue to grow at an exponential rate until environmental factors limit the rate. Eventually the balance between the birthrate and death rate reach a stable state which is the carrying capacity for that area. Even though a chart of the population growth may show peaks and valleys, over time the population growth is described as steady. The logistic model can be described in three steps:

1. Exponential growth where the birthrate > death rate. This occurs when there are minimal environmental factors that limit growth.
2. Density-dependent and independent limiting factors level the birthrate : death rate ratio as these factors deplete the population.
3. The birthrate and death rate reach a steady state over time.

Graphically, the logistic model can be represented by a flattened *J* curve or *S* curve as seen in the following graph.

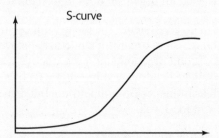

Interestingly, the growth of the human populations was at first controlled during the hunter-gatherer stages by density-dependent factors. However, when *Homo sapiens* became more agricultural the population began the *J* curve. The density dependent limiting factors struck again during the Middle Ages when several bouts with the bubonic plague or Black Death depleted 25 percent of the European and Mediterranean population. The Industrial Revolution and Great Awakening that followed led to advances in medicine and crop/animal production which temporarily lifted us from density-dependent factors and increased the human population exponentially. Sensing the nearness of the carrying capacity, some industrialized countries have either instituted or are considering voluntary birth reduction rates.

Social Behavior

Social behavior describes the interactions of individuals in a population and is characterized by behaviors established by the population and transmitted to successive generations. Social behaviors are necessary to minimize conflicts and training time while increasing the likelihood of survival and successfully finding a mate. There are eight types of social behaviors: agnostic, altruistic, communication, courtship, defensive, dominance, migration, and territorial. These behavior types are expanded in Chapter 4.

Life history patterns or evolutionary ecology is the predictable sequence and timing of events that occur between life and death that are shaped by natural selection. Life history traits are features of a species that can be described and measured such as the gestation time for mammals, reproductive season, and median death age. Summed together, the life history traits construct the life history for an organism or species which reflects lengthy natural selection events. Organisms with similar life histories may be more closely linked in an evolutionary sense.

Life history patterns are useful in predicting the life cycle for organisms. For instance, how long will it take the bugs in your garden to rebound and proliferate after spraying them with insecticide? On a more global level, how long must the ban on commercial and sport fishing for certain fishes stay in effect before the population replenishes itself? The answer often depends on whether the organism exhibits a short or long life history pattern. A short history life pattern is one where the life cycle is rapid. Short history life patterns are typical of areas characterized by organisms from changeable environments. Typically the organisms are small in structure, like rodents, and mature quickly, reproduce early, and rapidly pass through their short life cycle. Short life history organisms are defined as "live fast and die young." Long life history organisms, like trees and elephants tend to be large and proceed through their life cycle more slowly. A product of a slow changing environment, long life history organisms do not replenish their populations as quickly as short life history organisms. Long life history organisms are defined as "live long and prosper." It is interesting to note that long life history species are slightly more susceptible to population decline or extinction because of their slow reproduction response time.

Communities

A **community** is one or more species of plants, animals, and other organisms living and interacting in the same habitat. Communities can be found in virtually every biome including deserts, forests, tundra, and grasslands. Within each community every population has a distinct habitat and niche. The habitat is the location where a particular population lives. The niche is what an organism does in its habitat.

The **niche** is the role an organism plays in an ecosystem. The niche for a population describes its function and position within the ecosystem. For instance, is the organism a nocturnal scavenger or a diurnal herbivore? A niche further defines the diet, methods of food procurement, reproductive season, and periods of activity and inactivity for the species. An organism's niche is influenced by abiotic factors such as temperature and food requirements as well biotic factors such as intraspecific competition and density. A niche also includes the location of a population in the food chain and food web.

A food chain is a simplified linear description that displays the flow of energy through an ecosystem by showing which organism consumes or is consumed by another organism. Complete food chains begin with a plant and terminate with the top carnivore as seen in the following graphic.

Food webs are a more realistic magnification of food chains. Food webs show the complex interaction and energy flow between all or most members of the community. The more complex design still shows the flow of energy from the plant or sun to the top carnivore as seen in the following graphic.

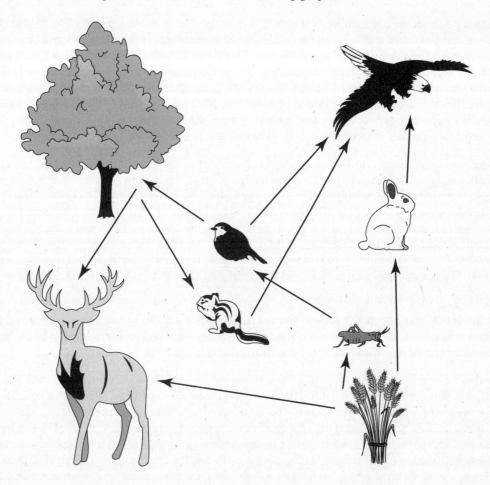

Interspecific relationships are symbiotic behaviors that have evolved over time that allow the members of a community to survive and successfully reproduce. Symbiotic behaviors or symbiosis occurs when two or more species live in close proximity over long periods of time, such as in the same community. There are four main types of species symbiotic behavior: commensalism, mutualism, parasitism, and predator-prey.

Commensalism is a relationship between two species in which one species benefits and the other species is unaffected. A typical commensalism relationship exists between domesticated cattle and egrets. As cattle forage for food in the grasslands, they scare up hidden insects. Hungry egrets monitor the movement of the cattle and prey upon any insect that shows itself. The egrets are fed and the cattle are unaffected. The goby fish receives protection from the poisonous sea urchin. The sea urchin is unaffected.

Mutualism is a symbiotic relationship in which both species benefit from their interaction. An interesting mutual behavior occurs between the ant and acacia trees in Central America. The ants burrow into the thorns of the acacia tree and live there while extracting a complete diet of plant fluids from the tree. The tree is unharmed but gains the protection of the ants from intruders. The ants release a foul-smelling odor and physically attack any intruding herbivore.

Parasitism occurs when one species benefits but the host organism is harmed by their interaction. Most people have heard of human tapeworms (endoparasite) and ticks (ectoparasite) because they warm themselves and dine at human expense. An orchid anchored and growing in a tree lives off of the fluids provided by the host tree.

Predator-prey relationships are a life and death event. The predator lives and benefits from the interaction while the prey dies because of the interaction. The bats that eat the mosquitoes in your yard every warm evening serve as predators and the mosquitoes are the prey.

Species diversity is a measure of the number of different species that live in an area. Species diversity helps to maintain the resiliency and productivity of a community. The more different types of species present in a community, the greater the resiliency and productivity of that community. Researchers conducted an experiment that measured the productivity of 207 separate land areas that yielded two concluding statements. They found that the greatest amount of plant material was produced in those experimental sites where the species diversity was the greatest. They also recorded that the sites with the greatest diversity also recovered faster after a drought. Interestingly, in some cases, species diversity is a bad thing. Airports maintain a monoculture of a local plant around the landing zone to discourage birds and other animals from interfering with the take-off and landing of aircraft.

Ecological succession is the orderly and predictable replacement of plant and animal populations in a given area over time as better adapted species populate the area. The process of succession is based on abiotic and biotic factors changing the environment. Changes in the environment allow better adapted organisms to reproduce at a faster rate and replace the existing species. Change in an environment will happen sooner or later. For instance, the growth of plants creates habitat for animals and more plants; the plants and animals grow, multiply, and change their environment by their life functions. Subtle changes caused by the existing plant and animal species allow better adapted plants and animals to replace them. Succession can also be described as a change in an ecosystem over time. Try not mowing your yard for several years and see what new plants and animals arrive.

The climate for a given area determines which plants can survive. The plant species found in a given area affect the type of animals that may are able to survive there. The somewhat regular succession or change of both plant and animal species in a given area continues until the most well adapted species dominate the area. At that point, a climax community is established and succession no longer occurs unless there is a disturbance.

Ecological succession begins with the growth of plants. Herbivores soon follow with carnivores next. Assuming that there are no drastic changes in climate or natural disasters, it is the plant and animal species that cause succession to occur. Each species changes the ecosystem allowing better-adapted organisms a chance to enter and dominate. The succession of species can be demonstrated on a beach after a hurricane strips the area of life. The first organisms to recolonizes the area are the beach grasses along with the invertebrates. Beach grasses soon stabilize the area and begin to proliferate, attracting herbivores and arthropods. Over time, the beach grasses create pockets of soil in protected areas that allow woody shrubs to grow. The woody shrubs attract birds and small mammals which in turn attracts predators such as snakes and hawks. The woody shrubs increasingly stabilize the area so that woody trees can grow. The graphic here depicts a simplified disturbed-area-to-forest ecological succession.

Natural disasters such as wildfires and volcanic eruptions may erase a climax community. When that happens, the process of primary succession begins. **Primary succession** is the colonization of an area occurs where life has not existed before. Primary succession is characterized by producing life without the assistance of soil. For instance, after a volcanic eruption, the lava cools and forms new land. Because no life has existed there before, primary succession begins as pioneer plants and animals form **pioneer communities.** Pioneer communities are the first to colonize a disturbed or new area. Through their life processes they change the area so that other plants and animals may gain a foothold. For instance, lichens or moss are pioneer plants and may begin growing on new or bare rock. Over time, the accumulation and decomposition of their dead parts and the trapping of additional soil sediments creates a small area of soil where a larger plant can gain a start. The larger plant shades the moss and minimizes its ability to photosynthesize. The moss dies, but the larger plant is now home for a species of bird that transports seeds that begin other new plants, which attracts other animals and so on. Primary succession begins as a slow process. As an example, algae may gain a foothold on a bare rock and grow there for decades before creating an environment that supports another plant or animal. The process of primary succession begins when a plant, such as lichens, algae, or moss begins to grow on a bare rock.

Secondary succession is more common than primary succession because it occurs in areas that have previously supported life, such as a meadow after a forest fire. Compared to primary succession, secondary succession is also faster. For instance, the massive wind-aided forest fires in California burn everything, but the soil remains intact. Likewise a bulldozer can clear a field of all plant and animal life. However in both scenarios, dormant seeds in the soil germinate and grow immediately after a disturbance. Secondary succession is faster than primary succession because the soil provides a starting point for new growth. In primary succession, there is usually no soil. Secondary succession reaches a stable or climax community sooner than primary succession.

Ecosystems

An **ecosystem** is the community of organisms and the abiotic factors with which they interact. Biotic factors include the types of vegetation and animals, their niches, the interspecies relationships, and the amount of species diversity in a given area. Interestingly, the long-term interaction of plants and animals in a given area allows both to co-evolve.

Abiotic factors include average temperature, amount of sunlight, season characteristics, and rainfall total, type, and seasonal dispersion. Interestingly, the tilt of the earth and your latitude location on the earth determines the length of the seasons and helps define the climate. The proximity of large bodies of water and large mountains influences the local weather and the climate for an area. Ecosystems are molded by the prevailing climate.

Terrestrial ecosystems are land-based ecosystems which vary in size. A terrestrial ecosystem may be as small as an island in a river or as large as a continental land mass. Large ecosystems are called biomes. A **biome** is a geographic region that is characterized by a certain climate and the climax vegetation. Although scientists differ in the classification of terrestrial biomes, there is general agreement to eight terrestrial biomes and three aquatic biomes.

Aquatic ecosystems are water-based ecosystems that include both fresh water and marine areas. Aquatic ecosystems, like terrestrial ecosystems vary in size. An aquatic ecosystem may be as small as a farm pond or as large as an ocean. There are three aquatic ecosystems that are also considered biomes. Terrestrial and aquatic biomes are classified separately, however in reality, nutrients, energy flow, and organisms trespass freely between the two types of biomes.

The following graphic is helpful in analyzing the elements that determine the major biomes.

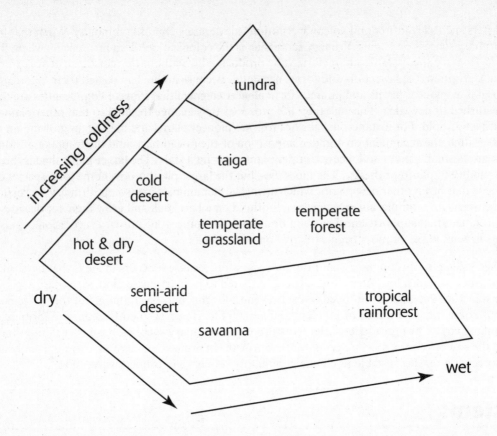

Terrestrial biomes are large land-based ecosystems. They vary greatly in their features such as climate, and the types of plant and animal life found there. The eight major terrestrial biomes are listed alphabetically:

- **Chaparral** is loosely defined Spanish for "a place where green shrubs always grow." The chaparral biome is characterized as having hot and dry summers with rainy but temperate winters, which makes ideal year-around growing conditions for certain shrubs like buckbrush and white-leaf manzanita. Plants in this area are mostly shrubs that have adapted to hot and dry conditions and shallow soils. Chaparral plants provide a plentiful food source and habitat sites for large bird populations. Most shrubs have waxy leaves to prevent evaporation and may contain volatile oils that help spread wildfires. Dry chaparral summers increase the threat of wildfires. Interestingly, the wildfires are an important part of the ecology of the chaparral. The hot burning fires periodically burn off invasive, non-native plant species. But, scrub oaks and other native-adapted shrubs survive. In fact some plants need fire to promote seed release and germination. The climate is dictated by cold ocean currents such as are found on the coastal areas of Chile, parts of the Mediterranean, and the middle of California. The climate is considered pleasant as more and more humans migrate to these areas and minimize the habitat for native species. Smaller, camouflaged animals such as mice and birds as well as bush-eaters, like deer, dominate the chaparral.

- **Desert** biomes receive less than 10 inches (25 cm) of precipitation annually. They are characterized as either hot or cold and extremely dry. The arid conditions do not support much if any plant growth, which forces the native plants and animals to adapt water collection and conservation features. For instance, CAM or Crassulacean Acid Metabolism plants (see Chapter 4) are well adapted to dry conditions and modify the collection of carbon dioxide for photosynthesis to minimize the opening of their stomata. Succulent plants have a waxy coating and cacti have modified leaves that minimize evaporation. The short rainy season causes desert plants to grow shallow and fibrous roots that greedily absorb water, allowing the plant to grow fast, bloom early, and disperse next season's seeds before the dry season. Desert animals avoid direct sunlight by adjusting their active periods to nighttime or remaining in shade whenever possible. Some animals burrow into the soil and enter a form of hibernation called estivation until the dry season passes. A structural modification of their kidneys allows the kangaroo rats to concentrate their urine to minimize water loss.

- **Savanna** is the great dry grasslands. In Spanish, *savanna* means "meadow." A better description would be dry meadow. The savanna biome is a transition area between a desert and grassland. The long dry summers and low seasonal precipitation prevents most tree growth but does allow some types of grasses to grow. Savanna plants have a shallow and fibrous root system like desert plants to absorb as much water as quickly as possible. Herds of herbivores populate the savanna as well as their predators. The grazing herbivores continually move to known water areas as the seasonal drought approaches. The herds of zebras, gazelles, giraffes, and bison time their reproductive cycle to give birth at the beginning of the rainy season as do the predatory cats, wolves, hyenas, and scavengers. The African savanna is the most well known but expansive savanna exists in large parts of Australia, South America, and a small north-south strip from east Texas into Canada.

- The **taiga biome** is characterized by wet and cold climates and is ideal for the growth of massive coniferous forests. In fact, *taiga* is a Russian word that when loosely translated means "pine forest." Taiga ranks second in coldest average temperatures behind the tundra biome. The taiga biome is also the largest terrestrial biome covering large portions of Siberia, inland Canada, and the northern inland United States; most of the Lapland area; and northern Japan and Mongolia. Taiga is a northern biome that adjoins with the tundra biome which surrounds the North Pole. In fact, taiga areas are often called boreal (northern) forests and contain mostly spruce and fir trees. These coniferous trees have developed two environmental adaptations to deal with the climate. Hemlocks, pines, and fir trees have developed needles (which are modified leaves to help reduce water loss) and protective cones for sheltering gametes. Taiga winters are cold, wet, and long which creates snow layers large enough for burrowing animals, such as snowshoe hares and rodents, to create pathways under the snow to escape predation from wolves, bears, and lynxes. Larger herbivore mammals like elk, moose, and deer graze on the vegetation. Taiga animals have developed cold adaptations such as longer fur and thicker layers of fat tissue. Some animals simply avoid the severe weather by migrating to warmer areas like the Canadian Goose or hibernating through it like the native bears.

- **Temperate deciduous forests** are areas where the hardwood trees lose their leaves in preparations for winter. Temperate deciduous forests are located between 35° and 50° latitudes where a relatively mild climate and plentiful rain promote the growth of huge forests of oak, poplar, hickory, beech, and maple trees. Deciduous trees are adapted hardwood trees that drop their leaves before the cold season and regrow them during the photosynthetic season. The deliberate shedding of leaves prevents water loss and adds to the forest litter which decomposes into fertile humus. The forest animals have some of the same adaptation as animals from colder areas such as hibernation, extra fur, and fat. A wide range of animals are typical of the temperate deciduous forest including amphibians, reptiles, birds, and mammals. The temperate deciduous forests are located along the eastern coastal areas of North America and Eastern Europe. In the autumn, the green pigment, chlorophyll, is degraded by the sun and cooler temperatures which allow the display of beautiful auxiliary pigments in final preparation for leaf drop. This biome features some of the most breathtaking fall colors because of the diversity of deciduous hardwoods.

- **Temperate grasslands** exist in dry areas but in almost the same latitude band as temperate deciduous forests all over the world. In North America temperate grasslands are called prairie; in Africa, veldt; in Eurasia, steppe; in South America, pampas. Temperate grasslands once covered most of the central parts of Canada and the United States. The deep fibrous roots systems of the grasses created a rich loamy soil that was several feet deep in some areas. Pioneer farmers capitalized on this wealth and plowed the native grasses into cultivated fields of cash crops. Unfortunately, the roots of the cash crops and uninformed farming techniques were insufficient to hold much of the top soil which blew away during the great Dust Bowl that plagued the United States and parts of Canada from 1930 to 1936. Temperate grasslands support grazing herbivores such as sheep, bison, pronghorns, and zebras. These herbivores have adapted large flat molar teeth for crushing and chewing the prairie grasses. The grasslands are maintained by periodic wildfires which burn hot enough to destroy everything in its path. Grasses have a meristematic region throughout their stem so they are able to regrow quickly, plus they have the fertile ash left behind for fertilizer. Trees and woody shrubs have an apical meristem that when burnt does not allow the trees to regrow. So the grasslands are maintained by regular fires. Burrowing animals simply go underground away the fire for safety while herding herbivores are usually able to run away for safety. The grasslands are home to a healthy insect population which eats the plants and is preyed upon by rodent, birds, and snakes in a complex food web. The absence of trees is a characteristic of the grasslands.

- **Tropical rainforests** are located on or near the equator where the weather is consistently warm and wet. Tropical rainforests are noted as the richest life biome because of the number of plant and animal species found there, perhaps up to half of the known plant and animal species worldwide. The climate and day length, which seldom is less than 11 hours per day, produces immense forests of tall trees that provide a stratified canopy over the forest floor. So deep is the canopy that direct light penetration on the forest floor is minimal. With an annual rainfall near 180 inches (457 cm) nutrients in the soil are constantly drawn into the plants, leaving a thin layer of poor topsoil. A characteristic of tropical rain forests is that most of the nutrients are contained within in the biotic (plants) part of the ecosystem, not the abiotic (soil). Plants have adapted to the poor soil by growing large root systems that anchor the huge plants and the organisms that live symbiotically on them. The canopy stratification creates vertical habitat diversity, which allows for greater numbers of species by increasing the amount of living area, much like humans in high rise condos. Animals have several tropical adaptations but the most unique adaptations allow the owner to be noticed or be hidden. Elaborate camouflage protects countless herbivores while equally expensive coloration draws particular attention to poison frogs or native birds.

- The **tundra** biome is huge covering about 20 percent of the terrestrial surface. *Tundra* is a Russian word meaning "marshy plain," which is an accurate description of the tundra during the warm season. The short warm seasons melt the very top layers of soil which creates pools of water that cannot be absorbed through the permafrost layer. Permafrost is the always-frozen layer of soil located a couple of inches beneath the thawed top layer that creates a barrier preventing the absorption of water. The liquid water is available for plant growth and animal usage and gives the area the characteristic "marshy" appearance. However, most of the time, it is cold. Located between the taiga and permanent ice of the North Pole, the tundra biome is bitterly cold and dry, with less than 10 inches of annual precipitation. The long winters also mean long nights and short days that add little to the warmth. Although the tundra biome appears desolate and unproductive, both plant and animal life survives. Plants are typically short and have cold-adapted to the area by producing shallow fibrous roots that rapidly absorb water, allowing a rapid reproductive cycle, and anchor the plant. Mosses and lichens are a dominant plant form. Herbivorous herding animals like the caribou migrate into the tundra during the short growing season to feed on the vegetation while predatory wolves follow. Year-round residents include predatory birds and arctic foxes that prey on lemmings, arctic snowshoe hares, and other burrowing rodents. An interesting seasonal adaptation is the coat color change that the arctic fox and snowshoe hare undergo as the seasons change. Their genome contains genes for fur color that are inactivated in cold weather so their fur grows with an absence of color (meaning white), which helps camouflage them during the snowy winter.

Aquatic biomes cover about 70 percent of the earth's surface and contain biotic and abiotic factors that greatly influence the terrestrial biomes. The immense amount of water on this planet influences climatic patterns, affects nutrient and energy flow, and provides habitat for an interesting variety of life forms. The three aquatic biomes are freshwater, estuary, and marine.

Fresh water is ecologically defined as containing less than 0.005 percent salt. Typical sources of fresh water are rivers, ponds, and lakes. Freshwater areas characteristically have an extended shoreline area, compared to oceans, which allows greater interaction with the terrestrial biomes. Nutrients continually erode from terrestrial biomes into aquatic systems, creating nutrient rich freshwater habitats. Nutrient enrichment creates abundant plant growth, which provides food and cover for invertebrates, arthropods, mollusks, amphibians, and fish. Overly enriched, or eutrophicated, freshwater areas cause algae blooms that become life-threatening as the algae die and their decomposers consume all of the oxygen.

Large impounded water like large ponds and lakes have three life zones: littoral, limnetic, and profundal. The littoral zone is the shallow, nonmoving area that connects to the shore. The littoral zone reaps the benefit of nutrient run-off and aquatic plants abound. This highly productive area is home for a variety of plant life including algae, cattails, and arrowplants. The dense vegetation provides a safer habitat for young fish, arthropods, and amphibians as well as housing for certain birds, like the red wing blackbird. Swampy areas that are only deep enough to be considered littoral are known as wetlands. Wetlands are highly productive areas that contain a large diversity of life. Wetlands, like bogs and marshes, serve to clean freshwater, absorb excess water thereby preventing flooding, and store water. The limnetic zone or euphotic or photic area connects to the littoral zone, but only includes the upper water layer. The limnetic zone receives enough light and nutrients to support photosynthesis, so algae and other floating plants are common as are fish. The profundal zone or benthic zone or aphotic zone, only occurs in the deep water areas that do not receive enough light for photosynthesis to occur. Shallow ponds and lakes do not have a profundal zone. Waste materials and dead organisms sink into the profundal zone and are decomposed or scavenged by the microorganisms, aquatic worms, and scavenger fish unique to that ecosystem. In certain cases, like eutrophicated waters, the profundal zone may become anaerobic because the decomposers have consumed all of the oxygen during cellular respiration.

Estuaries are brackish waters that are a mixture of salt and fresh water. Most estuaries are highly productive because they are shallow enough so that the limnetic zone reaches to the bottom, allowing photosynthesizing plants to grow. Estuaries also benefit from the oceanic tidal flow and fresh water input that brings a mixture of additional nutrients. The vegetative productivity creates an energy source for a well-developed food web that includes an abundance of top consumers like shore birds. Mangrove trees have developed a salt-adaptation with specialized structures that secrete salt out of their leaves.

Estuaries are also among the most threatened biomes because of natural and human interference. Hurricanes, cyclones, tsunamis, and tropical storms regularly alter the salt content in the water. A number of major urban centers, like New York City and Tokyo were built next to an existing estuary to make life easier. Unfortunately, humans often release their wastes, both biological and industrial, into the estuaries thereby making the living conditions intolerable for the life that makes an estuary so productive. In a typical estuary the waters are shallow and near human activity.

Marine or oceanic biomes are the largest biome. The marine biome is divided into three zones: intertidal, neritic, and pelagic.

The intertidal zone is the shallow water near shore where tidal fluctuations create alternating wet and dry areas. The intertidal zone creates environmental challenges for organisms living there. Alternating high and low tides create times of hydration and dehydration as well as alternating in-out, and up-down currents. Echinoderms like the sea cucumber and starfish have strong specialized structures that can hold them in place and waterproof exteriors that prevent water loss.

The neritic or coastal zone or sublittoral zone is the shallow water between the intertidal zone and the edge of the continental shelf. The neritic or photic or euphotic zone is the most productive of the marine zones because light penetration allows photosynthesis to occur at all depths. The neritic zone is heavily populated with plankton and zooplankton because of the sun penetration, dissolved oxygen, surface nutrient runoff, and the marine nutrients provided by ocean upwelling. Plankton and zooplankton are a community that includes microbes, algae, invertebrates, and fish larvae that form the base of the food. The intricate food web makes the neritic zone home for some of the world's best sport and commercial fishing areas. In the warmer tropical waters, invertebrate corals create huge coral reef communities.

The pelagic zone is any water that is not close to the bottom or shore. Pelagic is loosely translated from Greek to mean "open sea." The pelagic zone is the vast ocean. It includes the greatest vertical range and the largest volume of any biome. The pelagic vertical column is not very productive except for the surface photic layer. Increasing water depth leads to decreasing productivity because of decrease light, temperature, dissolved oxygen levels, and increasing water pressure. Surface animals like sharks, whales, migratory fish, and squid do not need special deep water adaptations, but the deep ocean critters have several specialized structures. Most have a flexible cartilaginous skeleton that will not break under extreme pressure and a reduced metabolism. Certain fish, like the angler fish, have developed a symbiotic relationship with luminescent bacteria that light up to attract prey. The graphic here shows the location of each zone.

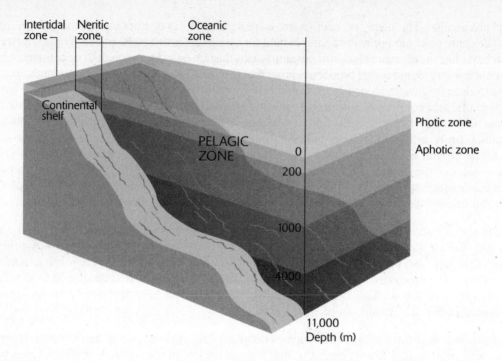

Energy flows in one direction within an ecosystem from the producers (plants, algae, bacteria) to consumers (animals) to decomposers (microbes). Energy is transformed from solar energy into various forms of chemical and heat energy as it is transferred from organism to organism. The ultimate source of all energy, except for some thermal vents, is the sun.

Producers or autotrophs trap the solar energy and change it into the chemical energy of carbohydrates and other biomolecules. Herbivores or heterotrophs transfer the chemical energy and transform it into useful biochemicals for their life functions. Consumers eat herbivores and other consumers transferring and transforming the energy again. In each energy transfer, approximately 90 percent of the original available energy is lost and unavailable to the next trophic level. (*Note:* To be clear, only 10 percent of the energy is transferred to the next trophic level, i.e., 90 percent is lost.) For instance, if the sun hypothetical releases 1,000 calories of energy that are absorbed and assimilated by the producers, then only 100 calories are available to the herbivore, and only 10 available to the first carnivore, and only 1 to a carnivore that feeds on the first carnivore. Each level, such as producer or consumer, is a trophic level and allows ecologists to study the flow of energy in a more realistic method. The pathway of energy through the various trophic levels is called a food chain, mentioned earlier in the chapter. Food chains show the order that organisms feed on other organisms and transfer their energy. Food chains may include four trophic levels but a fifth level is rare because of the meager amount of energy available to the top consumer. In the simple food chain shown here, the sun is the energy input, the grass (producer) represents the first tropic level; the second trophic level is occupied by a deer (herbivore); while the third trophic level contains a lion (carnivore).

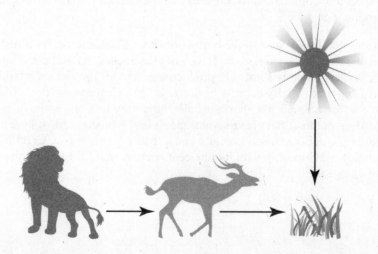

The energy flow through an ecosystem often has more than one option. A more realistic view of energy transfer is depicted by a food web, also mentioned earlier in the chapter. A food web shows the interconnection between all of the life forms that transfer energy. A food web is the combination of multiple food chains that show all energy flow options for an ecosystem. Food webs also show the change of energy flow direction that may result when the growth of a population becomes high or low. The food web shows that a population change in one or more species has a ripple effect through the web.

The transfer of energy can also be diagrammed using an energy pyramid. An energy pyramid is a graphic model that shows the relative amount of energy available in each trophic level. Each trophic level is represented by a stacked block and the amount of energy available is depicted as the width of the block. Because producers contain the most available energy, their block is the widest and on the bottom. Primary consumers (herbivores) are the next largest block located on top of the producers. Secondary consumers receive less energy and have a smaller block with tertiary consumers receiving even less. This has a profound effect on the relative abundance of primary consumers and tertiary consumers. For example it would take 1 million, 1 gram–size grasshoppers (1,000 kg) to sustain 2 to 5 Kg of owls. Examine the simplified energy pyramid shown here and note the amount of energy that is lost as it is transferred within a food chain.

Energy Pyramid

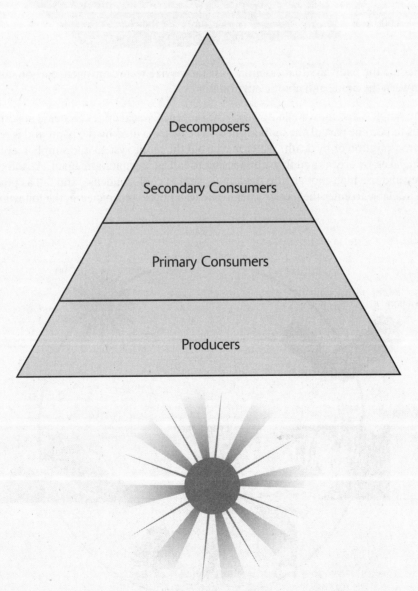

Sometimes energy pyramids combine the organisms found in the food chain or web to provide even more information. Note the simplified energy pyramid shown here that integrates the organisms found at the trophic level.

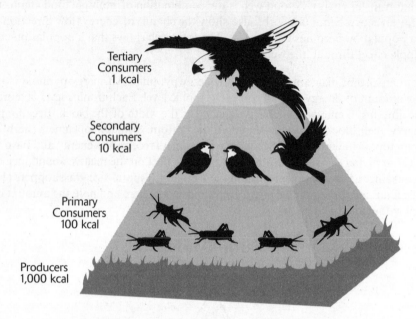

Biogeochemical cycles are the pathways that essential substances like water, nitrogen, carbon, and phosphorus take as they pass between the biotic and abiotic environment.

The water cycle is the simplest and most well known of the biogeochemical cycles. Water is absorbed by plants and unicellular organisms to become part of the biotic system. The water is used by the plant and is released to the abiotic atmosphere by transpiration or by death. Water may avoid the biotic system and simply recycle by evaporating from puddles, stream, lakes, or oceans and then condensing to fall as precipitation again. At some point the water molecules gain energy and rise high enough into the atmosphere to cool, condense, and fall as precipitation. The precipitation is then available to enter the biotic system. The water cycle is depicted in the following graphic.

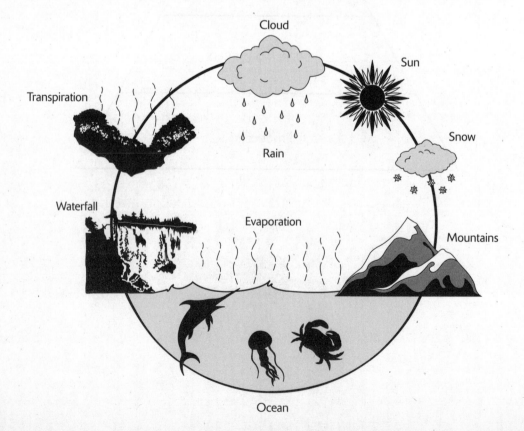

The carbon cycle follows the flow of elemental carbon. Recall that carbon is used in every biomolecule and forms the framework for all organic molecules. Carbon exists in the abiotic environment as carbon dioxide in the atmosphere or dissolved in water. Carbon dioxide is absorbed by plants as a raw material for photosynthesis. Photosynthesis creates carbon-based biomolecules which enter the biotic system when used by plants and consumed by animals. Carbon dioxide is released from all aerobic organisms as a result of their aerobic respiration of food and decomposition after death. Carbon dioxide is also returned to the atmosphere by combustion and erosion. The combustion or burning of organic materials, such as wood and fossil fuels, gives off carbon dioxide as a waste gas. Carbon eroded from the terrestrial ecosystems into the aquatic communities may be absorbed by corals or mollusks and other shell forming organisms to create a calcium carbonate shell or exoskeleton. Over years the deposited calcium carbonate is compressed into limestone which when exposed to the atmosphere, offers the carbon in the carbonate for use by organisms. Limestone is often sold as lime for use as a soil amendment to neutralize acidic soils. The following graphic shows the recycling pathway of carbon.

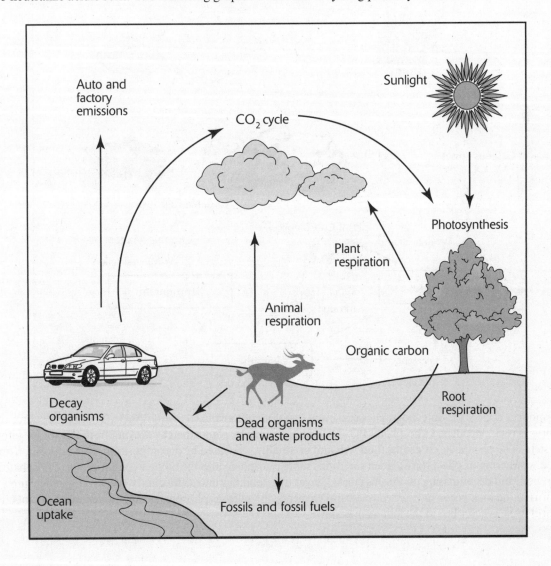

The nitrogen cycle is unique because it relies heavily on microbial action. Our atmosphere is mostly (78 percent) elemental nitrogen (N_2) which is a form that is not directly usable by humans or plants. However, the atmospheric nitrogen is converted into ammonia (NH_3) by nitrogen-fixing bacteria. Ammonia readily reacts with water in the environment to form ammonium (NH_4^+). Another type of bacteria called nitrifying bacteria convert ammonium to nitrate (NO_3), the usable form of nitrogen. Plants absorb the nitrate changing it from the abiotic to the biotic environment, incorporating it into proteins and nucleic acids. Plants and animals transfer the nitrogen in the food web until acted upon by decomposers which change nitrogen products into ammonium (NH_4). The ammonium can be recycled by nitrifying bacteria for reuse by plants or it can be converted back into atmospheric nitrogen (N_2) by denitrifying bacteria. Interestingly, the nitrogen balance is maintained by bacteria in the soil. The model of the nitrogen cycle shown here displays the involvement of bacteria in the process.

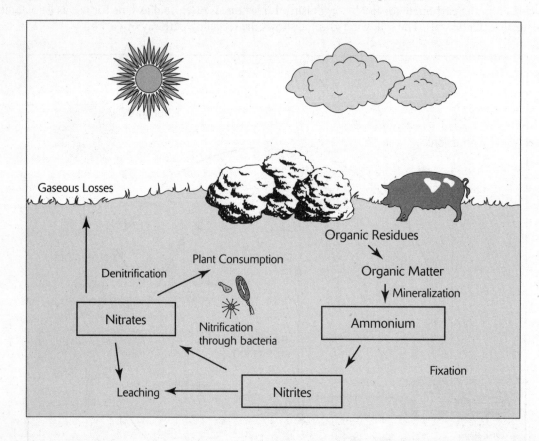

The phosphorus cycle is the only biogeochemical cycle that does not involve the atmosphere. The abiotic source of phosphorus is rock. Weathered phosphate (PO_4^{-3}) becomes useable by plants thereby moving from the abiotic into the biotic system. The phosphate enters the food web and eventually is released by decomposition. Decomposition and continued weathering of phosphorus-laden rock adds more phosphate into the biotic world of plants. Phosphate from surface runoff and decomposing organisms create a layer that solidifies into sedimentary rock over geologic time. The phosphorus in the rock becomes exposed to erosive elements and releases phosphates that are useable by plants. The phosphorus cycle is described in the following graphic.

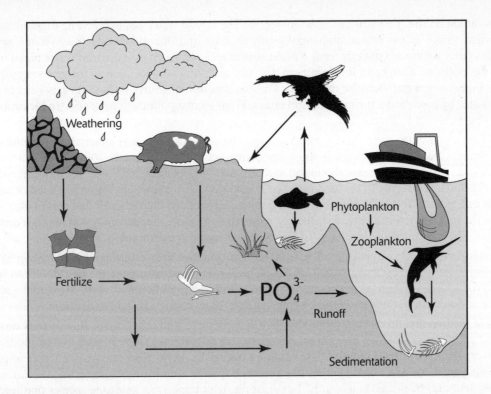

Ecological stability and disturbances are both natural and man-made. A stable ecosystem is one that is characterized by a biotic community that efficiently uses the abiotic resources. The energy flow through a stable ecosystem is constant and biological diversity is maintained. A stable ecosystem is also resilient to natural disasters that temporarily change an area. A disturbance can be any biotic or abiotic factor that changes the stability of the ecosystem. Some disturbances are natural, such as a wildfire or volcanic eruption; but others are man-made, such as bulldozing a forest or releasing air pollutants. Ecosystem disturbances are common and can result in a loss of biodiversity and affect the balance that supplies human food, medicine, and pleasure. Stable ecosystems tend to recover quickly from natural disturbances. Man-made disturbances vary greatly and the ability of the ecosystem to stabilize afterward depends on the severity of the disruption.

The **human impact** on ecosystem stability falls into eight broad categories: air pollution, the greenhouse effect, water pollution, soil pollution, habitat destruction, loss of biodiversity, invasive species, and extinction:

- **Air pollution** is mostly caused by human activities. The bulk of the harmful air pollutants, carbon dioxide (CO_2), sulfur dioxide (SO_2), nitrites (NO_2), and nitrates (NO_3) are released as a result of burning fossil fuels for industrial and transportation purposes. Fossil fuel pollutants are largely responsible for acid rain, usually in the form of sulfuric or nitric acid. Other air pollutants are classified as chlorofluorocarbons (CFCs) that are used as refrigerants and aerosol propellants. CFCs released in the atmosphere react with the ozone and contribute to the destruction of the protective ozone layer. Smoke (particulate material) from industrial chimneys contributes to air pollution.

- The **greenhouse effect** occurs when excessive amounts of atmospheric CO_2 and H_2O allow solar radiation to penetrate to the earth's surface but reflect the resulting heat waves back to the earth's surface thereby warming the planet. Although scientists think that periods of global warming and cooling are natural, many think that the process has been accelerated and perhaps intensified by increasing amounts of air pollution. The gradual warming of the planet is documented and may have serious consequences. Global warming will continue to melt the ice in polar areas thereby increasing water levels causing flooding in coastal areas but also changing the salinity of the oceans which may cause a shift in ocean currents. Shifting ocean currents will have a dramatic effect on climatic conditions worldwide. Global warming is likely to spawn more hurricanes because of increased ocean temperatures while bringing drought conditions to other areas. Note that the solar radiation reaches the surface but the heat waves are contained near the planet.

- **Water pollution** is mostly a man-made phenomenon. The largest water polluters come from agricultural and homeowner runoff, industrial and municipal waste, unlined landfills, and leaky septic systems. Sometimes pollutants enter waterways directly from a point source location, such as industrial waste piped into a local stream. Or, pollutants can enter local water systems by nonpoint sources such as the gross runoff of fertilizers after homeowners over-fertilize their yard. Point and nonpoint source pollutants can also enter the ground water by percolating through the soil layers. Point source pollutants are easier to locate and identify than nonpoint source pollutants.

- **Soil pollution** and damage occurs in two primary ways. The depositing of waste materials or harmful substances onto the ground creates soil problems. In most cases, whatever is deposited on the soil ends up in a waterway sooner or later. Also, certain chemicals kill soil microbes and invertebrates that power the nitrogen cycle, increase soil fertility, and add diversity to the food web. Soil is damaged when agents of erosion like wind or water remove the biotic or top layer. Top soil is alive and teeming with microbes and invertebrates that contribute to the overall health of the soil. When that layer is disturbed or removed by erosion, the remaining soil may be completely depleted of nutrients and biotic reservoirs to replenish and regrow the community.

- **Habitat destruction** is the elimination of natural habitat. Massive deforestation in the Amazon valley and other locations has destroyed nearly half of the tropical rain forest biomes of the world. Urban sprawl has added to the amount of habitat destruction in areas of human population growth. Most ecologists agree that habitat destruction is currently the leading cause of biodiversity loss and extinction.

- The **loss of biodiversity** affects the sustainability of communities and ecosystems. Biodiversity describes the variety of species that inhabit a given area. An ecosystem disturbance that causes a loss of biodiversity affects every member of the food web. The resulting change in energy flow may have a ripple impact on the population growth for additional species. If a keystone species is unfavorably impacted, the entire food web and ecosystem may be placed in jeopardy. For example, sea otters, are a keystone species that feed on sea urchins which feed on the lower stalks of kelp. Sea urchins, if unchecked by the sea otters, create "urchin barrens" that are considerably less productive.

- **Invasive species** are species that have moved from their native to a nonnative habitat and allowed to flourish. Invasive species often have an ecological advantage over native species because they do not have natural predators and their population growth curve is only limited by food sources and habitat. Invasive species compete with native species for food and habitat, but their reproductive success gives them an advantage. In some cases, the invasive species, like the trumpeter swan, is pushing out the local swan species. How serious is the problem? Currently, there are 92 invasive bird species, 192 invasive pathogenic species, and 472 invasive insect species listed for North America by the Center for Invasive Species and Environmental Health.

- **Extinction** lasts forever. It is the loss of every member of a species including their genome. The loss of the genetic diversity may deprive humanity of a medicinal benefit, industrial substance, or delightful fragrance. The loss of a keystone species (as in the example of the sea otter earlier) can have profound effects on the structure and productivity of an entire ecosystem. Some species have faced extinction because of natural forces like the climate change that killed off the dinosaurs, but most recently man's intervention has been the cause. All of the ecosystem disturbances listed in this section has contributed to the extinction or near extinction of one or more species. So precarious is the condition of certain species that they are listed on an endangered species list. There are currently 2,269 organisms on the endangered species list for the United States, including popular animals like the alligator snapping turtle, American crocodile, Apache trout, and moon coral. Passenger pigeons were once the predominant bird in North America. A sighting in Ontario noted that a migratory flock of passenger pigeons was a mile wide, 300 miles long, and took 14 hours to pass overhead. The estimated number of birds in that flock alone was 3.5 billion birds. That sighting was made in 1866. By the 1890s most were gone and the last one died in 1914 in the Cincinnati zoo. Unfortunately for the passenger pigeon, they became a source of cheap food and were hunted into extinction.

Interrelationships among ecosystems encompass all biotic and abiotic factors that inhabit and maintain balance in an ecosystem. The interactions can be classified as involving the climate, soil, topography, plants, and animals. It has been said that everything in an ecosystem affects everything else. To an extent that statement is true, but in varying degrees. For instance, the climate influences all components of the ecosystem. Topography and plants can also influence climate, such as a mountain chain may have a wet and dry side. Topography can also influence animals. For instance, the top of Pike's Peak is not a premier agricultural area or a place to find warm-weather animals. Plants and animals influence each other as part of the food web and in interspecies relationships described throughout this chapter. Plants, animals, and soils affect each other; plants and topography also interact as the growth of certain plants is limited by topography. The graphic here shows the various interrelationships that occur among ecosystems.

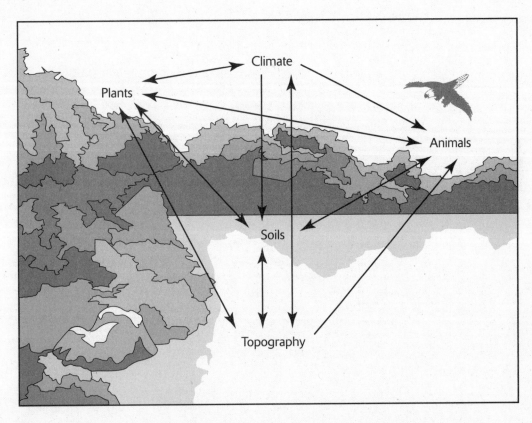

Ecosystems are the functional unit of the biosphere. Healthy ecosystems are a benefit to man.

Chapter 6

Science, Technology, and Society

Science, Technology, and Society (STS) is the study of how social, cultural, and political values affect scientific research and technological innovation and how these factors then in turn affect society and politics. STS is the integration of science, technology, and society.

Although STS is a recent addition to most secondary and collegiate curricula, STS began when the first invention, perhaps fire, had a ripple effect on society and the technology associated with it. Harnessing fire changed the technology of food preparation, the defense against hostile predators, and created new ways of keeping warm, at a minimum. The application of "fire technology" changed the existing society by making life safer, more comfortable, and extended food choices, which allowed the population to increase. Changes in technology and scientific thinking produce changes in society. In turn, cultural shifts in society change the need for science and technology. STS is not linear, but is best described as an intersection. So what are the components of STS?

- Science is the process in which facts and truth are determined. Science is also the summation of what is known, what is theorized, and ideas yet to come.
- Technology is the application of scientific processes, tools, and knowledge to solve a problem.
- Society is you and me. We reflect the cultural, economic, and political aspirations of our social group of community.

Society is often the catalyst that drives changes provided by science and technology. For instance, at present various mobile communication devices significantly dwarf the capabilities of earlier telephones. The technology of communication is advanced by a pressing need from society.

Impact of Science and Technology on the Environment and Human Affairs

One of the best examples of the dynamic nature of STS is the affect of science and technology on the environment. As in most cases, a societal or cultural need generates scientific discoveries which create the need for new technology that change the existing social pattern.

The social push for more conveniences led to an expansion of power-producing industries. Water wheels were replaced by coal, oil, and nuclear fired turbines that produce enough electricity to meet most social desires and needs. In the haste to design and produce more electricity, several environmental factors were not sufficiently weighed. Coal and oil deposits were/are mined with techniques that greatly alter the local environment. Strip mines remove coal from near the earth's surface and until recently, were not returned to their natural state. Oil drilling and transportation accidents threaten offshore aquatic areas, pristine tundra ecosystems, and supplies of fresh water. Both oil and coal have increased the amount of pollutants in the air and water to a point where the global climate may be affected, most surface fresh water is not potable, and clean air is a luxury. The combustion of oil and coal for powering turbines also changes the carbon balance in the global ecosystem by bringing carbon deposits from inside the earth and thereby adding carbon into the earth's atmosphere, land, and water. Nuclear energy may be "carbon-cleaner" than oil and coal, but the danger of uncontrolled radiation may be greater than oil and coal. Nuclear energy also presents the technological problem of what to do with spent fuel rods. Recently, social pressure has affected the science and technology behind energy production. The Clean Air Act of 1970 and Clean Water Act of 1972 placed restrictions on the release of pollutants into the environment. The Resource and Recovery Act of 1976 legally defined hazardous waste and prevented the unsafe and illegal dumping of hazardous wastes on land. In addition the Energy Reorganization Act of 1974 created the Nuclear Regulatory Commission to oversee the safe use of nuclear energy.

Beyond environmental concerns, STS has greatly influenced the course of human affairs. The lifestyle of someone living today is vastly different from a person living 100 or even 20 years ago. Notably, one of the biggest changes is the availability of information to everyone via the Internet and the social connections provided by high tech communication devices such as cell phones and their descendents. Access to information has allowed the common person to expand their understanding in areas that extend beyond their formal education and keep pace with scientific discoveries. High speed mass communication devices are now used as a form of social networking and political awareness. People find mates, locate restaurants, and start social uprisings using their personal communication technology. The use of computers has also opened new worlds of efficiency in manufacturing, transportation, and health services. Computers are universal and connect with the Internet to solve problems and increase social interaction. What next? Several social issues have arisen since the rapid advent of this personalized technology. For instance, most states have some ban on driving an automobile while texting or talking on a phone. Parents worry that their children spend too much time in front of video games instead of learning to enjoy the great outdoors or life time sports. Other parents are concerned that an overuse of communication devices may create a generation of social misfits because they lack the live interaction with their peers. Governments worry that bomb-making directions are easily found on the Internet.

The social and cultural issues that stem from a change in technology generate a need for more scientific investigation. The scientific investigation produces a need for technology to apply the newly discovered scientific principles. Social and cultural practices change with the new technology. The cycle repeats.

Human and Nature-Induced Hazards

Natural hazards are varied and common. On a macro-level, hurricanes, earthquakes, and floods cause massive damage and loss of life. On a more local level, volcanic eruptions, tornadoes, droughts, and wildfires are fearsome and the localized damage can be excessive. The societal need is for a means to predict and prevent natural catastrophes. Unfortunately at this time, the scientific knowledge is inadequate to completely understand and therefore predict and prevent most of these natural forces. While teams of scientists experiment to determine the cause(s) of natural disasters, the science of natural disasters is still relatively young. For instance, scientists do not know how to accurately predict the timing of an earthquake, volcanic eruption, or tsunami. Even less is known about preventing them. However, there is some progress. Scientists do understand how some natural disasters like hurricanes, tornadoes, and volcanoes form. The need for an answer to natural disasters is currently beyond the knowledge of the scientific community and the related technology.

As if natural disasters aren't bad enough, man-made disasters add to the consternation. In the constant quest for improvement in the quality of life, man-made catastrophes are often common. These catastrophes sometimes occur because of the rush to implement new ideas without first considering all potential hazards and collateral damage. Sometimes the economic short-term gains outweigh the longer-term overall benefits. The cycle of society-science-technology is often amended because of societal need and human greed.

Everyone knows about the Dust Bowl that occurred during the "dirty thirties" (1930–36), which created an ecological and agricultural disaster in the American and Canadian prairies. A combination of poor farming techniques and dry weather combined to dry out and loosen the topsoil so that prevailing winds from the west blew huge clouds of top soil hundreds of miles to the east. The remaining depleted soil was unable to sustain even marginal crop farming so thousands of people became penniless and homeless in what became another large human migration in American history. This man-made disaster prompted scientific investigations that revealed several simple truths: deep plowing of the virgin grasses that held the soil in place for centuries followed by a lack of cover crops, crop rotation, and fallow fields created an ideal scenario for wind erosion. The recovery of the prairies began as farmers began using these techniques. Some scientists fear that modern day farming of the prairies may cause another dust bowl as the economic pressure for increased crop production may cause farmers to violate one or more of the simple truths about dry climate farming. The social pressure to produce more crops is forcing additional scientific research that will ultimately lead to new technologies, such as climate-controlled drip irrigation and genetically modified crops. The Dust Bowl of the dirty thirties caused considerable damage in human terms as well as agricultural, environmental, and economic that was not resolved by political means.

The generation of electricity that is needed to power homes, factories, and other human services is made by burning hydrocarbons or splitting atoms. In all cases, the creation of the electricity has also created long-term problems with air, water, and land pollution. Some scientists also affirm that increased air pollution has dramatically affected global weather patterns. Industrial areas contribute to the same problems by adding their waste products to the environment as opposed to recycling, collecting, or neutralizing them. The products of technology have created a social response that is prompting more scientific investigations to create new technologies to solve another problem.

Issues and Applications

Since the end of World War II, the standard of living has significantly increased in North America heralding an escalation of consumer demands and the industrial responses. Along with the social pressure for new and better commodities to improve the quality of life, came a number of ancillary problems.

Production and Disposal

The proliferation of items for general sale and distribution has skyrocketed and paralleled the economic growth of North America. New products that make life easier, more efficient, or more fun spring up as social needs and desires change. The technology to produce these products also creates environmental and energy production issues. Scientific investigation has unlocked several useful production standards that will greatly minimize production disposal and waste:

- Create products that use less material and energy by redesigning manufacturing processes. For instance, the gas crisis forced car makers to create cars with lighter steel and more plastic to reduce their overall weight by 25 percent.
- Implement eco-industrial measures to produce low waste products. Pollution and waste are considered eco-industrial design flaws. Eco-industrial products are designed to produce no waste because they are consumed, recycled, or composted.
- Reinvent products that are easy to repair, reuse, remanufacture, recycle, or compost. Consumers have lost the ability to work on products that fail. Instead, consumers trash the product and buy a new one to replace it. Rather than adding to the community waste pile, reinventing products with the end in mind keeps them in use instead of in the dump.
- Eliminate or minimize packaging by creating recyclable or compostable packing materials. Some packaging is necessary to prevent theft, keep items organized, or prevent them from perishing. In some cases, excessive individual packaging was a technological response to the social need of lowering prices by preventing shoplifting. New displaying techniques may eliminate the need for packaging certain items. The use of biodegradable "peanuts" as a packing material has minimized the need for paper and plastic packing materials. Interestingly, European countries must recycle 55 to 80 percent of their packaging waste.
- Directly influence the production process as a consumer by refusing to purchase items that are produced without sufficient thought of the future of the product.

Some scientists think that the production of materials must be linked with their disposal as well. This "cradle to grave" social initiative requires scientific investigation to produce a technological response.

Use and Storage

In a wealthy society such as exists in North America, items are purchased at an accelerated rate compared to the rest of the world in a spirit of "affluenza." The seemingly insatiable desire for new products often runs ahead of their actual use. Consumers often buy something they want rather than something they need and then find the item unuseful after a short period of time. The problem is compounded when a consumer purchases more than is required because they got a good deal. A number of stored items are seasonal in nature, such as lawn care equipment and clothing. Some people also choose to hold onto items for sentimental reasons or for use at a later time, perhaps. The modern-day phenomenon of "hoarding" is prevalent in affluent areas. The social need of more storage becomes a problem. People rent storage sites; buy additional storage for their house; pile their garages with stuff; and sometimes leave unwanted items as urban debris or country ravine-fillers. Landfills become the final storage place for unwanted products.

Industries have a storage problem as well. The nuclear industry has to store spent fuel rods that are radioactive and dangerous. The scientific concepts of half-life, distance, dilution, and shielding offer solutions. Some nuclear power plants employ the technology of temporarily storing spent fuel rods in concrete bunkers on a remote site. Most industrial storage problems have to do with storage of waste materials. The harmful chemicals that are dumped into the environment are easy examples, but what about the remnants of hazardous chemicals that are stored and then forgotten? In some cases, this problem is solved by releasing the waste into the environment or by declaring a Superfund site at taxpayers' expense. The Superfund is the common name for the Comprehensive Environmental Response, Compensation, and Liablity Act (CERCLA) of 1980. The Superfund is designed to clean up areas contaminated with hazardous substances.

What can be done to minimize or eliminate use and storage problems? There are several suggestions proposed by scientists:

- Consumers should examine the long-term nature of the product. Will it be around for more than a season? If so, where will it be stored? Can it be reused, recycled, or repurposed for additional uses?
- Industries might adopt a cradle-to-grave mentality about the processes that are used to make their product. Are there economically sensible options that eliminate the need for storage? Who will be responsible for the storage of dangerous products, such as spent fuel rods or the litany of harmful chemicals?
- Government regulations may include cradle-to-grave standards for all stored items and declare responsibility.
- Everyone should read the directions and use products correctly and never over-purchase.

Management and Disposal of Consumer Products and Energy

As the proliferation of consumer products and energy escalate with increased wealth and population, the social problem of management and disposal become a scientific concern. What are the recommended procedures for handling this situation?

Scientists agree that there are several strategies that consumers, industries, and governments can do to improve the situation.

Consumer strategies include:

- Escape from affleunza by not purchasing short-term fads or unnecessary items
- Voluntarily determine ways to simplify and consume less, such as walking, bicycling, or using mass transit
- Avoid purchasing or using throw-away items, such as plastic or paper grocery bags in favor of reusable containers
- Repurpose items for a different use before disposing of them
- Recycle or compost rather than dispose
- Get an energy audit for house; superinsulate dwellings

Industrial strategies include:

- Improve energy efficiency in the production, storage, and distribution of products
- Develop methods to prevent pollution and eliminate waste
- Investigate alternative sources of local environmentally friendly energy
- Repurpose and recycle waste into a profitable venture such as rubber mulch or filler from used tires

Government strategies include:

- Mandate purchase of electric, hybrid, biofuel, natural gas, or fuel-efficient vehicles
- Provide and continue tax credits for buying environmentally friendly vehicles, appliances, and housing or making environmentally friendly home improvements
- Offer tax and other incentives for the development of local renewable energy resources and new energy producers
- Phase out subsidies on industries, etc., that burn fossil fuels
- Increase monitoring and penalties for violators of environmental quality acts
- Favor pollution prevention instead of pollution clean-up
- Emphasize protection of habitat rather than protection of species
- Encourage local or industrial efforts to repurpose materials such as unwanted plastic containers to make materials that replace metals, wood, and other plastics
- Increase composting opportunities, such as used Christmas trees

Although the list of potential management and disposal changes extends in greater detail and to more specific situations, the fundamental premise is to examine all products and energy in a cradle-to-grave lifespan.

Management of Natural Resources

Simply speaking, a natural resource is any natural material that is used by humans. Natural resources may be renewable or nonrenewable. Renewable natural resources are ones that can be regenerated by nature in a relatively short time, like trees. Nonrenewable natural resources like fossil fuels and minerals require substantial amounts of time to regenerate. Depleted renewable resources rebound quickly but depleted nonrenewable resources may not regenerate for centuries or longer. However, if social demands for a renewable natural resource exceed its ability to regenerate, then the natural resource is considered inadequate.

Natural capital includes the goods and services produced by the earth's natural resources. Natural capital supports every economy and all life. Examine the abridged table below that indicated how natural capital is the sum of the natural resources and their natural good or service.

Natural Resource	Natural Good or Service
Air	Air purification
Water	Water purification
Soil	Soil renewal, water, and nutrient storage
Nonrenewable minerals	Vegetative support and waste treatment
Renewable energy	Climate stability and energy sustainability

The concept of sustainability has gained increasing acceptance in the environmental community. **Sustainability** is the condition whereby social needs are achieved by scientific and technological interaction to allow the human population to survive indefinitely in a changing world. There are several considerations that describe an environmentally sustainable economic development program:

- The emphasis on production shifts from quantity to quality.
- Natural resources are considered as natural capital.
- Renewable resources are favored over nonrenewable.
- Materials are recycled, reused, or composted rather than discarded.
- Pollution prevention becomes the mantra rather than pollution cleanup.
- Human populations are kept below the carrying capacity. The carrying capacity is the maximum species population load that can be sustained indefinitely given availability of food, water, habitat in that area.

The pathway to sustainability begins with an understanding of the natural capital for the local and worldwide community and how it may be simultaneously used and protected. The sustainable model is one that demonstrates that humans can live in such a way that invests in natural capital and does not compromise life in the future by aimlessly consuming natural capital.

Social, Political, Ethical, and Economic Issues in Biology

Issues that surface in the local and worldwide news are often entangled with social, political, ethical, cultural, and economic interests. Sorting through the varying interests is sometimes a long and tedious task.

Economics is the study of the choices that humans make in their use of limited resources. Markets are described as self-contained economic systems in which products, services, and money flow in a predictable cycle. The monetary value of a product or service is determined by the consumer based on its cost and benefit. The producer of the product or service also determines the monetary value based on the cost or time involved in its production and distribution. The monetary values for the producer and consumer change as priorities shift. **Economic growth** is described as an economic system where an increase in the flow of money and products or services is noted. In most economic models, collateral effects are not considered. For instance, the effect on existing native habitat may not be considered before establishing a new industrial zone. In fact, economists often view external factors such as subsequent environmental problems as a form of market failure. A market failure occurs when the actual cost of an item is different from its true cost. As an example, the cost of a leather belt is influenced by market failures such as the cost of drilling a new well to water the livestock because the previous impoundment of water was removed because it blocked the natural movement of local fish.

When a market appears to be overstepping a boundary, social forces are exerted on the politicians. Politicians then spend political capital encouraging governments to influence the market based on societal pressures. In response, governments sometimes impose regulations on economic systems. The regulations often provide guidelines based on social pressure and institute fines for failure to follow them. Likewise governments establish economic incentives to reward the market for a new initiative. Governments have tried both the carrot and the stick approach to regulating economic systems. Unfortunately, regulations interfere with the fundamentals of capitalism and are often difficult to enforce. The best solutions occur when the government and economists collaborate on a long-term solution to an issue.

What are some of the major biological issues? The following abbreviated list contains issues that society is wrestling with at this time. Societal indecision may affect the resulting scientific investigations and technological innovations in the following areas: environmental quality or industrial expansion; genetic engineering or natural breeding; global warming—fact or fiction; bioterrorism or invasion of personal privacy; nuclear power or alternative energy; stem cell research or not; pregnancy or abortion; human health or medical advances; and life or death.

Ethics is a branch of philosophy that addresses the morality of issues and is often referred to as moral philosophy. Ethical considerations probe right or wrong, good or evil, virtue or vice, and fair or unfair for controversial issues. **Bioethics** is a subset of ethics that deals with questions arising from advances in biology and medicine. Typically the issues overlap cultural preferences, social demands, political ramifications, economic interests, legal precedent, and scientific progress. Advancements in science and technology are met with a degree of ethical filtering. In some areas the ethical considerations create heated debates, such as in the scientific progress in the human health and medical field.

Societal Issues with Health and Medical Advances

Next to ethical concerns about the environment, scientific and technological progress has created the most discussion. It is likely that the emphasis placed on health and medical advances are due to rapid and continual scientific discoveries in the area. Within the field of medicine and health is the blossoming field of genetic engineering, which has formed a large data base of new concepts. The rush of recent discoveries has created a general lack of public education in the fundamentals regarding each breakthrough. This lack of understanding is often translated into negative feelings, distrust, and antagonistic responses. The role of the biology educator is often seen as a mediator or facilitator of discussions regarding ethical considerations. Some of the more prominent health and medical issues are defined next:

- **Biometrics** is the analysis and cataloging of genetic traits, such as fingerprints and iris patterns, to identify individuals. It is thought that databases containing this type of personal information is an invasion of privacy and may make people more susceptible to identity theft. Others feel that this level of identification is necessary to prevent terrorist attacks and security breaches.

- **DNA manipulation** or **genetic engineering** is the deliberate altering of an organism's DNA so as to produce a useful product. A genetically modified organism (GMO) poses several health problems such as what happens when there is an accidental or purposeful release of GMOs into the environment? GMOs may alter the food web and interfere with the human food supply, interbreed with native species to form unwanted genetic combinations, or mutate into a harmful organism. Ethical issues surrounding DNA manipulation include creating new organisms that may ultimately have a detrimental effect versus the positive aspect of curing existing diseases and providing more efficient food sources.

- **Cloning** is a process that occurs in nature and can also be replicated in the laboratory. Cloning is a natural form of asexual reproduction, like the budding or mitotic division of unicellular organisms. In the laboratory, the process of cloning large animals occurs when in a process called somatic-cell nuclear transfer (SCNT), whereby the nucleus of an adult cell is inserted to replace an existing egg cell. The egg cell then grows into an embryo. In 1997, a cloned sheep named Dolly was the first successful clone. Is it ethical to continue to clone animals? What about plants? Humans? Interestingly, most countries have made human cloning illegal. On the other side, cloned plants and animals provide an efficient means to supply needed foods and medicines to a bulging population.

- **Stem cells** are undifferentiated cells that can develop into different types of tissues. The tissues can then be used for medical purposes or for further scientific investigations. Multipotent stem cells can be harvested from adult bone marrow but multipotent stem cells can only produce a few tissue types, such as blood cells. Totipotent stem cells can develop into virtually any tissue type and are harvested from new human embryos. Is it right or wrong to harvest stem cells from a human embryo to conduct scientific investigations that may produce a cure for a disease?

- **Human genetics** is a sensitive issue for many people. An analysis of an individual's genome may help prevent genetic diseases. However, the fear that this information may "brand" or discriminate against certain people, interfere with employment opportunities, insurance coverage, and matrimonial interests is a drawback. Is it a good idea to have your personal genome examined? Should everyone be forced to submit to this procedure?

- The **environment** is directly and indirectly linked to human health. Disrupting a balanced ecosystem to increase potential crop areas may lead to the loss of a food web that we depend upon. The release of toxic or hazardous wastes into the air, water, and onto the land increases the likelihood of a potential problem with human health or the health of an ecosystem. Is it fair to interrupt the normal energy flow of the environment to create jobs for the unemployed?

- **New medicines** are created at a profitable rate. But how safe are they? Is it acceptable to test them on animals before human use? Is it permissible to use them on humans without their prior approval? What about experimenting with a new treatment on a group of human volunteers or paid participants? Is it considered proper to try a new medicine as a first treatment on a patient who is dying knowing that this medicine may help save them?

- Most states allow citizens to become **organ donors** and note that request on their driver's license. Blood banks rely on blood donors. Should this practice continue? Is it possible that a new industry may flourish that grows humans to harvest their organs? Currently people are paid to donate a kidney and blood plasma. Is this a virtue or a vice?

The cycle of social need and scientific and technological response intersects at various points with economic, political, ethical, and cultural interests. A lack of understanding in any of these areas will confound the issue and may escalate and lead to frustration and anger. It is therefore essential that educators respect every aspect of any issue. In the case of biological issues, biology educators need to provide at a minimum the fundamentals so that all citizens become informed voters and effective stewards of the earth.

PART II

FULL-LENGTH PRACTICE TESTS

Praxis II Biology Content Knowledge

1 Ⓐ Ⓑ Ⓒ Ⓓ	41 Ⓐ Ⓑ Ⓒ Ⓓ	81 Ⓐ Ⓑ Ⓒ Ⓓ	121 Ⓐ Ⓑ Ⓒ Ⓓ
2 Ⓐ Ⓑ Ⓒ Ⓓ	42 Ⓐ Ⓑ Ⓒ Ⓓ	82 Ⓐ Ⓑ Ⓒ Ⓓ	122 Ⓐ Ⓑ Ⓒ Ⓓ
3 Ⓐ Ⓑ Ⓒ Ⓓ	43 Ⓐ Ⓑ Ⓒ Ⓓ	83 Ⓐ Ⓑ Ⓒ Ⓓ	123 Ⓐ Ⓑ Ⓒ Ⓓ
4 Ⓐ Ⓑ Ⓒ Ⓓ	44 Ⓐ Ⓑ Ⓒ Ⓓ	84 Ⓐ Ⓑ Ⓒ Ⓓ	124 Ⓐ Ⓑ Ⓒ Ⓓ
5 Ⓐ Ⓑ Ⓒ Ⓓ	45 Ⓐ Ⓑ Ⓒ Ⓓ	85 Ⓐ Ⓑ Ⓒ Ⓓ	125 Ⓐ Ⓑ Ⓒ Ⓓ
6 Ⓐ Ⓑ Ⓒ Ⓓ	46 Ⓐ Ⓑ Ⓒ Ⓓ	86 Ⓐ Ⓑ Ⓒ Ⓓ	126 Ⓐ Ⓑ Ⓒ Ⓓ
7 Ⓐ Ⓑ Ⓒ Ⓓ	47 Ⓐ Ⓑ Ⓒ Ⓓ	87 Ⓐ Ⓑ Ⓒ Ⓓ	127 Ⓐ Ⓑ Ⓒ Ⓓ
8 Ⓐ Ⓑ Ⓒ Ⓓ	48 Ⓐ Ⓑ Ⓒ Ⓓ	88 Ⓐ Ⓑ Ⓒ Ⓓ	128 Ⓐ Ⓑ Ⓒ Ⓓ
9 Ⓐ Ⓑ Ⓒ Ⓓ	49 Ⓐ Ⓑ Ⓒ Ⓓ	89 Ⓐ Ⓑ Ⓒ Ⓓ	129 Ⓐ Ⓑ Ⓒ Ⓓ
10 Ⓐ Ⓑ Ⓒ Ⓓ	50 Ⓐ Ⓑ Ⓒ Ⓓ	90 Ⓐ Ⓑ Ⓒ Ⓓ	130 Ⓐ Ⓑ Ⓒ Ⓓ
11 Ⓐ Ⓑ Ⓒ Ⓓ	51 Ⓐ Ⓑ Ⓒ Ⓓ	91 Ⓐ Ⓑ Ⓒ Ⓓ	131 Ⓐ Ⓑ Ⓒ Ⓓ
12 Ⓐ Ⓑ Ⓒ Ⓓ	52 Ⓐ Ⓑ Ⓒ Ⓓ	92 Ⓐ Ⓑ Ⓒ Ⓓ	132 Ⓐ Ⓑ Ⓒ Ⓓ
13 Ⓐ Ⓑ Ⓒ Ⓓ	53 Ⓐ Ⓑ Ⓒ Ⓓ	93 Ⓐ Ⓑ Ⓒ Ⓓ	133 Ⓐ Ⓑ Ⓒ Ⓓ
14 Ⓐ Ⓑ Ⓒ Ⓓ	54 Ⓐ Ⓑ Ⓒ Ⓓ	94 Ⓐ Ⓑ Ⓒ Ⓓ	134 Ⓐ Ⓑ Ⓒ Ⓓ
15 Ⓐ Ⓑ Ⓒ Ⓓ	55 Ⓐ Ⓑ Ⓒ Ⓓ	95 Ⓐ Ⓑ Ⓒ Ⓓ	135 Ⓐ Ⓑ Ⓒ Ⓓ
16 Ⓐ Ⓑ Ⓒ Ⓓ	56 Ⓐ Ⓑ Ⓒ Ⓓ	96 Ⓐ Ⓑ Ⓒ Ⓓ	136 Ⓐ Ⓑ Ⓒ Ⓓ
17 Ⓐ Ⓑ Ⓒ Ⓓ	57 Ⓐ Ⓑ Ⓒ Ⓓ	97 Ⓐ Ⓑ Ⓒ Ⓓ	137 Ⓐ Ⓑ Ⓒ Ⓓ
18 Ⓐ Ⓑ Ⓒ Ⓓ	58 Ⓐ Ⓑ Ⓒ Ⓓ	98 Ⓐ Ⓑ Ⓒ Ⓓ	138 Ⓐ Ⓑ Ⓒ Ⓓ
19 Ⓐ Ⓑ Ⓒ Ⓓ	59 Ⓐ Ⓑ Ⓒ Ⓓ	99 Ⓐ Ⓑ Ⓒ Ⓓ	139 Ⓐ Ⓑ Ⓒ Ⓓ
20 Ⓐ Ⓑ Ⓒ Ⓓ	60 Ⓐ Ⓑ Ⓒ Ⓓ	100 Ⓐ Ⓑ Ⓒ Ⓓ	140 Ⓐ Ⓑ Ⓒ Ⓓ
21 Ⓐ Ⓑ Ⓒ Ⓓ	61 Ⓐ Ⓑ Ⓒ Ⓓ	101 Ⓐ Ⓑ Ⓒ Ⓓ	141 Ⓐ Ⓑ Ⓒ Ⓓ
22 Ⓐ Ⓑ Ⓒ Ⓓ	62 Ⓐ Ⓑ Ⓒ Ⓓ	102 Ⓐ Ⓑ Ⓒ Ⓓ	142 Ⓐ Ⓑ Ⓒ Ⓓ
23 Ⓐ Ⓑ Ⓒ Ⓓ	63 Ⓐ Ⓑ Ⓒ Ⓓ	103 Ⓐ Ⓑ Ⓒ Ⓓ	143 Ⓐ Ⓑ Ⓒ Ⓓ
24 Ⓐ Ⓑ Ⓒ Ⓓ	64 Ⓐ Ⓑ Ⓒ Ⓓ	104 Ⓐ Ⓑ Ⓒ Ⓓ	144 Ⓐ Ⓑ Ⓒ Ⓓ
25 Ⓐ Ⓑ Ⓒ Ⓓ	65 Ⓐ Ⓑ Ⓒ Ⓓ	105 Ⓐ Ⓑ Ⓒ Ⓓ	145 Ⓐ Ⓑ Ⓒ Ⓓ
26 Ⓐ Ⓑ Ⓒ Ⓓ	66 Ⓐ Ⓑ Ⓒ Ⓓ	106 Ⓐ Ⓑ Ⓒ Ⓓ	146 Ⓐ Ⓑ Ⓒ Ⓓ
27 Ⓐ Ⓑ Ⓒ Ⓓ	67 Ⓐ Ⓑ Ⓒ Ⓓ	107 Ⓐ Ⓑ Ⓒ Ⓓ	147 Ⓐ Ⓑ Ⓒ Ⓓ
28 Ⓐ Ⓑ Ⓒ Ⓓ	68 Ⓐ Ⓑ Ⓒ Ⓓ	108 Ⓐ Ⓑ Ⓒ Ⓓ	148 Ⓐ Ⓑ Ⓒ Ⓓ
29 Ⓐ Ⓑ Ⓒ Ⓓ	69 Ⓐ Ⓑ Ⓒ Ⓓ	109 Ⓐ Ⓑ Ⓒ Ⓓ	149 Ⓐ Ⓑ Ⓒ Ⓓ
30 Ⓐ Ⓑ Ⓒ Ⓓ	70 Ⓐ Ⓑ Ⓒ Ⓓ	110 Ⓐ Ⓑ Ⓒ Ⓓ	150 Ⓐ Ⓑ Ⓒ Ⓓ
31 Ⓐ Ⓑ Ⓒ Ⓓ	71 Ⓐ Ⓑ Ⓒ Ⓓ	111 Ⓐ Ⓑ Ⓒ Ⓓ	
32 Ⓐ Ⓑ Ⓒ Ⓓ	72 Ⓐ Ⓑ Ⓒ Ⓓ	112 Ⓐ Ⓑ Ⓒ Ⓓ	
33 Ⓐ Ⓑ Ⓒ Ⓓ	73 Ⓐ Ⓑ Ⓒ Ⓓ	113 Ⓐ Ⓑ Ⓒ Ⓓ	
34 Ⓐ Ⓑ Ⓒ Ⓓ	74 Ⓐ Ⓑ Ⓒ Ⓓ	114 Ⓐ Ⓑ Ⓒ Ⓓ	
35 Ⓐ Ⓑ Ⓒ Ⓓ	75 Ⓐ Ⓑ Ⓒ Ⓓ	115 Ⓐ Ⓑ Ⓒ Ⓓ	
36 Ⓐ Ⓑ Ⓒ Ⓓ	76 Ⓐ Ⓑ Ⓒ Ⓓ	116 Ⓐ Ⓑ Ⓒ Ⓓ	
37 Ⓐ Ⓑ Ⓒ Ⓓ	77 Ⓐ Ⓑ Ⓒ Ⓓ	117 Ⓐ Ⓑ Ⓒ Ⓓ	
38 Ⓐ Ⓑ Ⓒ Ⓓ	78 Ⓐ Ⓑ Ⓒ Ⓓ	118 Ⓐ Ⓑ Ⓒ Ⓓ	
39 Ⓐ Ⓑ Ⓒ Ⓓ	79 Ⓐ Ⓑ Ⓒ Ⓓ	119 Ⓐ Ⓑ Ⓒ Ⓓ	
40 Ⓐ Ⓑ Ⓒ Ⓓ	80 Ⓐ Ⓑ Ⓒ Ⓓ	120 Ⓐ Ⓑ Ⓒ Ⓓ	

CUT HERE

CUT HERE

Time—120 minutes

150 Questions

Directions: Each of the questions or incomplete statements below is followed by four possible answer choices or completions. Select the best response and then fill in the corresponding lettered space on the answer sheet.

1. Barnacles are crustaceans that sometimes attach to the skin of a whale. The barnacle benefits because it is continually transported to new food sources. The whale remains unaffected. Which of the following best describes this association?

   A. Parasitism
   B. Predation
   C. Mutualism
   D. Commensalism

2. A researcher was given an unknown cell from a crime scene for identification. Using an electron microscope, the biologist observes the presence of a nucleus, cell wall, and numerous ribosomes. What is the likely source of this cell?

   A. Human
   B. Plant
   C. Animal
   D. Virus

3. A segment of DNA has the following structure: 5'-CAT GAT TAG-3'. Which of the following would represent the transcripted RNA?

   A. 3'-GUA CUA AUC-5'
   B. 5'-TAC GAT TUA-3'
   C. 3'-UAC GUA UAG-5'
   D. 5'-TAG UGA GAT-3'

4. The bones in a human arm are analogous to which of the following structures?

   A. Bird wing
   B. Whale flipper
   C. Reptile forelimb
   D. Butterfly wing

5. Which of the following best describes the action of a wave of depolarization across a mammalian synaptic gap?

   A. Sodium ions diffuse into the synapse in response to nervous stimulation of specialized cells in the dendrite.
   B. Action potentials cross the synapse in the form of mild direct electrical currents to depolarize the cells in the axon.
   C. The synapse is bridged by specialize cells in the dendrite that carry the wave of depolarization to the axon.
   D. Nervous stimulation releases neurotransmitters into the synapse, which transmit the wave of depolarization.

6. Starch is the stored form of carbohydrates in plants and glycogen is stored carbohydrates found in animals. Which of the following is a common feature of both biomolecules?

   A. Polymers of glucose
   B. Fat soluble disaccharides
   C. Structural components of chlorophyll
   D. Contain alternating monomers of fructose and galactose

159

7. The Law of Superposition states that older rock layers are found beneath younger rock layers. Two vertebrate fossils were uncovered in separate undisturbed rock layers. It is their first appearance in the fossil record. If the fossilized remains of an early snake were found in a layer of sedimentary rock and the other fossil was located in a rock layer above that stratum, which of the following is likely the vertebrate that formed the other fossil?

   A. Amphibian
   B. Hominid
   C. Dinosaur
   D. Fish

8. The reaction that combines the amino acid glycine with another amino acid, alanine, to form the dipeptide glycylalanine, releases which of the following?

   A. Water
   B. Oxygen
   C. Carbon dioxide
   D. Amine group

9. Geese that are raised in captivity by humans think that their human caregiver is their parent or leader of their group. This phenomenon is an example of which type of behavior?

   A. Habituation
   B. Conditioning
   C. Imprinting
   D. Operant conditioning

Questions 10–12

The graph here shows the results of an experiment conducted to determine the effects of introducing a lynx population to prevent the agricultural destruction caused by an introduced hare population. Both populations were counted at the same time on a predetermined annual date.

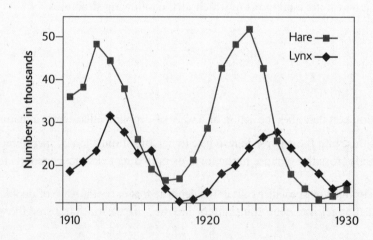

10. What is the independent variable for this experiment?

    A. Hare population
    B. Lynx population
    C. Prevention of agricultural destruction
    D. Time

11. What factor would be graphed on the Y axis?

    A. Time
    B. Degree of agricultural destruction
    C. Hare population
    D. Lynx population

12. Counting both populations at the same time on a predetermined date is an example of which of the following?

    A. Dependent variable
    B. Independent variable
    C. Controlled variable
    D. Uncontrolled variable

13. After transcription, the additional changes that the eukaryotic mRNA undergoes before leaving the nucleus can be described as

    A. linked to other mRNA molecules to form large chains.
    B. a cap and tail are added and introns removed.
    C. introns added and exons removed and linked to histones.
    D. histones and cap added, and formed into plasmids.

14. What is the function of carbon dioxide in photosynthesis?

    A. Absorb and convert light energy into chemical energy.
    B. Supply electrons in the light reaction.
    C. Provide oxygen for the light-independent reaction.
    D. Form carbohydrates.

15. Varieties of skin color exist in the human population. No Mendelian explanation of this phenomenon provides the same pattern of results. The inheritance of skin color is due to which of the following?

    A. Polygenic dominance
    B. Codominance
    C. Sex-linked dominance
    D. Incomplete dominance

Questions 16–17

The following age structure graphs show the number of male and female laboratory mice used in an ongoing population growth study.

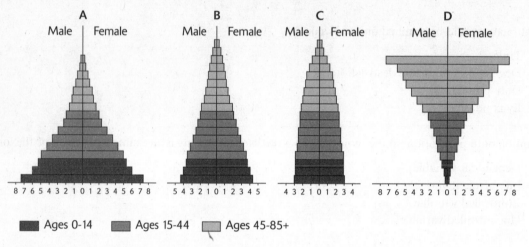

Ages 0-14   Ages 15-44   Ages 45-85+

Note: X-axis represents the population (percent)

16. Which age structure graph shows a sustained population that is closest to the zero growth level?

    A. A
    B. B
    C. C
    D. D

17. Which population represents an aging population that is declining in growth?

    A. A
    B. B
    C. C
    D. D

18. The relative distance between the loci of four different genes located on the same chromosome has been mapped from the following crossover frequencies. Arrange the four genes in their order on the chromosome.

Genes	% Crossover Frequency
A and B	65
C and B	25
A and D	15
C and D	55

    A. ABCD
    B. BCDA
    C. BCAD
    D. DACB

19. The chordates represent a variety of organisms that have a number of similarities during their embryonic development. What is the best explanation for this phenomenon?

    A. Common ancestor.
    B. All animals have similar embryonic stages.
    C. Same analogous structures found in adults.
    D. All organisms have the same embryonic pathway from fertilization to the blastula stage.

20. California wildfires often destroy over 90 percent of the local vegetation. Which of the following describes the wildfire microevolution pattern that results?

    A. Genetic drift
    B. Bottleneck effect
    C. Pioneer effect
    D. Speciation

Questions 21–22 refer to the following gases

    I.   Sulfur dioxide
    II.   Oxygen
    III. Carbon monoxide
    IV. Chlorofluorocarbons

21. Social pressure to generate more electrical power may have contributed to the release of which gas that also is mostly responsible for acid rain?

    A. sulfur dioxide
    B. oxygen
    C. carbon monoxide
    D. chlorofluorocarbons

22. Consumer overuse of certain aerosol propellants has increased which gas that is also thought to be destroying the ozone?

    A. sulfur dioxide
    B. oxygen
    C. carbon monoxide
    D. chlorofluorocarbons

23. Which structure provides food for the developing embryo before germination?

    A. Cotyledon
    B. Vacuole
    C. Nucleus
    D. Endoplasmic reticulum

24. Which of the following is the most effective method to determine the degree of evolutionary kinship in organisms?

    A. Habitat
    B. Food preference
    C. Niche
    D. Genetic compliment

25. Species diversity is best increased in an aquatic ecosystem by which strategy?

    A. Increasing the fertilizer load in the water
    B. Increasing the food web by adding additional producers and introducing foreign predators
    C. Creating more and diverse habitats
    D. Decreasing the number of predators

26. Which individual demonstrates the best Darwinian evolutionary fitness?

    A. A beautiful child who excelled in academics and athletics
    B. A 90-year-old woman with no children
    C. A healthy grandmother with 5 children and 23 grandchildren
    D. An unhealthy grandfather with 7 children and 44 grandchildren

27. Which of the following is an example of a density-dependent factor?

    A. Average temperature
    B. Herd size
    C. Annual rainfall
    D. Climate zone

28. Which of the following is considered a prokaryote based on their cellular structure?

    A. Human
    B. Blue-green bacteria
    C. Blue-green mold
    D. Any multicellular organism

29. Which of the following regulations governing human research is *not* true?

    A. The rights of human subjects were not protected through federal regulations prior to 1974.
    B. An Institutional Review Board (IRB) must approve all human research prior to experimentation for all organizations receiving federal funding.
    C. Human subjects must provide informed consent before any research is conducted by any agency that receives federal funding.
    D. The rights of human subjects are the top priority unless experimentation is designed to resolve an emergency situation.

30. The genome for a particular species of insect is described as

    A. the sum total of the genetic information for that species.
    B. the number of chromosomes that are species-specific.
    C. the specific order of the genes on the chromosomes.
    D. the actual rate of mutation for each allele unique to that species.

31. Each of the following statements regarding meiosis is true except:

    A. Chromosomes are duplicated during the first stages of Meiosis I.
    B. Meiosis II produces four haploid daughter cells with the same genetic information.
    C. Meiosis I reduces the ploidy from diploid to haploid.
    D. Meiosis creates both male and female sex cells.

32. What unique feature of the water molecule provides cohesion and surface tension?

   A. Covalent bonding between hydrogen atoms
   B. Pyramidal geometric shape
   C. Polarity
   D. Ionic bonding between hydrogen and oxygen atoms

33. Some plants undergo an alternation of generation life cycle. Which part of this cycle is haploid?

   A. Seed
   B. Adult
   C. Sporophyte
   D. Gametophyte

34. Which of the following characteristics identifies a prokaryote cell?

   A. Identifiable nucleus
   B. Organelles protected by membranes
   C. DNA suspended in the cytoplasm
   D. DNA organized into chromosomes

35. Which of the following is *not* a true plant stem?

   A. Node
   B. Corm
   C. Rhizoid
   D. Tuber

36. The ability of a cell to grow larger is limited mostly by which of the following?

   A. Diffusion of nutrients and wastes
   B. Phospholipid linkages within the cell membrane
   C. Cell surface area to volume ratio
   D. Genetic predisposition

37. Plants obtain nitrogen in a form that is usable by which process?

   A. Lightning
   B. Direct absorption from the air
   C. Nitrogen-fixing bacteria
   D. Denitrifying bacteria

38. *Felis catus* is the common housecat. Which of the following explains this term?

   A. *Felis* is the species, *catus* is the genus
   B. Binomial nomenclature for genus/species
   C. Kingdom/species classification
   D. Cladistic classification of a species

39. Which of the following are more closely related?

    I.   *Canus lupis* (gray wolf)
    II. *Canus familiaris* (domesticated dog)
    III. *Canus latrans* (coyote)
    IV. *Canus rufus* (red wolf)

    A. I and II
    B. II and IV
    C. III and IV
    D. All equally related

40. Which of the following best explains the concept and driving force of evolution?

    A. Natural selection
    B. Hardy-Weinberg equilibrium
    C. Speciation
    D. Directional selection

41. The presence of mammary glands at some point in their development is a characteristic of which phylum?

    A. Mammalia
    B. Aves
    C. Amphibia
    D. Reptilia

42. Potable freshwater has become an increasingly difficult ecological and economic problem for certain parts of the world. Globally the greatest freshwater consumption is generated by which of the following?

    A. Households
    B. Industry
    C. Recreation
    D. Agriculture

43. In a research experiment, two organisms were mated (P_1) that produced offspring (F_1) that showed an intermediate coloring. When the F_1 offspring were mated, the F_2 generation exhibited the coloration of the parents in almost equal numbers with no intermediate coloring. This type of inheritance is characteristic of which of the following?

    A. Mutation
    B. Codominance
    C. Incomplete dominance
    D. Sex-linked dominance

44. Some organisms increase their likelihood of continuing the species by reproducing in vast numbers. Which of the following deposits hundreds of fertilized eggs at a single event with very few surviving long enough to reproduce?

    A. Humans
    B. Salamanders
    C. Birds
    D. Dolphins

45. Flowers are the reproductive parts of an angiosperm. Which flower parts are necessary for sexual reproduction in plants?

    A. Root, stem, and leaf
    B. Carpel and stamen
    C. Seed and sepal
    D. Petal, carpel, stamen, and sepal

46. Which phase of the cell cycle is pictured here?

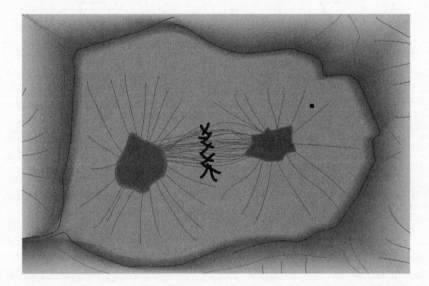

    A. Interphase
    B. Prophase
    C. Metaphase
    D. Anaphase

47. Whales and elephants are among the largest animals on Earth. They are both herbivores. Why are the largest animals usually herbivores?

    A. The amount of available energy is greater for herbivores.
    B. Herbivores are higher on the food web.
    C. The trophic level of consumers contains more free energy.
    D. Consumers are preyed upon more extensively than herbivores and seldom reach large sizes.

48. In a small population of rabbits, the loss of certain alleles due to random changes in their allele frequency is defined as which of the following?

    A. Natural selection
    B. Bottleneck
    C. Speciation
    D. Genetic drift

49. Primary succession is uniquely associated with which of the following?

    A. Climax community
    B. Recolonizing an area after a major fire
    C. Tree growth
    D. Pioneer species

50. Which process is depicted in the graphic below?

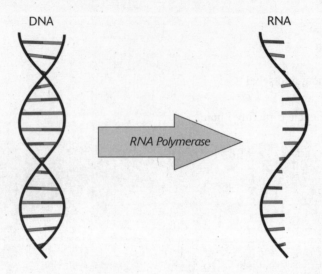

A. Mitosis
B. Meiosis
C. Transcription
D. Translation

51. A biology student massed the same beaker with a salt precipitate four times. Which describes the following four measurements?

First measurement = 23.0 g

Second measurement = 23.1 g

Third measurement = 23.0 g

Fourth measurement = 23.0 g

A. Accurate but not precise
B. Precise
C. Accurate
D. Precise but not accurate

Questions 52–54

A student wanted to determine the effect of fertilizer X on the growth of iceberg lettuce. The student planted 20 lettuce plants in container A and placed 20 lettuce plants in a similar container B. Fertilizer X was added to container B as described by the manufacturer. Both containers were placed next to each other in the greenhouse and watered regularly. The student measured and recorded the growth daily.

52. What experimental error is likely to confound the data?

A. No experimental error is present.
B. Fertilizer should have been added to both groups of lettuce.
C. There is no control group.
D. The independent variable is not measureable

53. What is the control for this experiment?

    A. Iceberg lettuce
    B. Fertilizer X
    C. Identical conditions for both containers
    D. Container A

54. What is the dependent variable for this experiment?

    A. Fertilizer X
    B. Iceberg lettuce
    C. Container B
    D. Amount of growth

55. Which type of biomolecule has a hydrophobic and hydrophilic end making it useful as a membrane component?

    A. Protein
    B. Enzyme
    C. Phospholipid
    D. Carbohydrate

56. What is the best way for a classroom teacher to find specific information about a chemical before using it?

    A. Material safety data sheets
    B. E-mail the vendor
    C. Call the manufacturer
    D. Contact the chemistry teacher

57. Extinction has many causes. What is the primary cause of modern day species extinction?

    A. Climate change
    B. Habitat destruction
    C. Water, land, and air pollution
    D. Unrestricted hunting, over-predation, and dwindling food supplies

58. In 1975, Race and Sanger checked the M and N blood type of 1,279 individuals in London. They found 363 MM, 634 MN, and 282 were NN. If the gene frequency for the M allele is 0.53167, what is the frequency of the N allele?

    A. 0.46833
    B. 1.06334
    C. 0.26587
    D. Cannot be determined from the information provided

59. Beavers are known to flap their tails on water as a warning to other beavers about an impending danger. Although the sound may attract predators or danger to the one who made the noise, the action is effective at alerting other beavers. What type of behavior is demonstrated in this phenomenon?

    A. Habituation
    B. Social
    C. Altruistic
    D. Territorial

60. Which of the following is matched with the appropriate chromosome number?

    A.   Embryo—haploid
    B.   Gamete—haploid
    C.   Sporophyte—haploid
    D.   Gametophyte—diploid

61. Amylase and pepsin are both enzymes that help digest food. Pepsin is active in the stomach and amylase is active in the mouth and small intestine. The following graph shows how quickly an enzyme(s) works on a food type. The lower the pH, the faster the enzyme activity. Which enzyme or enzymes are described?

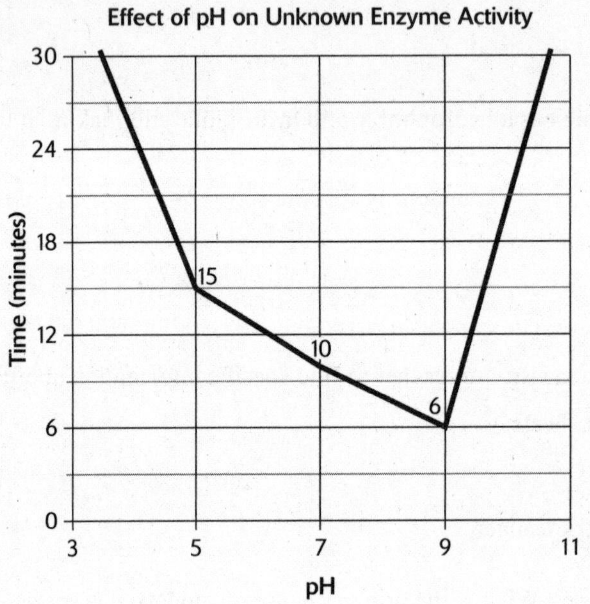

Effect of pH on Unknown Enzyme Activity

    A.   Amylase
    B.   Amylase and pepsin
    C.   Pepsin
    D.   Neither enzyme

62. DNA replication is initiated by which of the following?

    A.   RNA
    B.   mRNA
    C.   Plasmids
    D.   DNA polymerase

63. Thermophile bacteria have been discovered in underwater volcano vents and scalding hot geysers where no other organism is known to live. In which taxonomic group are they members?

    A.   Eubacteria
    B.   Fungi
    C.   Virus
    D.   Archaea

64. Which of the following describes the correct sequence of blood flow?

   A.   Right atrium → left atrium → lungs → heart
   B.   Lungs → left atrium → left ventricle → body
   C.   Vena cava → left atrium → right atrium → right ventricle
   D.   Left atrium → mitral valve → left ventricle → lungs

Questions 65–67

The list below contains organelles that may be found in both plants and/or animals. Assign one or more organelle to one or more of the following questions.

   I.   Ribosome
   II.   Nonmembrane bound nucleus
   III. Mitochondria
   IV.   Cell wall

65. Which organelle(s) are found in both plants and animals?

   A.   I and IIII
   B.   I, II, III
   C.   I, IV
   D.   IV

66. Which of the following is a distinguishing characteristic of prokaryotes?

   A.   I and II
   B.   II
   C.   II and III
   D.   IV

67. RNA is a primary component of which organelle(s)?

   A.   II and III
   B.   IV
   C.   I
   D.   I and IV

Questions 68–70 refer to the following biomes.

   I.   Tundra
   II.   Taiga
   III. Tropical rain forest
   IV.   Deciduous forest
   V.   Grassland

68. This biome is recognized because of permafrost.

   A.   I
   B.   I and II
   C.   II
   D.   IV

69. This biome is often called prairie, steppe, or pampas.

    A. I
    B. III and IV
    C. V
    D. III and V

70. This biome is known for containing the greatest species diversity.

    A. II
    B. II and III
    C. I and IV
    D. III

Question 71–73

Researchers applied two types of fertilizer onto hybrid corn plants and measured their growth height and graphed their data here.

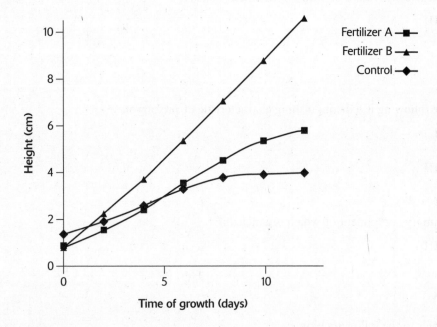

71. What is the likely characteristic of the group symbolized by the diamond line?

    A. A mixture of fertilizer A and fertilizer B
    B. Tested fertilizer
    C. Natural fertilizer
    D. No fertilizer

72. What is the dependent variable in this experiment?

    A. Growth
    B. Type of fertilizer
    C. Length of the experiment
    D. Type of plant grown as the treatment group

73. What hypothesis references this graph?

    A. Which concentration of fertilizer works best?
    B. What is the effect of light on plant growth?
    C. If fertilizer affects plant growth, then the best fertilizer will produce the most plant growth.
    D. How is time dependent on plant growth?

Questions 74–77

In a particular cat, one pair of alleles determine the fur length, short (S) or long (s) and another pair of alleles determines eye color, blue (B) or brown (b). A particular male cat with blue eyes and short fur was repeatedly mated to a female cat with brown eyes and long fur. All of the offspring from these matings had blue eyes and short fur. A different male cat with brown eyes and short hair was mated one time to the same female cat, but most of the offspring had brown eyes and long hair as seen in the data table here:

F₁ Cross	F₂ Results
brown eyes, short hair × brown eyes, long hair	3 brown eyes and short fur
	3 brown eyes and long fur
	1 blue eyes and short fur
	1 blue eyes and long fur

74. Which of the following describes the interaction between the alleles for blue eyes and brown eyes?

    A. Blue eyes are dominant.
    B. Brown eyes are dominant.
    C. Codominance with both eye colors.
    D. Incomplete dominance for both alleles.

75. What is the genotype of the male cat in the first mating?

    A. SB
    B. SsBb
    C. SSBB
    D. Ssbb

76. What is the genotype of the female cat?

    A. SB
    B. SsBb
    C. SSBB
    D. Ssbb

77. Predict the phenotypic ratio of the offspring when the male cat in the first mating is crossed with a female cat with an ssbb genotype.

    A. 100 percent blue eyes and short hair
    B. 75 percent brown eyes and short fur; 25 percent brown eyes and long fur
    C. 75 percent blue eyes and short fur; 25 percent blue eyes and long fur
    D. 50 percent brown eyes and short fur; 50 percent blue eyes and long fur

78. In humans the incidence of infant mortality are higher for heavy and light birth weight infants. This phenomenon is an example of which of the following?

    A. Disruptive selection
    B. Stabilizing or normal selection
    C. Directional selection
    D. Preferential selection

79. The two seed leaves that store carbohydrates for a dicotyledon embryo are called

    A. sepals.
    B. cotyledons.
    C. dicots.
    D. seeds.

80. The first cells on Earth were likely to have been

    A. eukaryotes.
    B. autotrophs.
    C. formed for anaerobic conditions.
    D. formed for locomotion by pseudopodia.

81. Fruit farmers use which plant hormone to speed up the ripening of fruit to maximize whole crops ripening times for economic purposes?

    A. Ethylene
    B. Benzene
    C. Auxin
    D. Cytokinin

82. In the modern day classification of animals, which category is least inclusive?

    A. Phylum
    B. Order
    C. Family
    D. Genus

83. Bone marrow is found in the larger mammalian bones. What is the main function of bone marrow?

    A. Provide nutrients for the bones.
    B. Secrete hemoglobin into the bones.
    C. Synthesize bone hormones.
    D. Create red blood cells.

84. Which atmospheric gas is removed by photosynthesis and replenished by aerobic respiration?

    A. Carbon dioxide
    B. Carbon monoxide
    C. Oxygen
    D. Nitrogen

85. Which zone denotes the bottom of the Pacific Ocean?

    A. Oceanic
    B. Photic
    C. Aphotic
    D. Benthic

86. Which structure is responsible for the translocation of water and nutrients in a tall tree?

    A. Vascular
    B. Dermis
    C. Epidermis
    D. Meristem

87. Which plant part has the highest rate of mitosis?

    A. Root
    B. Stem
    C. Dermis
    D. Meristem

88. What happens during the contraction of skeletal muscles?

    A. The sarcomere shortens
    B. The sarcomere lengthens
    C. Myosin fibers overlap each other
    D. Actin filaments and myosin fibers remain stationary

89. The first action of receptor-mediated endocytosis is best described by which of the following?

    A. Receptors in the blood stream locate a specific antigen.
    B. Extracellular molecules diffuse through the membrane.
    C. ADP is converted into ATP.
    D. Receptor proteins bind to specific molecules.

90. Which of the following must *not* take place in order for Hardy-Weinberg Equilibrium to happen in a population?

    A. Mutation
    B. Sexual reproduction
    C. Immigration
    D. Emigration

91. The extinction of the dinosaurs gave rise to a proliferation and diversification of mammals. This type of population growth is known as

    A. adaptive radiation.
    B. allopatric speciation.
    C. sympatric speciation.
    D. bottleneck speciation.

92. Snakes belong to which phylum?

    A. Chordata
    B. Nematode
    C. Annelid
    D. Aves

93. The field of science and technology offers many career opportunities. Which characteristic is often the first characteristic that fits the profile of this career?

    A. Skepticism
    B. Reasoning ability
    C. Strong scientific knowledge base
    D. Artistic ability

94. Polar compounds are generally formed by which type of chemical bond?

    A. Hydrogen
    B. Ionic
    C. Covalent
    D. Polar covalent

95. Most algae and all protozoans are classified into which kingdom?

    A. Plant
    B. Animal
    C. Protist
    D. Archaea

96. Which condition prevents osmosis?

    A. Isotonic
    B. Hypertonic
    C. Hypotonic
    D. Exothermic

97. Which biochemical process creates the most ATPs per glucose molecule?

    A. Glucogenesis
    B. Glycolysis
    C. Fermentation
    D. Electron transport system

98. What is the longest part of the cell cycle, which occurs when the cell is carrying out its primary function?

    A. Interphase
    B. Prophase
    C. Telophase
    D. Metaphase

99. What is the SI unit for mass?

    A. Gram
    B. Pound
    C. Meter
    D. Liter

100. On the first day of school, a biology teacher notices that there is no eye wash station in the laboratory. Which of the following should the teacher *not* do?

    A. Contact the school administration.
    B. Document the situation.
    C. Conduct a scientific investigation with the students.
    D. Consider relocating to a different room on lab day.

101. Which marine zone supports the most growth of autotrophs?

    A. Photic
    B. Aphotic
    C. Benthic
    D. Shoreline

102. Which of the following is *not* known as an energy storage molecule?

    A. ATP
    B. Starch
    C. Glycogen
    D. RNA

103. Specialized stacked plants cells that transfer nutrients and are joined together at sieve plates are known as

    A. xylem.
    B. phloem.
    C. meristematic.
    D. dermis.

104. Which of the following is *not* true about pH?

    A. The human stomach has a pH below 6.
    B. Buffers can act to minimize pH changes.
    C. Pancreatic juice raises the pH of chime.
    D. Neutral pH is below 6.

105. The final product of gametogenesis in humans produces

    A. spermatagonia.
    B. ovaries and testes.
    C. sperm and eggs.
    D. a zygote.

106. Developing cells in the gastrula differentiate into germ layers that develop into tissues and organs. Which germ layer forms the skin and nervous system?

   A. Endoderm
   B. Epidermis
   C. Ectoderm
   D. Mesoderm

107. Scarecrows are initially effective at keeping some varmints out of a garden area. Over time, the tactic becomes less useful as the varmints learn not to be afraid. This type of learning is called

   A. habituation.
   B. imprinting.
   C. altruistic.
   D. conditioning.

108. Which of the following may be composed of amino acid polymers?

   A. Amylase
   B. Fructose
   C. Cellulose
   D. Steroids

109. The original energy input is our sun. From then on energy is transferred between organisms in trophic levels. What happens to the free energy as it is transferred through an ecosystem?

   A. Free energy is restored by the producers.
   B. The amount of unusable energy increases.
   C. Entropy decreases as usable energy decreases.
   D. The remaining usable energy is consumed by the decomposers.

Questions 110–113

The pedigree below shows the inheritance of hemophilia, a sex-linked genetic disorder. Affected persons are shaded red.

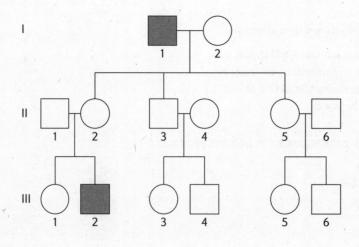

110. Which of the females in row two are likely heterozygous for this genetic disorder?

    A. II-2
    B. II-4
    C. II-2, II-5
    D. All

111. Which of the females in row III cannot be carriers?

    A. III-1
    B. III-3
    C. III-5
    D. III-3 and III-5

112. What is the phenotype of individual II-3?

    A. Carrier
    B. Homozygous recessive-hemophiliac
    C. Normal
    D. Heterozygous

113. Which allele from parent II-I caused the offspring to inherit hemophilia?

    A. X
    B. Y
    C. Both
    D. Neither

114. Which important discovery is credited to Rudolph Virchow?

    A. Plants are made of cells.
    B. Cells can only arise from pre-existing cells.
    C. Germ theory of disease.
    D. Smallpox vaccine.

115. Which of the following determines the radius of an atom?

    A. Nucleus
    B. Electron
    C. Proton
    D. Neutron

116. How is the Periodic Table of Elements constructed?

    A. Elements are listed in ascending order of atomic number.
    B. Atoms are ordered by their number of ions.
    C. Elements are listed in descending order of their reactivity.
    D. Elements are listed in ascending order of their atomic mass.

117. Carbohydrate subunits, or monomers, are chemically bonded in a series of reactions that release water and form large carbohydrate molecules. What type of reaction describes this biochemical event?

   A. Neutralization
   B. Decomposition
   C. Condensation
   D. Synthesis

118. Which type of molecule is identified by always containing an amino group?

   A. Protein
   B. Carbohydrate
   C. Lipid
   D. Fat

119. Some enzymes require nonprotein cofactors to bind with the active site to facilitate the binding with the substrate. Organic cofactors are more commonly called

   A. metal ions.
   B. inhibitors.
   C. prosthetic groups.
   D. coenzymes.

120. An overabundance of sugar in the blood stimulates the release of insulin from the Islets of Langerhans in the pancreas. Insulin is what type of biomolecule?

   A. Structural protein
   B. Hormone
   C. Transport protein
   D. Cofactor

121. Photosynthetic green algae are thought to have provided the evolutionary pathway leading to the domination of plants on land. Which of the following does *not* support this theory?

   A. Land plants and green algae contain the photosynthetic pigments chlorophyll A and chlorophyll B.
   B. Both store their excess glucose as starch.
   C. They have a cellulose cell wall.
   D. They both perform photosynthesis.

122. Mosses, hornworts, and liverworts are the only major groups of which plant type?

   A. Nonvascular
   B. Vascular
   C. Angiosperm
   D. Gymnosperm

123. Which of the following is *not* one of the three main types of vascular plants or tracheophytes?

 A. Angiosperms
 B. Gymnosperms
 C. Flowering plants
 D. Ferns

124. What structure often develops into the fruit of the plant?

 A. Endosperm
 B. Pollen
 C. Flower
 D. Phloem

125. Plants with two or more cotyledons are called dicotyledons (dicots). Which of the following is *not* true of dicots?

 A. Dicots represent 25 percent of the flowering plants and are characterized as having leaves with parallel veins.
 B. Dicots are evolutionarily younger than monocots.
 C. Dicots are characterized by branched or networked leaves.
 D. Dicots have a vascular bundle in rings, and flower petals in multiples of four or five.

126. What type of tissue is located between the vascular and dermal tissues and is responsible for storing the carbohydrates produced by the plant?

 A. Parenchyma
 B. Ground
 C. Sclerenchyma
 D. Meristematic tissue

127. Disaccharides are formed when two monosaccharides are chemically bonded together in a condensation reaction which liberates a molecule of water. The most common disaccharide is which of the following?

 A. Fructose
 B. Glucose
 C. Starch
 D. Sucrose

128. Which is *not* a characteristic of lipids?

 A. The ratio of hydrogen to oxygen is always greater than 2:1.
 B. Lipids are not polymers.
 C. Lipids provide long term energy storage (fats).
 D. Lipids are structural components of cell membranes (phospholipids).

129. What type of bond is shown in the previous diagram?

    A.   Hydrogen

    B.   Phosphodiester

    C.   Ionic

    D.   James

130. Chargaff's Rule is summarized in which of the following statements?

    A.   Adenosine (A) matches with cytosine (C); guanine (G) with uracil (U).

    B.   The number of purines is equal to the number of pyrimidines in a nucleic acid.

    C.   The total number of purines and pyrimidines is determined by the formula $p + q = 1$.

    D.   Purines and pyrimidines form the "backbone" of the DNA molecule.

131. The reproductive cycle in plants includes both a gametophyte and sporophyte stage. What is this cycle called?

    A.   Haploid-diploid generation

    B.   Gametophyte-sporophyte stage

    C.   Sexual reproduction

    D.   Alternation of generations

132. Which of the following is true about the endosymbiotic theory?

    A.   Prokaryotes on the primitive Earth photosynthesized and added significant amounts of oxygen into the atmosphere.

    B.   During the Paleozoic Era about 600 million years ago multicellular marine animals appeared in abundance.

    C.   Bacteria were engulfed and formed a mutualistic relationship with larger cells.

    D.   Describes the evolution of the first prokaryotes.

133. Which of the 10 animal phyla are mostly marine animals that exhibit tissue-level organization and possess nematocysts or stinging cells that are used for defense and prey capture?

    A. Porifera
    B. Cnidaria
    C. Nematode
    D. Annelida

134. Which phyla are somewhat similar because they both have a one-way gut with a mouth and anus?

    A. Annelida and Arthropoda
    B. Platyhelminthes and Porifera
    C. Porifera and Annelida
    D. Chordata and Arthropoda

135. Which structure prevents the acid reflux from the stomach from backwashing into the esophagus?

    A. Epiglottis
    B. Esophagus
    C. Cardiac sphincter
    D. Pyloric sphincter

136. The Clean Air Act of 1970 and Clean Water Act of 1972 placed restrictions on the release of pollutants into the environment. This legislation is an example of which of the following?

    A. Class action lawsuit
    B. Technological intervention
    C. A scientific breakthrough in the tertiary treatment of air and water wastes
    D. Social backlash

137. What caused the Dust Bowl that occurred during the "dirty thirties"?

    A. A combination of poor farming techniques and dry weather
    B. Better farming tools and a decade of wet summers
    C. Using horses instead of tractors to plow large tracts of land
    D. Creating legislation, which allowed industrial pollution that covered and destroyed native plants and crops preventing them from holding the soil during rain and wind storms

138. Which is *not* a recommended method for minimizing production disposal and waste?

    A. Redesign manufacturing processes to create products that use less material and energy.
    B. Implement eco-industrial measures to produce low waste products.
    C. Reinvent products that are easy to repair, reuse, remanufacture, recycle, or compost.
    D. Eliminate the production of all plastic storage units.

139. The social problem of management and disposal of waste has become a scientific concern. Which is *not* a recommended procedure for consumers in handling this situation?

    A. Avoid purchasing or using throw-away items.
    B. Repurpose items for a different use before disposing of them.
    C. Recycle or compost rather than dispose.
    D. Store waste rather than dispose of it.

140. Which biome is characterized as having hot and dry summers with rainy but temperate winters, which makes ideal year-around growing conditions for certain shrubs that have adapted to hot and dry conditions and shallow soils?

    A. Chaparral
    B. Taiga
    C. Grasslands
    D. Temperate deciduous forests

141. Which population growth model is more realistic than the exponential growth model because it takes into account both density-dependent and independent limiting factors? Graphically, this model can be represented by a flattened J curve or S curve.

    A. Exponential growth
    B. Carrying capacity
    C. Logistic
    D. Competition

142. What concept do the following statements describe? The emphasis on production shifts from quantity to quality. Natural resources are considered as natural capital. Renewable resources are favored over nonrenewable. Materials are recycled, reused, or composted rather than discarded.

    A. Industrial-political complex
    B. Sustainability
    C. Resource management
    D. Eco-agriculture

143. What structure contains microvilli and absorbs most of the foods consumed by humans?

    A. Illium
    B. Jejunum
    C. Duodenum
    D. Stomach

144. A double circulation system includes the extra pulmonary circulation that delivers oxygen-rich blood from the lungs to the heart and removes wastes. Which phylum is first to exhibit a double circulatory system?

    A. Platyhelminthes
    B. Chordate
    C. Reptiles
    D. Mammals

145. The atrioventricular node (AV) is so dense that the contraction message is delayed by 0.1 seconds. Why is this delay important?

    A. To ensure the ventricles do not contract at the same time as the atria
    B. To give the Purkinje fibers time to relay the message to the ventricles
    C. To allow both atria to drain completely
    D. To allow both ventricles to fill completely

146. What happens if the change in Gibbs Free Energy is negative?

   A.   The reaction is not spontaneous.
   B.   The reaction is not spontaneous but the overall reaction is spontaneous.
   C.   The reaction is spontaneous.
   D.   The reaction is spontaneous but the overall reaction is not spontaneous.

147. Which stage of photosynthesis is endergonic?

   A.   Krebs' Cycle
   B.   Dark reaction
   C.   Calvin Cycle
   D.   Photolysis

148. Which biogeochemical cycle is unique because it relies heavily on microbial action?

   A.   Water
   B.   Carbon
   C.   Phosphorus
   D.   Nitrogen

149. How do the functions of endocrine and exocrine glands differ?

   A.   Endocrine glands produce hormones.
   B.   Exocrine glands produce neurotransmitters.
   C.   Exocrine glands secrete substances that affect targeted glands.
   D.   Endocrine glands secrete pancreatic juice into the small intestine for digestion.

150. Following meiosis I, the unequal dividing of the cytoplasm of a primary oocyte creates a large and small cell. What happens to the larger cell?

   A.   It becomes an egg cell.
   B.   It becomes the first polar body.
   C.   It dies.
   D.   It becomes the second polar body.

Biology Content Knowledge Practice Test 1
Answer Key

1. D	31. B	61. A	91. A	121. D
2. B	32. C	62. D	92. A	122. A
3. A	33. D	63. D	93. D	123. C
4. D	34. C	64. B	94. D	124. A
5. D	35. A	65. A	95. C	125. A
6. A	36. C	66. B	96. A	126. B
7. B	37. C	67. C	97. D	127. D
8. A	38. B	68. A.	98. A	128. A
9. C	39. D	69. C	99. A	129. B
10. B	40. A	70. D	100. C	130. B
11. D	41. A	71. D	101. A	131. D
12. C	42. D	72. A	102. D	132. C
13. B	43. C	73. C	103. B	133. B
14. D	44. B	74. A	104. D	134. A
15. A	45. B	75. C	105. C	135. C
16. C	46. C	76. B	106. C	136. D
17. D	47. A	77. A	107. A	137. A
18. C	48. D	78. B	108. A	138. D
19. A	49. D	79. B	109. B	139. D
20. B	50. C	80. C	110. A	140. A
21. A	51. B	81. A	111. B	141. C
22. D	52. A	82. D	112. C	142. B
23. A	53. D	83. D	113. D	143. B
24. D	54. D	84. A	114. B	144. B.
25. C	55. C	85. D	115. B	145. A
26. D	56. A	86. A	116. A	146. C
27. B	57. B	87. D	117. C	147. D
28. B	58. A	88. A	118. A	148. D
29. D	59. C	89. D	119. D	149. A
30. A	60. B	90. B	120. B	150. A

Practice Test 1 Detailed Answers and Explanations

Praxis II Biology Content Knowledge (0235)

1. **D.** (ecology) Commensalism is the interaction where one species is unaffected and the other receives a benefit. A parasite and predator (choices A and B) receive a benefit but their respective host is injured; in a mutualistic situation (Choice C), both receive a benefit.

2. **B.** (diversity of life) The presence of a cell wall is the key; none of the other choices have a cell wall.

3. **A.** (molecular and cellular biology) The 3'-5' order is correct; A-U, G-C; uracil (U) replaces thymine (T) in RNA.

4. **D.** (diversity of life) All of the other selections are homologous to a human arm.

5. **D.** (diversity of life) Sodium ions (Choice A) and direct electrical current (Choice B) do not cross the synapse; there are no specialized cells that bridge the synaptic gap, so Choice C is wrong as well.

6. **A.** (molecular and cellular biology) Glycogen is not found in plants; alternating fructose and galactose monomers (Choice D), and fat soluble disaccharides (Choice B) is not a common characteristic because neither biomolecule contains either feature.

7. **B.** (diversity of life) The hominids were the only vertebrate listed thought to have evolved after reptiles.

8. **A.** (molecular and cellular bio) Polymerization of amino acids is a condensation reaction, which releases water only.

9. **C.** (diversity of life) Imprinting is the behavior that occurs at birth when the offspring identify their parents. Habituation is the lack of a response to a false alarm; conditioning and operant conditioning are types of learning.

10. **B.** (basic principles) The independent variable is the one controlled and tested by the experimenter; the hare population (Choice A) is the dependent variable; prevention of agricultural destruction (Choice C) is the problem; and time(Choice D) is a controlled variable.

11. **D.** (basic principles) The dependent variable (hare population) is always graphed on the Y axis; lynx is the independent variable (Choice B); degree of agricultural destruction (Choice C) is the problem; and time (Choice A) is a controlled variable.

12. **C.** (basic principles) A controlled variable (Choice C) is one where the researcher prevents experimental error by removing any effect that may be caused by a variable—counting procedures; an uncontrolled variable (Choice D) may affect the results of the experiment; and the dependent and independent variables (choices A and B) are what is being tested and measured.

13. **B.** (molecular and cellular biology) Remember that mRNA is never linked to form larger mRNA units or plasmids; introns (choices A and C) are always removed, and histones (Choice D) are not added.

14. **D.** (molecular and cellular biology) Carbon dioxide forms the carbon backbone for larger carbohydrate molecules; water supplies the electrons for the light reaction; pigments absorb solar energy.

15. **A.** (classical genetics and evolution) In codominance (Choice B), both genes are expressed; in incomplete dominance (Choice D), a blending of traits occurs; and sex-linked dominance (Choice C) would affect males and females differently.

16. **C.** (ecology) Choice A represents a fast growing population; Choice B represents a slower growing population; and Choice D represents a decreasing growth population.

17. **D.** (ecology) Choice A represents a fast growing population; Choice B represents a slower growing population; and Choice C represents a zero population growth.

18. **C.** (molecular and cellular biology) The crossover frequency is directly related to the distance between genes; A and D are the closest; C and D are most distant; and B and C are almost as close as A and D.

19. **A.** (diversity of life) It is thought that embryonic commonalities occur because of a common ancestor; animals and organisms (this includes plants) do not have a similar embryonic development (Choice B); analogous structures may or may not be found in humans (Choice C); and all organisms may not have the same embryonic pathway from fertilization to the blastula stage (Choice D).

20. **B.** (classical genetics and evolution) Genetic drift and the pioneer effect (choices A and C) normally apply to the colonization of new territories; there is no evidence or reason for new species to form because of the disaster (Choice D).

21. **A.** (science, technology and society) Oxygen is released as a waste product of photosynthesis; carbon monoxide is only a slight contributor to air pollution; CFCs destroy the ozone.

22. **D.** (science, technology and society) Oxygen is released as a waste product of photosynthesis; carbon monoxide is only a slight contributor to air pollution; sulfur dioxide is the main pollutant that creates acid precipitation.

23. **A.** (diversity of life) The vacuole (Choice B) is used for water storage; the nucleus (Choice C) is the control center; and the endoplasmic reticulum (Choice D) is mostly used as a transport structure.

24. **D.** (classical genetics and evolution) Habitat, food preference, and niche are valuable data but the most effective is the analysis of the gene similarities.

25. **C.** (ecology) Decreasing the number of predators (Choice D) will allow more producers to grow but will not increase the number of species; introducing foreign predators (Choice B) temporarily increases the species diversity, but usually ends with the new species growing unchecked and outcompeting existing species especially if they have no known predator and feed at the same food source as existing predators; and increasing the fertilizer load in certain nutrient (Choice A) exhausted areas may work to maintain existing species, but may actually decrease the species diversity as in the case of eutrophication.

26. **D.** (classical genetics and evolution) Darwin was only concerned about the ability to survive and reproduce.

27. **B.** (ecology) Temperature, rainfall, and climate occur regardless of how crowded the organisms are in the question.

28. **B.** (cellular and molecular biology) Prokaryote are the simplest type of cell; molds (Choice C) have a sophisticated cell; any multicellular organism (Choice D) would include humans (Choices A).

29. **D.** (basic principles of science) The 1974 Common Rule established protection for human subjects as the top priority (Choice A); IRB review (Choice B) and informed consent (Choice C) were part of this regulation.

30. **A.** (classical genetics and evolution) The chromosomes, genes, and alleles determine the characteristics of the organism; the genome is the sum total of the genetic information.

31. **B.** (molecular and cellular biology) The four haploid cells created have a different allele configuration so they contain different genetic information.

32. **C.** (molecular and cellular biology) The polarity of water adheres other water molecules to form surface tension.

33. **D.** (diversity of life) The gametophyte stage is the only haploid stage represented, the rest are diploid.

34. **C.** (diversity of life) Prokaryote are simpler than eukaryotes having free floating DNA rather than DNA organized into chromosomes (Choice D); membrane bound organelles (Choice B) and a nucleus (Choice A) are characteristics of eukaryotes.

35. **A.** (diversity of life) Corms, rhizoids, and tubers are stems, albeit underground in some cases.

36. **C.** (molecular and cellular biology) A cell remains stable when the volume of the cytoplasm is balanced by the surface area of the cell; diffusion (Choice A) is not a limiting factor in fact the more surface area, generally the greater the diffusion; phospholipids (Choice B) can be added or subtracted as directed by the cell nucleus via genetics.

37. **C.** (ecology) Denitrifying bacteria (Choice D) convert nitrogen back into unusable nitrogen gas; atmospheric- and lightning-released nitrogen (choices B and A) are unusable by plants.

38. **B.** (diversity of life) *Felis* is the genus, *catus* is the species; kingdoms (Choice C) are not expressed via binomial nomenclature (Choice B); and cladistics (Choice D) refers to evolutionary family tree.

39. **D.** (diversity of life) The binomial nomenclature places all of the subjects in the same genus (*Canus*), so they are equally related.

40. **A.** (classical genetics and evolution) Hardy-Weinberg (Choice B) predicts population trends under idealized conditions; speciation (Choice C) is a part of evolution; and directional selection (Choice D) is a type of natural selection.

41. **A.** (diversity of life) Only mammals have mammary glands.

42. **D.** (science, technology, and society) Although all choices consume freshwater, agricultural freshwater usage is the greatest.

43. **C.** (classical genetics and evolution) In codominance (Choice B) both alleles are expressed; a mutation (Choice A) would not recreate the P_1 coloration; and sex-linked dominance (Choice D) would show a differentiation between males and females.

44. **B.** (ecology) Salamanders lay huge clusters of eggs whereas humans and dolphins (choices A and D) do not deposit eggs; birds (Choice C) deposit fewer eggs that have a greater chance of survival.

45. **B.** (diversity of life) Roots, stems and leaves (Choice A) are not flower parts; seeds are plant embryos and sepals and petals are not reproductive organs, making choices C and D incorrect.

46. **C.** (cell structure and function) The cell is dividing and the chromosomes are aligned along the equatorial plate. Interphase (Choice A) is the functioning, nondividing phase; the chromosomes become visible during prophase (Choice B); in anaphase the daughter chromosomes move to opposite ends of the dividing cell.

47. **A.** (ecology) Herbivores are lower on food chains (Choice B) and webs than consumers; consumers are located at higher trophic levels (Choice C); consumers are predators (Choice D).

48. **D.** (classical genetics and evolution) Natural selection (Choice A) is not a random change in allele frequency; speciation (Choice C) does not remove alleles; and bottleneck (Choice B) is a phenomenon where a small population has a limited gene pool.

49. **D.** (ecology) Climax community, recolonization, and tree growth are characteristics of secondary succession.

50. **C.** (molecular and cellular biology) Mitosis and Meiosis (choices A and B) involve cell division; translation (Choices D) changes mRNA into a specific protein.

51. **B.** (basic principles) Accuracy cannot be determined because the correct number is not available.

52. **A.** (basic principles) Choice C is incorrect because a control group (untreated lettuce) is present; the independent variable should not be measured, so Choice D is also incorrect; and adding fertilizer to both removes the control, making Choice B incorrect.

53. **D.** (basic principles) Iceberg lettuce (Choice A) is the experimental subject; the fertilizer (Choice B) is the independent variable; and the identical conditions are controlled variables (Choice C).

54. **D.** (basic principles) Fertilizer X (Choice A) is the independent variable; Iceberg lettuce (Choice B) is the experimental subject; Container B (Choice C) is the experimental or treatment group.

55. **C.** (molecular and cellular biology) Enzymes are a type of proteins along with carbohydrates; none consistently have hydrophobic/hydrophilic characteristics.

56. **A.** (basic principles) The MSDS sheets accompany all chemicals and contain all of the vital information about a particular chemical; thoughtful chemistry teachers, vendors, and manufacturers will use their copy of the MSDS to answer any question.

57. **B.** (ecology) All of the choices affect survival, but loss of habitat is the greatest threat to extinction.

58. **A.** (classical genetics and evolution) The answer can be calculated by subtracting q from 1.0, recall that p (M) $+ q$ (N) $= 1.0$.

59. **C.** (diversity of life) Habituation (Choice A) is the ignoring of a false stimulation; social (Choice B) is a combination of many behaviors; and territorial (Choice D) references behavior for a particular area usually in regards to mating or preserving a food source.

60. **B.** (cellular and molecular biology) The gametophyte stage (Choice D) of plants is haploid and the sporophyte (Choice C) is diploid; and embryos (Choice A) are the result of egg fertilization.

61. **A.** (diversity of life) The amylase works in a basic small intestine environment as described by a pH of 9; pepsin (Choice C) works in an acidic stomach environment.

62. **D.** (molecular and cellular biology) RNA (Choice A) and mRNA (Choice B) are products of DNA replication; plasmids (Choice C) are circular DNA found in certain bacteria.

63. **D.** (diversity of life) Viruses (Choice C) are not bacteria; Fungi (Choice B) do not include bacteria; and Eubacteria (Choice A) contain nonextreme bacteria.

64. **B.** (diversity of life) Returning blood flows from vena cava to right atrium to right ventricle to the lungs returning to left atrium, left ventricle, and then to the body.

65. **A.** (diversity of life) Prokaryotes have a nucleus with no membrane; a cell wall is found only in plants.

66. **B.** (diversity of life) Ribosomes, mitochondria, and cell walls are found in eukaryotes.

67. **C.** (diversity of life) Ribosomes are mostly made of ribosomal RNA.

68. **A.** (ecology) Permafrost is only found in the tundra biome. Taiga is typified by coniferous forests, being infertile, and acidic soil.

69. **C.** (ecology) Tundra and taiga biomes are too cold for with a short growing season to be called prairie; the rainforest and deciduous forest are dominated by trees, not grasses.

70. **D.** (ecology) Tropical rain forests have the best climate to encourage the growth and sustainability of both plant and animal species.

71. **D.** (basic principles) The control is always the group that does not contain the independent variable; the treatment groups are compared to the control group to determine an effect caused by the treatment group.

72. **A.** (basic principles) The dependent variable is always graphed on the Y axis and is the variable that is measured.

73. **C.** (basic principles) The hypothesis includes the independent and dependent variable; fertilizer concentration (Choice A) is not part of the experiment; light (Choice B) is not part of the experiment; and time (Choice D) is not the dependent variable.

74. **A.** (classical genetics and evolution) Blue eyes are seen as dominant in the first mating series; codominance is evident when both alleles are represented; and incomplete dominance provides a blending of the traits.

75. **C.** (classical genetics and evolution) A genotype is represented by two alleles in normal situations; the fact that all offspring had the male's genotype indicated a homozygous dominant genotype because the female had to be heterozygous for both traits to give the results in the second mating.

76. **B.** (classical genetics and evolution) The results of both matings indicate that the female cat had to be heterozygous for both alleles.

77. **A.** (classical genetics and evolution) The cross between a homozygous dominant and a homozygous recessive always gives 100 percent heterozygous dominant offspring.

78. **B.** (ecology) Stabilizing selection is the most common form of natural selection and favors the intermediate factors; directional (Choice C) and disruptive (Choice A) favor extreme phenotypes; preferential (Choice D) does not exist and serves as a distracter.

79. **B.** (diversity of life) Sepals (Choice A) are a flower structure; dicot (Choice C) is short for dicotyledon; and seeds (Choice D) produce embryos.

80. **C.** (diversity of life) The atmosphere and water contained little oxygen; eukaryotes (Choice A) are too complex to be the first cells; autotrophs (Choice B) likely followed heterotrophs; and pseudopodia (Choice D) developed later in evolutionary history.

81. **A.** (diversity of life) Benzene (Choice B) is not a plant hormone; auxins (Choice C) stimulate tropisms; and cytokinins (Choice D) prepare the plant for winter.

82. **D.** (diversity of life) Genus is the most specific classification listed. The appropriate order of the seven levels are kingdom, phylum, class, order, family, genus, and species.

83. **D.** (diversity of life) No hormones (Choice C) are made in the bone barrow; hemoglobin (Choice B) and nutrients (Choice A) are not secreted into the bones from the marrow.

84. **A.** (diversity of life) Carbon dioxide is a raw material for photosynthesis and a waste product of aerobic respiration; carbon monoxide (Choice B) is not a product of aerobic respiration; oxygen (Choice C) is a product of photosynthesis and a raw material for aerobic respiration; and nitrogen (Choice D) is not part of either process.

85. **D.** (ecology) The photic and aphotic zones (choices B and C) are near the surface; oceanic (Choice A) is the global term for all zones.

86. **A.** (diversity of life) Dermis (Choice B) and epidermis (Choice C) are the covering; meristem (Choice D) is the growing area.

87. **D.** (diversity of life) The dermis, roots and stems do not grow as fast as the meristem region.

88. **A.** (diversity of life) The sarcomere shortens when the action and myosin filaments contract.

89. **D.** (diversity of life) Receptors are not located in the blood so Choice A is incorrect; diffusion is not receptor-mediated, making Choice B incorrect; and ATP is not created as indicated in Choice C.

90. **B.** (ecology) Hardy-Weinberg Equilibrium is a theoretical construct that can only happen when allele frequencies are not affected.

91. **A.** (classical genetics and evolution) Allopatric speciation (Choice B) occurs when two species are geographically isolated; sympatric speciation occurs (Choice C) when two populations become reproductively separated in the same geographic location; and bottleneck (Choice D) occurs when only a few members of a population survive to reproduce.

92. **A.** (diversity of life) The chordates have a backbone-like structure; nematodes and annelids (choices B and C) are worm-like organisms with no backbone; aves (Choice D) represents birds.

93. **D.** (science, technology, and society) Scientists and engineers are expected to have all characteristics but artistic ability.

94. **D.** (molecular and cellular biology) Hydrogen bonds (Choice A) only form when Hydrogen is involved; ionic and covalent bonds (choices B and C) create neutral compounds.

95. **C.** (diversity of life) Archaea contain the extreme organisms.

96. **A.** (molecular and cellular biology) Hyper- and hypotonic solutions (choices B and C) contain a concentration gradient that powers osmosis; exothermic (Choice D) refers to energy leaving a reaction.

97. **D.** (molecular and cellular biology) The ETS creates 34 ATPs; fermentation and glycolysis (choices C and B) create 2 ATPs; glucogenesis (Choice A) is the formation of glucose.

98. **A.** (molecular and cellular biology) Time wise, interphase is the main part of the cell cycle; the remaining parts are quicker because the cell is dividing.

99. **A.** (basic principles) Pound (Choice B) is English for weight; meter (Choice C) is distance; and liter (Choice D) is volume.

100. **C.** (basic principles) The teacher is responsible and liable for all instruction that occurs.

101. **A.** (ecology) The aphotic zone (Choice B) has no light penetration; the benthic zone (Choice C) is the deep water beyond light penetration; and the shoreline (Choice D) is not a zone and does not always have an abundance of plant growth.

102. **D.** (molecular and cellular biology) Glycogen (Choice C) is stored energy for animals; starch (Choice B) is stored energy for plants; and ATP (Choice A) is stored energy.

103. **B.** (diversity of life) Xylem tissue (Choice A) conducts water; meristem (Choice C) is the growth region of plants; dermis (Choice D)is the covering beneath the epidermis.

104. **D.** (molecular and cellular biology) The pH of your stomach is below 6 (Choice A); the small intestine is alkaline because of pancreatic juice (Choice C); buffers resist pH change (Choice B); and neutral pH is 7-only, making Choice D correct.

105. **C.** (diversity of life) Gametogenesis is the production of gametes, sperm and eggs (Choice C); testes and ovaries (Choice B) are the structures that produce the gametes; spermatagonia (Choice A) are pre-sperm that may develop into sperm; a zygote (Choice D) is a fertilized egg.

106. **C.** (diversity of life) The mesoderm (Choice D) forms most of the organ systems; the endoderm (Choice A) forms the GI lining; and the epidermis (Choice B) is the upper layer of skin.

107. **A.** (diversity of life) Altruism (Choice C) benefits the group at the individual's expense; conditioning (Choice D) is learning from others; and imprinting (Choice B) is identifying with something as a parent upon birth.

108. **A.** (molecular and cellular biology) Amylase is an enzyme and all enzymes are made of protein and all protein is made from amino acids. Cellulose and fructose (choices C and B) have a carbohydrate background while steroids (Choice D) are made from lipids.

109. **B.** (molecular and cellular biology) Producers do not make energy (Choice A); decomposers do not consume energy (Choice D); and the total amount of energy does change as it passes through the ecosystem.

110. **A.** (classical genetics and evolution) The genetic disorder is sex-linked, so all II-male children are not affected and not carriers, but all females inherit the carrier X chromosome from their father.

111. **B.** (classical genetic and evolution) The Punnet square shows that III-I and III-5 have a 50 percent chance of being a carrier, while III-3 is 0.

112. **C.** (classical genetics and evolution) The Punnet square shows that all males from this mating will be normal.

113. **D.** (classical genetics and evolution) The Punnet square shows that the male only contributes the Y chromosome which does not contain the allele for hemophilia.

114. **B.** (basic principles) Jenner discovered the smallpox vaccine (Choice D); Pasteur the germ theory (Choice C); and Schleiden discovered that plants are made of cells (Choice A).

115. **B.** (molecular and cellular biology) The nucleus (Choice A) contains the protons and neutrons; protons and neutrons (choices C and D) contain the greatest mass, but the volume or size of an atom is determined by the energy levels created by the pathways of the electrons.

116. **A.** (molecular and cellular biology) Originally elements were listed in ascending order by their atomic mass (Choice D); atoms are not listed (Choice B); and reactivity (Choice C) is consistent within families and periods.

117. **C.** (molecular and cellular biology) Neutralization (Choice A) reactions occur between acids and bases; decomposition (Choice B) is the breakdown of a compound into smaller units; and synthesis (Choice D) is the opposite of decomposition, smaller units are added together to form a larger compound. Condensation always releases water, making Choice C correct.

118. **A.** (molecular and cellular biology) Carbohydrates (Choice B) are identified by the $C(H_2O)$ formula; lipids (Choice C) are similar to carbs, but do not have their formula; and fats (Choice D) are a type of lipid.

119. **D.** (molecular and cellular biology) Metal ions (Choice A) are inorganic cofactors; prosthetic groups (Choice C) are cofactors that are chemically bonded to the protein; and inhibitors (Choice B) are substances that attach to the active site of an enzyme thereby preventing the catalyzing of a reaction.

120. **B.** (molecular and cellular biology) Cofactors (Choice D) are proteins that bind with the active site to facilitate the binding with the substrate; transport proteins (Choice C) moves smaller particles throughout the body and through cell membranes; and structural proteins (Choice A) form materials that cells use for structural purposes such as fur, hair, feathers, or wool.

121. **D.** (diversity of life) All of the answers are true; however photosynthesis (Choice D) is not unique to these examples.

122. **A.** (diversity of life) Vascular plants (Choice B) are more complex than the Bryophytes; angiosperms and gymnosperms (choices C and D) are vascular plant types.

123. **C.** (diversity of life) Flowering plants are angiosperms.

124. **A.** (diversity of life) Pollen (Choice B) is the male gamete; flowers (Choice C) contain the reproductive structures; and phloem (Choice D) is part of the vascular bundle and transports nutrients.

125. **A.** (diversity of life) Choice A is a feature of monocots.

126. **B.** (diversity of life) Parenchyma (Choice A) and sclerenchyma (Choice C) are cell types found in ground tissue; and meristem (Choice D) is the growth area.

127. **D.** (molecular and cellular biology) Fructose and glucose (choices A and B) are monosaccharides; starch (Choice C) is a polysaccharide.

128. **A.** (molecular and cellular biology) The ratio of hydrogen to oxygen is always greater than 2:1; carbs are 2:1.

129. **B.** (molecular and cellular biology) Hydrogen bonds (Choice A) must include a hydrogen atom; they are covalently bonded, not ionic (Choice C); James Bond (Choice D) is 007.

130. **B.** (molecular and cellular biology) Choice A is incorrect because the correct order of the nucleotide bases should be A-T, G-C; $p + q = 1$ (Choice C) the $p + q$ describes Hardy-Weinberg Equilibrium, not purines and pyrimidines; and sugar-phosphate linkages form the backbone rather than purines and pyridimines, making Choice D incorrect.

131. **D.** (diversity of life) Haploid-diploid generation (Choice A), gametophyte-sporophyte stage (Choice B), and sexual reproduction (Choice C) are all true of this process, but the name is alternation of generations.

132. **C.** (diversity of life) Prokaryotes on the primitive Earth photosynthesized and added significant amounts of oxygen into the atmosphere (Choice A) and during the Paleozoic Era about 600 million years ago multicellular marine animals appeared in abundance (Choice B) are true, but not the correct answer. For Choice D, endosymbiosis, not endosymbiotic theory, describes the evolution of eukaryotes.

133. **B.** (diversity of life) Porifera (Choice A) are sponges; Nematoda (Choice C) are roundworms; and Annelida (Choice D) include earthworms.

134. **A.** (diversity of life) Porifera do not have an anus, making choices B and C incorrect; chordates (Choice D) have a complete digestive system.

135. **C.** (diversity of life) The epiglottis prevents food from entering the airways, making Choice A incorrect; the esophagus is the tube that connects the mouth and stomach and thereby receives the acid reflux and does not have prevention capabilities (Choice B); the pyloric sphincter (Choice D) regulates the flow of food from the stomach into the small intestine.

136. **D.** (science, technology, and society) There were no national class action lawsuits (Choice A) over these problems; technology (Choice B) was seen as the problem and the solution, but events were not caused by an intervention; and the breakthroughs (Choice C) came *after* the legislation.

137. **A.** (science, technology, and society) The weather was unusually dry (not wet) with a prolonged drought in most areas, so Choice B is incorrect. The use of horses may have helped because farmers would have turned over less soil to add to the erosion problem, making Choice C incorrect. Pollution was minimal at this time in the Midwest, making Choice D irrelevant.

138. **D.** (science, technology, and society) Choices A, B, and C are recommended methods of minimizing production of wastes The elimination of plastic may be helpful, but it is not practical at this time and is not a recommendation.

139. **D.** (science, technology, and society) Choices A, B, and C are recommended consumer methods of disposing wastes. Storing waste may not be practical and only serves to postpone the problem.

140. **A.** (ecology) Taiga (Choice B) is a coniferous forest; grasslands (Choice C) are dominated by grasses; and temperate deciduous forests (Choice D) are dominated by trees.

141. **C.** (ecology) Exponential growth (Choice A) is a *J* curve; carrying capacity (Choice B) is how many of a species can live successfully in an area; and competition (Choice D) is a density-dependent factor.

142. **B.** (science, technology, and society) Cooperation between industrial-political concerns (Choice A), eco-agriculture (Choice D), and resource management are parts of sustainability (Choice C).

143. **B.** (diversity of life) The illium (Choice A) is a pelvic bone; the duodenum (Choice C) is the location where pancreatic juices and bile continue digestion; the stomach (Choice D) does absorb some substances, but not in bulk.

144. **B.** (diversity of life) Platyhelminthes (Choice A) does not have a closed circulatory system; reptiles and mammals (choices C and D) are more complex than amphibians, and mammals are not a phylum.

145. **A.** (diversity of life) The AV node amplifies the impulses and relays them through the Purkinje fibers to the muscular ventricles; The first systolic action takes about 0.1 second and is a slight contraction of the atria to drain any remaining blood into the ventricles. Choices B, C, and D are partial answers and may describe the function of certain structures, only Choice A is correct.

146. **C.** (molecular and cellular biology) The amount of energy capable of doing work in any chemical reaction is quantitatively measured by the change in the Gibbs Free Energy formula; positive GFE = spontaneous; a positive and negative GFE reactions are often coupled so they will proceed spontaneously when the positive is greater than the negative GFE. Choices A, B, D indicate a negative GFE or are labeled as not spontaneous-all of which are incorrect answers

147. **D.** (molecular and cellular biology) The Krebs' Cycle (Choice A) is part of aerobic respiration; the dark reaction (Choice B) does not require an energy input; and the Calvin Cycle (Choice C) is a method of carbon fixation.

148. **D.** (ecology) The water (Choice A), carbon (Choice B), and phosphorus (Choice C) cycles are independent of microbes.

149. **A.** (diversity of life) Endocrine glands produce hormones and exocrine glands make secretions, making Choice A incorrect. Exocrine glands do not produce neurotransmitters (Choice B); and exocrine glands secrete pancreatic juice, making Choice D wrong as well.

150. **A.** (diversity of life) The smaller cell becomes the first polar body and dies, making choices B and C incorrect. The second polar body occurs after Meiosis II, making Choice D incorrect as well.

Praxis II Biology Content Knowledge

1 Ⓐ Ⓑ Ⓒ Ⓓ	41 Ⓐ Ⓑ Ⓒ Ⓓ	81 Ⓐ Ⓑ Ⓒ Ⓓ	121 Ⓐ Ⓑ Ⓒ Ⓓ
2 Ⓐ Ⓑ Ⓒ Ⓓ	42 Ⓐ Ⓑ Ⓒ Ⓓ	82 Ⓐ Ⓑ Ⓒ Ⓓ	122 Ⓐ Ⓑ Ⓒ Ⓓ
3 Ⓐ Ⓑ Ⓒ Ⓓ	43 Ⓐ Ⓑ Ⓒ Ⓓ	83 Ⓐ Ⓑ Ⓒ Ⓓ	123 Ⓐ Ⓑ Ⓒ Ⓓ
4 Ⓐ Ⓑ Ⓒ Ⓓ	44 Ⓐ Ⓑ Ⓒ Ⓓ	84 Ⓐ Ⓑ Ⓒ Ⓓ	124 Ⓐ Ⓑ Ⓒ Ⓓ
5 Ⓐ Ⓑ Ⓒ Ⓓ	45 Ⓐ Ⓑ Ⓒ Ⓓ	85 Ⓐ Ⓑ Ⓒ Ⓓ	125 Ⓐ Ⓑ Ⓒ Ⓓ
6 Ⓐ Ⓑ Ⓒ Ⓓ	46 Ⓐ Ⓑ Ⓒ Ⓓ	86 Ⓐ Ⓑ Ⓒ Ⓓ	126 Ⓐ Ⓑ Ⓒ Ⓓ
7 Ⓐ Ⓑ Ⓒ Ⓓ	47 Ⓐ Ⓑ Ⓒ Ⓓ	87 Ⓐ Ⓑ Ⓒ Ⓓ	127 Ⓐ Ⓑ Ⓒ Ⓓ
8 Ⓐ Ⓑ Ⓒ Ⓓ	48 Ⓐ Ⓑ Ⓒ Ⓓ	88 Ⓐ Ⓑ Ⓒ Ⓓ	128 Ⓐ Ⓑ Ⓒ Ⓓ
9 Ⓐ Ⓑ Ⓒ Ⓓ	49 Ⓐ Ⓑ Ⓒ Ⓓ	89 Ⓐ Ⓑ Ⓒ Ⓓ	129 Ⓐ Ⓑ Ⓒ Ⓓ
10 Ⓐ Ⓑ Ⓒ Ⓓ	50 Ⓐ Ⓑ Ⓒ Ⓓ	90 Ⓐ Ⓑ Ⓒ Ⓓ	130 Ⓐ Ⓑ Ⓒ Ⓓ
11 Ⓐ Ⓑ Ⓒ Ⓓ	51 Ⓐ Ⓑ Ⓒ Ⓓ	91 Ⓐ Ⓑ Ⓒ Ⓓ	131 Ⓐ Ⓑ Ⓒ Ⓓ
12 Ⓐ Ⓑ Ⓒ Ⓓ	52 Ⓐ Ⓑ Ⓒ Ⓓ	92 Ⓐ Ⓑ Ⓒ Ⓓ	132 Ⓐ Ⓑ Ⓒ Ⓓ
13 Ⓐ Ⓑ Ⓒ Ⓓ	53 Ⓐ Ⓑ Ⓒ Ⓓ	93 Ⓐ Ⓑ Ⓒ Ⓓ	133 Ⓐ Ⓑ Ⓒ Ⓓ
14 Ⓐ Ⓑ Ⓒ Ⓓ	54 Ⓐ Ⓑ Ⓒ Ⓓ	94 Ⓐ Ⓑ Ⓒ Ⓓ	134 Ⓐ Ⓑ Ⓒ Ⓓ
15 Ⓐ Ⓑ Ⓒ Ⓓ	55 Ⓐ Ⓑ Ⓒ Ⓓ	95 Ⓐ Ⓑ Ⓒ Ⓓ	135 Ⓐ Ⓑ Ⓒ Ⓓ
16 Ⓐ Ⓑ Ⓒ Ⓓ	56 Ⓐ Ⓑ Ⓒ Ⓓ	96 Ⓐ Ⓑ Ⓒ Ⓓ	136 Ⓐ Ⓑ Ⓒ Ⓓ
17 Ⓐ Ⓑ Ⓒ Ⓓ	57 Ⓐ Ⓑ Ⓒ Ⓓ	97 Ⓐ Ⓑ Ⓒ Ⓓ	137 Ⓐ Ⓑ Ⓒ Ⓓ
18 Ⓐ Ⓑ Ⓒ Ⓓ	58 Ⓐ Ⓑ Ⓒ Ⓓ	98 Ⓐ Ⓑ Ⓒ Ⓓ	138 Ⓐ Ⓑ Ⓒ Ⓓ
19 Ⓐ Ⓑ Ⓒ Ⓓ	59 Ⓐ Ⓑ Ⓒ Ⓓ	99 Ⓐ Ⓑ Ⓒ Ⓓ	139 Ⓐ Ⓑ Ⓒ Ⓓ
20 Ⓐ Ⓑ Ⓒ Ⓓ	60 Ⓐ Ⓑ Ⓒ Ⓓ	100 Ⓐ Ⓑ Ⓒ Ⓓ	140 Ⓐ Ⓑ Ⓒ Ⓓ
21 Ⓐ Ⓑ Ⓒ Ⓓ	61 Ⓐ Ⓑ Ⓒ Ⓓ	101 Ⓐ Ⓑ Ⓒ Ⓓ	141 Ⓐ Ⓑ Ⓒ Ⓓ
22 Ⓐ Ⓑ Ⓒ Ⓓ	62 Ⓐ Ⓑ Ⓒ Ⓓ	102 Ⓐ Ⓑ Ⓒ Ⓓ	142 Ⓐ Ⓑ Ⓒ Ⓓ
23 Ⓐ Ⓑ Ⓒ Ⓓ	63 Ⓐ Ⓑ Ⓒ Ⓓ	103 Ⓐ Ⓑ Ⓒ Ⓓ	143 Ⓐ Ⓑ Ⓒ Ⓓ
24 Ⓐ Ⓑ Ⓒ Ⓓ	64 Ⓐ Ⓑ Ⓒ Ⓓ	104 Ⓐ Ⓑ Ⓒ Ⓓ	144 Ⓐ Ⓑ Ⓒ Ⓓ
25 Ⓐ Ⓑ Ⓒ Ⓓ	65 Ⓐ Ⓑ Ⓒ Ⓓ	105 Ⓐ Ⓑ Ⓒ Ⓓ	145 Ⓐ Ⓑ Ⓒ Ⓓ
26 Ⓐ Ⓑ Ⓒ Ⓓ	66 Ⓐ Ⓑ Ⓒ Ⓓ	106 Ⓐ Ⓑ Ⓒ Ⓓ	146 Ⓐ Ⓑ Ⓒ Ⓓ
27 Ⓐ Ⓑ Ⓒ Ⓓ	67 Ⓐ Ⓑ Ⓒ Ⓓ	107 Ⓐ Ⓑ Ⓒ Ⓓ	147 Ⓐ Ⓑ Ⓒ Ⓓ
28 Ⓐ Ⓑ Ⓒ Ⓓ	68 Ⓐ Ⓑ Ⓒ Ⓓ	108 Ⓐ Ⓑ Ⓒ Ⓓ	148 Ⓐ Ⓑ Ⓒ Ⓓ
29 Ⓐ Ⓑ Ⓒ Ⓓ	69 Ⓐ Ⓑ Ⓒ Ⓓ	109 Ⓐ Ⓑ Ⓒ Ⓓ	149 Ⓐ Ⓑ Ⓒ Ⓓ
30 Ⓐ Ⓑ Ⓒ Ⓓ	70 Ⓐ Ⓑ Ⓒ Ⓓ	110 Ⓐ Ⓑ Ⓒ Ⓓ	150 Ⓐ Ⓑ Ⓒ Ⓓ
31 Ⓐ Ⓑ Ⓒ Ⓓ	71 Ⓐ Ⓑ Ⓒ Ⓓ	111 Ⓐ Ⓑ Ⓒ Ⓓ	
32 Ⓐ Ⓑ Ⓒ Ⓓ	72 Ⓐ Ⓑ Ⓒ Ⓓ	112 Ⓐ Ⓑ Ⓒ Ⓓ	
33 Ⓐ Ⓑ Ⓒ Ⓓ	73 Ⓐ Ⓑ Ⓒ Ⓓ	113 Ⓐ Ⓑ Ⓒ Ⓓ	
34 Ⓐ Ⓑ Ⓒ Ⓓ	74 Ⓐ Ⓑ Ⓒ Ⓓ	114 Ⓐ Ⓑ Ⓒ Ⓓ	
35 Ⓐ Ⓑ Ⓒ Ⓓ	75 Ⓐ Ⓑ Ⓒ Ⓓ	115 Ⓐ Ⓑ Ⓒ Ⓓ	
36 Ⓐ Ⓑ Ⓒ Ⓓ	76 Ⓐ Ⓑ Ⓒ Ⓓ	116 Ⓐ Ⓑ Ⓒ Ⓓ	
37 Ⓐ Ⓑ Ⓒ Ⓓ	77 Ⓐ Ⓑ Ⓒ Ⓓ	117 Ⓐ Ⓑ Ⓒ Ⓓ	
38 Ⓐ Ⓑ Ⓒ Ⓓ	78 Ⓐ Ⓑ Ⓒ Ⓓ	118 Ⓐ Ⓑ Ⓒ Ⓓ	
39 Ⓐ Ⓑ Ⓒ Ⓓ	79 Ⓐ Ⓑ Ⓒ Ⓓ	119 Ⓐ Ⓑ Ⓒ Ⓓ	
40 Ⓐ Ⓑ Ⓒ Ⓓ	80 Ⓐ Ⓑ Ⓒ Ⓓ	120 Ⓐ Ⓑ Ⓒ Ⓓ	

CUT HERE

CUT HERE

Time—120 minutes

150 Questions

Directions: Each of the questions or incomplete statements below is followed by four possible answer choices or completions. Select the best response and then fill in the corresponding lettered space on the answer sheet.

1. A new species of fruit fly has been discovered in Latin America. What will likely happen when the newly discovered species begins to occupy the habitat of existing species?

   A. Genetic variation will decrease as the new species is absorbed the existing species.
   B. Altruistic behavior will increase.
   C. Interspecies competition will increase.
   D. Species diversity will decrease as intraspecific mating condenses the genome.

2. The role that a species plays in the ecosystem is known as

   A. niche.
   B. territory.
   C. habitat.
   D. behavior pattern.

Questions 3–5

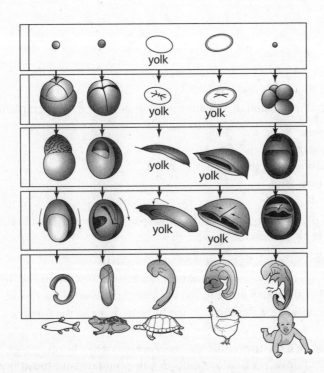

3. What explanation is given for differences between the embryologic development of the fish and chicken?

   A. Their development is based on their niche.
   B. Differences in development are due to different habitats.
   C. Embryological development is based on natural selection.
   D. They do not share a recent common ancestor.

Practice Test 2

4. Why does the last image of their embryological development look somewhat similar?

    A. They are vertebrates.
    B. They have a recent common ancestor.
    C. Cladistics indicates a close evolutionary relationship.
    D. Their rate of coevolution is similar.

5. Why does the embryological development of the turtle and chicken appear similar?

    A. They coevolved.
    B. They evolved from a common ancestor.
    C. They reproduce by external fertilization.
    D. Their life histories are similar.

6. Which of the following is a means of asexual reproduction in plants?

    A. Liverworts releasing sperm into the water
    B. Pollination in flowering plants
    C. Grafting desirable fruit tree buds onto rootstocks
    D. Gametogenesis during the gametophyte stage

7. Which of the following structures takes blood from your heart to the lungs?

    A. Pulmonary artery
    B. Left ventricle
    C. Right atrium
    D. Aorta

8. Fungi and simple plants appear similar. What is the main difference between plants and fungi?

    A. Plants are eukaryotes.
    B. Fungi are decomposers.
    C. Fungi have cell walls and cell membranes.
    D. Plants make their own food.

9. When a stem is cut and placed in colored ink, the flower of certain plants will take on a lighter shade of the ink. What causes this phenomenon?

    A. Turgor pressure moves the ink to the flowers via phloem tissue.
    B. Evaporation and transpiration pull the cohesive water-ink solution to the flower via xylem tissue.
    C. Root pressure pushes the water-ink solution via vascular tissue to the flower.
    D. Osmotic pressure draws the water through the phloem tissue to the flowers.

10. Sulfur dioxide (SO_2) is often a waste product that is generated when burning high sulfur coal to produce energy. Certain industries release massive amounts of this pollutant into the atmosphere.

    What is one effect associated with sulfur dioxide in the atmosphere?

    A. Acid precipitation
    B. Increased light penetration through the atmosphere
    C. Increased pH in certain lakes
    D. Decreased phosphorus cycling

11. What can governments do to limit or minimize air pollution caused by sulfur?

    A. Monitor sulfur emissions from offending industries.
    B. Require industries to self regulate their emissions.
    C. Support local cleanup efforts by detoxifying surface water and offering grants to help local agencies repair damage caused by air pollution.
    D. Offer tax incentives to develop environmental friendly power sources.

12. The microevolution that begins as lava creates new landforms is an example of which of the following?

    A. Sympatric speciation
    B. Secondary succession
    C. Primary succession
    D. Mutualism

13. Which of the following are required to accommodate the high metabolic rate of hummingbirds?

    A. Open circulatory system and extensive nervous control
    B. Central nervous system and multi-stage digestive system
    C. Internal fertilization and plentiful food source
    D. Lungs and four-chambered heart

14. What difference has been discovered between prions and viroids?

    A. Prions are harmful.
    B. Viroids contain RNA.
    C. Prions are nonliving proteins.
    D. Viroids are found in nature.

15. The joining of glucose and fructose to create sucrose has a positive 5.5 kcal/mole G value. This reaction will not take place spontaneously. However, if this reaction is coupled with the conversion of ATP to ADP, it will occur spontaneously because the ADP-ATP conversion has a negative 7.3 kcal/mole G value. Therefore the total G value is –1.8 kcal/mole, so the overall reaction will proceed spontaneously. What allows this reaction to proceed spontaneously?

    A. A negative G value
    B. Hess's Law
    C. Bioenergetics
    D. Second Law of Thermodynamics

16. What is the likely reason that plants with the dominant tall stems can produce plants with short stems?

    A. Incomplete dominance
    B. Gene linkage
    C. Heterozygous parents
    D. Multiple alleles

17. What is the main difference between viruses and viroids?

    A. Viruses are considered living.
    B. Viroids cause diseases in plants and animals.
    C. Viroids cause Hepatitis D.
    D. Viruses are microscopic.

18. The double helix structure of DNA is held together by which force(s)?

    A. Sugar-phosphate backbone
    B. Hydrogen bonding between bases
    C. Energy released by ATP
    D. Ionic attraction between nitrogen bases

19. Which of the following is *not* true regarding Darwinian evolution?

    A. All organisms survive and reproduce.
    B. More organisms are born that will survive to reproduce.
    C. The most fit organism survive to reproduce.
    D. The environment places stress on organisms.

Questions 20–23

A researcher suspected that isopropyl alcohol would cause seed germination in monocots faster than water. The researcher hoped to germinate weed seeds before crop seeds so herbicides would be more effective. A test was constructed by placing 100 noxious weed seeds in container A. 100 corn seeds were planted in container B. Both containers and their environment were exactly the same. The seeds in container A were soaked in isopropyl alcohol and the seeds container B received water. Germinated seeds were counted every day for two weeks and the germinated seeds were removed. At the end of the experiment, the data indicated a difference between germination times. The seeds soaked in isopropyl alcohol germinated on the average 2.4 times faster than the seeds germinated in water.

20. What was the dependent variable for this experiment?

    A. Number of seeds (100)
    B. Application of isopropyl alcohol
    C. Corn seeds
    D. Germination time

21. Which of the following was an experimental error?

    A. No control group existed.
    B. The independent variable was confounded with the dependent variable.
    C. The independent variable was not tested.
    D. The dependent variable was not measured fairly.

22. What would be graphed on the Y axis?

    A. Amount of isopropyl alcohol
    B. Time
    C. Seed type
    D. Germination rate

23. What change would make this a more fair experiment?

    A. Soak container A and B in isopropyl alcohol.
    B. Test corn seeds in container A as well as B.
    C. Measure the number of seeds in both containers that did not germinate.
    D. Test noxious weed seeds in both containers.

24. Which of the following supports the one gene-one polypeptide theory?

    A. Polypeptides are made of protein subunits.
    B. One gene makes every polypeptide.
    C. A single nitrogen base change in DNA may cause a faulty polypeptide to be produced.
    D. Each gene is made from a unique polypeptide.

Question 25–27 refer to the following graphic:

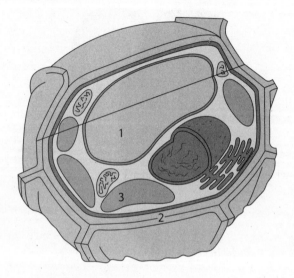

25. What is the large structure labeled #1?

    A. Nucleus
    B. Mitochondrion
    C. Golgi body
    D. Central vacuole

26. Structure #2 is most likely the

    A. Cell wall.
    B. Cell membrane.
    C. Endoplasmic reticulum.
    D. Phospholipid bilayer.

27. What function is performed by structure #3?

    A. Aerobic respiration
    B. Photosynthesis
    C. Glycolysis
    D. Krebs' Cycle

28. Aluminum is one of the most recycled metals. Which is *not* a benefit of recycling aluminum?

    A. It is cheaper to recycle than process raw ore.
    B. Aluminum waste reacts with water to dissolve in landfills.
    C. Aluminum biodegrades in temperate climates.
    D. Excessive aluminum cans add to litter and create unsightly areas.

29. Why are there fewer organisms in the highest trophic level compared to the other trophic levels for any ecosystem?

    A. Intraspecific competition limits population growth.
    B. Fewer food sources exist at the highest trophic level.
    C. The amount of available energy from food is lowest at the highest trophic level.
    D. Prey organisms adapt to predatory techniques faster than predators can adapt new strategies.

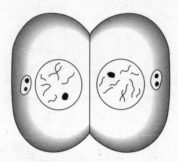

30. The cell in the figure is in which of the following mitotic phases?

    A. Anaphase
    B. Metaphase
    C. Prophase
    D. Telophase

31. Oak, hickory, and maple hardwood trees represent a climax community in certain temperate biomes. Which of the following is most closely related to this phenomenon?

    A. Succession ends
    B. Primary succession
    C. Secondary succession
    D. Tertiary succession

32. Which of the following is closest to the actual conversion efficiency that occurs when plants transfer solar energy to chemical energy?

    A. 1 percent
    B. 10 percent
    C. 50 percent
    D. 90 percent

33. A mating between an organism with an unknown genotype and a homozygous recessive organism to determine the unknown genotype is an example of which of the following?

    A. Pedigree mating
    B. Testcross
    C. Hybridization
    D. Dihybrid cross

34. Denitrifying bacteria perform which of the following functions in a grassland biome?

    A. Decompose and recycle nutrients.
    B. Change soil nitrate (NO_3) to atmospheric nitrogen (N_2).
    C. Degrade the protein in dead plants into usable nitrates (NO_3).
    D. Convert atmospheric nitrogen into a form that is usable by plants (NO_3).

35. What type of mutation is exemplified in the example?

    Original: The sky is a blue today.

    After mutation: The sky is yadot eulb.

    A. Deletion
    B. Point
    C. Frame shift
    D. Inversion

36. Which of the following genotypes is the simplest genotype that the genotype ABc could be from?

    A. AaBBC
    B. ABC
    C. AaBbCC
    D. AABbCc

37. At the beginning of the school year a biology teacher routinely holds up his right hand and states that the students need to come to attention and focus on the lesson. Over time, the students come to attention when the teacher raises his right hand with no verbal command. This is an example of which of the following?

    A. Child abuse
    B. Classical conditioning
    C. Operant conditioning
    D. Habituation

38. Which of the following is *not* a laboratory safety rule?

    A. Eating snacks of any kind is not permitted in the laboratory.
    B. Grooming and applying cosmetics is not allowed.
    C. Open-toed shoes are not permitted.
    D. In an emergency, students are expected to operate the fire extinguisher.

39. A joint venture between the governments of Brazil and Peru to dam the Inambari River to produce hydroelectric power has received both positive and negative reviews from their respective populations. Which of the following would help ease the tensions?

    A. Conducting a thorough review and solving any environmental, economic, and social problems before construction begins
    B. Relocating each resident from the affected areas
    C. Allowing business and industrial employment opportunities to convince all stakeholders of the future success of the project
    D. Taxing the associated electric companies to repair any damages that may occur during the dam construction

40. The theory of evolution has received the greatest support from which of the following?

    A. Analysis of analogous structures of existing organisms
    B. Similarities in phenotypes
    C. Fossil record
    D. Intelligent design

41. Which of the following best describes the function of the anticodon?

    A. Attach at the appropriate location on the codon
    B. Gene regulation
    C. Pre-mRNA cloaking
    D. Prion prevention

42. Pepsin is a stomach enzyme that helps digest proteins. Which of the following is *not* true about pepsin?

    A. Pepsin is active only in low pH environments.
    B. Pepsinogen is the precursor molecule.
    C. Pepsin is found in gastric juice.
    D. Pepsin is secreted by the exocrine segment of the pancreas.

43. At what level are organisms most closely related?

    A. Kingdom
    B. Phylum
    C. Genus
    D. Species

Questions 44–46

Cross-Section of an Animal Cell

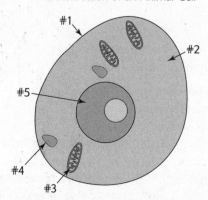

44. Structure #1 is which of the following?

    A. Cell wall
    B. Cell membrane
    C. Endoplasmic reticulum
    D. Golgi apparatus

45. Which structure performs aerobic respiration?

    A. 5
    B. 4
    C. 3
    D. 2

46. In prokaryotes, which structure is *not* contained by a double membrane as it is in eukaryotes?

    A. 1
    B. 2
    C. 4
    D. 5

47. Which of the following is evidence that this cell is *not* a plant cell?

    A. small vacuoles
    B. contains cytoplam
    C. nucleus and mitochondria are present
    D. multiple mitochondria

48. A mating between parents with type A ($I^A I^A$) and type B ($I^B I^B$) produced an offspring with type AB ($I^A I^B$) blood. This phenomenon is an example of what type of inheritance?

    A. Incomplete dominance
    B. Sex-linked
    C. Codominance
    D. Dominant and recessive genes

49. The phospholipid bilayer interspersed with proteins is a distinguishing feature of which of the following?

    A. Virus
    B. Prion
    C. Eukaryote cell membrane
    D. Prokaryote mitochondrial membrane

50. If placed in a horizontal position, gymnosperm roots bend downward in a process called

    A. geotropism.
    B. phototropism.
    C. hydrotropism.
    D. hormone contraction.

51. Which theory of evolution claims that there are long periods of relative evolutionary stability interrupted by intermittent bursts of speciation during brief time spans?

    A. Big bang
    B. Punctuated equilibrium
    C. Uniformity
    D. Linear

52. After a massive forest fire, a meadow ecosystem sprang up over the next several seasons. This phenomenon is an example of which of the following?

    A. Climax community
    B. Speciation
    C. Primary succession
    D. Secondary succession

53. Who was the first scientist to describe the appearance of cell walls in cork samples that he named "cells"?

    A. Schleiden
    B. Schwann
    C. Hooke
    D. Leeuwenhoek

54. Herbivores in savanna biomes have to temporarily and regularly move to find new sources of water in a process called

    A. migration.
    B. immigration.
    C. territoriality.
    D. genetic drift.

55. Food preferences and eating habits of Americans have changed dramatically over the last generation. Which is the least likely cause for this phenomenon?

    A. Advertising
    B. Cultural preferences
    C. Health concerns
    D. Agricultural practices

56. Which vertically aligned cells located in the mesophyll tissue contains the most chloroplasts?

    A. Palisade layer
    B. Columnar cells
    C. Dermis
    D. Stomata

57. The number of a particular organelle within a cell is dependent upon the function of that cell. Which organelle is found in abundance in cardiac cells?

    A. Lysosomes
    B. Mitochondria
    C. Vacuoles
    D. Chloroplasts

58. Binomial nomenclature is the scientific name for any organism which always contains two elements: genus and the "species modifier." Which scientist is given credit for this classification scheme?

    A. Whittaker
    B. Darwin
    C. Wallace
    D. Linnaeus

59. Which taxonomic scheme is based on the idea that organisms should be classified by their evolutionary relationships as determined by their primitive and derived characteristics?

    A. Evolutionary systematics
    B. Binomial nomenclature
    C. Cladistics
    D. Phylogeny

60. The evolution of plants to a terrestrial habitat required new adaptations. Which is *not* a prerequisite that plants faced before living on dry land?

    A. Absorbing nutrients from soil
    B. Preventing desiccation
    C. Photosynthesis
    D. Reproducing in a dry area

61. Which types of cells are stacked upon each other like joined water pipes and add structural support for the plant?

    A. Xylem
    B. Epithelial
    C. Phloem
    D. Palisade

Questions 62–64 refer to the following graphic.

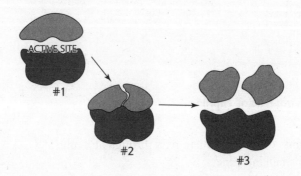

62. What is represented in #2?

    A. Enzyme
    B. Substrate
    C. Inhibitor
    D. Enzyme-substrate complex

63. What is the "active site"?

    A. The area of attachment located on the substrate
    B. The specific chemical address located on the enzyme
    C. The substrate receptor area
    D. The specific area where a mixture of enzyme and substrate are formed

64. What happens to the enzyme after this series of events?

    A. It is reused.
    B. A new active site forms.
    C. If needed, it reattaches to the substrate to continue the reaction.
    D. It is energized by the ATP→ADP reaction.

65. Gymnosperms are mostly woody trees with seeds that are not protected by an endosperm. Which of the following is *not* a gymnosperm?

   A.   Cycadophyta
   B.   Ginkgophyta
   C.   Flowering plants
   D.   Gnetophhyta

66. Which structure is located at the apex of the stem that contains the meristematic, or growing, cells?

   A.   Node
   B.   Terminal bud
   C.   Petiole
   D.   Leaf

67. Which phylum is the first to exhibit the extra pulmonary circulation that delivers oxygen-rich blood from the lungs to the heart and removes wastes?

   A.   Porifera
   B.   Aves
   C.   Amphibian
   D.   Reptilian

68. Which of the following is *not* true of capillaries?

   A.   Form capillary beds
   B.   Small diameter permits only one RBC to pass through at a time
   C.   Surround lungs and small intestine
   D.   Deliver deoxygenated blood to vena cava

69. Which are the most common WBC that also function to fight infections by engulfing invading bacteria?

   A.   Leukocytes
   B.   Platelets
   C.   Neutrophils
   D.   Basophils

70. The immune system is activated by the presence of foreign antigens. Which of the following statements is an accurate description of an antigen?

   A.   A polysaccharide molecule attached to the exposed surface of a cell
   B.   A blood plasma protein that binds with the receptor site and destroys the invading cell
   C.   Substances released into the bloodstream that flow to the site and destroy microbes
   D.   An enzyme that destroys the cell walls of most bacteria

71. Which of the following is *not* true of a desert biome?

   A.   Sparse vegetation
   B.   Low annual precipitation
   C.   High humidity
   D.   Extreme hot and cold temperatures

72. Which phyla diffuse gases directly from/into the environment?

   A.   Mollusks and Arthropods
   B.   Cnidarians and Porifera
   C.   Annelids and Echinoderms
   D.   Porifera and Mollusks

73. Which phylum represents the first animals to have an efficient internal waste collecting system?

   A.   Porifera
   B.   Unicellular organisms
   C.   Aquatic invertebrates
   D.   Mollusks

74. Which structure performs three functions: filtration, secretion and reabsorption, and urine formation?

   A.   Epiglottis
   B.   Nephron
   C.   Bowman's capsule
   D.   Alveoli

75. Which phylum is the first to exhibit cephalization and centralization?

   A.   Cnidarians
   B.   Echinoderms
   C.   Platyhelminthes
   D.   Unicellular animals

76. The stretching of the urinary bladder to signal muscle contractions is an example of which type of sensory receptor?

   A.   Baroreceptors
   B.   Mechanoreceptros
   C.   Chemoreceptors
   D.   Photoreceptors

77. Which of the following is a characteristic of the cytokinesis stage of mitosis?

   A.   Cytoplasm divides forming two daughter cells.
   B.   Chromatin condenses.
   C.   Centrioles migrate.
   D.   Nuclear membrane disappears.

78. In which phase of meiosis do the chromosomes align along the equator of the dividing cell?

   A.   Interphase
   B.   Prophase
   C.   Metaphase
   D.   Anaphase

79. Dendrites receive a signal and relay it to the cell body. The cell body contains a nucleus that determines the next action. Which of the following is *not* an option for the nucleus?

    A. The message may have no effect.
    B. The message may be translated and sent to other parts of the neuron.
    C. The message may be forwarded to the next neuron via the axon.
    D. The message may be deliberately scrambled and forwarded to the previous neuron.

80. The charge difference across the membrane when the membrane is not electrically active is called the **resting potential** and is measured at –70 millivolts. Which of the following is a cause of the resting potential?

    A. Calcium ions are actively transported into the cell.
    B. Potassium ions are diffused out of the cell.
    C. Calcium and sodium ions are moved into the cell.
    D. Sodium ions are actively transported out of the cell.

81. As the myosin and actin fibers slide past each other, what is drawn with them?

    A. Sarcomere
    B. Z-line
    C. Sliding filaments
    D. Muscle fibers

82. Which of the following are double membrane structures within cardiac muscle that synchronize the contraction for a normal heartbeat?

    A. Intercalated disks
    B. Pacemaker
    C. Smooth muscles
    D. Purkinje fibers

83. Which phylum(a) exhibit a hydrostatic skeleton that supports each segment by the force of the fluids in that segment?

    A. Porifera
    B. Arthropods
    C. Amphibians and Reptiles
    D. Cnidarians and Annelids

84. The change of leaf color during the autumn season shows the presence of which of the following?

    A. Chlorophyll A
    B. Auxiliary pigments
    C. Chlorophyll B
    D. Cytokinins

85. With the release of energy, ATP is broken down to ADP + a phosphate group. What type of reaction is represented?

    A.   Degradation
    B.   Condensation
    C.   Hydrolysis
    D.   Neutralization

86. The growth of a population of Drosophila that receives adequate space, food, and growing environment along with no predators is described by which of the following?

    A.   Moderate
    B.   *S* curve
    C.   *J* curve
    D.   Interstate curve

87. What is the main function of the periosteum?

    A.   Support of young plants
    B.   Protective tissue surrounding the mammalian heart
    C.   Provide a blood supply to bones
    D.   The site of Krebs' Cycle

88. Exocrine glands are glands that produce secretions through ducts directly to their target cells. Which of the following is both an endocrine and exocrine gland?

    A.   Bulbourethral glands
    B.   Pancreas
    C.   Thymus
    D.   Ovaries

89. Which of the following stimulates sperm production in the seminiferous tubules?

    A.   Luteinizing hormone (LH)
    B.   Estrogen
    C.   Testosterone
    D.   Testosterone and follicle-stimulating hormone (FSH)

90. What is the function of the endometrium?

    A.   Nourish the embryo
    B.   Serve as the site for fertilization
    C.   Location of spermatogenesis
    D.   Secrete estrogen

91. Human chorionic gonatotropin (HCG) stimulates estrogen and progesterone to prevent menstrual flow, and causes morning sickness. Pregnancy tests detect the presence of HCG. At what stage is the embryo when the body begins secreting HCG?

    A. Day 1
    B. Day 2
    C. Days 3–5
    D. Days 6–7

92. Which of the following non-embryonic features do you only have in common with other mammals?

    A. Gastrulation creates three germ layers: endoderm, mesoderm, and ectoderm.
    B. Amniotic sac is the tough and transparent layer of membranes that surround and protect the developing embryo and contain amniotic fluid.
    C. Gill pouches
    D. Mammary glands

93. Which is *not* a characteristic of the first trimester of human development?

    A. The head is large and out of proportion to the rest of the body.
    B. Bone replaces cartilage.
    C. Male or female anatomy is confirmed.
    D. A layer of fine hair appears.

94. Which of the following biomes is characterized as having warm temperatures, moderate and seasonal precipitation, and is mostly dominated by grasslands and migrating herbivores?

    A. Temperate deciduous forest
    B. Temperate coniferous forest
    C. Taiga
    D. Savanna

95. Which of the following best explains evolution?

    A. Advances toward a predetermined goal
    B. Represents the differential reproduction of certain phenotypes
    C. Represents the directed selection of acquired characteristics
    D. Stabilizing selection

96. What type of reaction joins two amino acids and releases a water molecule?

    A. Condensation
    B. Hydrolysis
    C. Replacement
    D. Degradation

97. Which of the following does *not* contain deoxygenated blood?

    A. Vena cava
    B. Right atrium
    C. Aorta
    D. Right ventricle

Question 98–100 refer to the diagram.

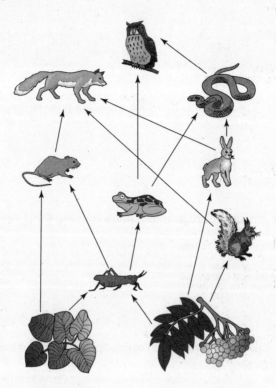

98. What would likely happen if the frog population suddenly became extremely small because the pond was drained?

    A.   The squirrel population decreases.
    B.   The fox population increases.
    C.   The plant population increases dramatically.
    D.   Snakes eat more rabbits.

99. What organism(s) have the greatest amount of usable energy available to them?

    A.   Producers
    B.   Owl
    C.   Foxes and snakes
    D.   Frogs

100. At what trophic level are the foxes located?

    A.   1
    B.   2
    C.   3
    D.   4

101. Which substance stimulates smooth muscle receptors in the uterine lining to rhythmically contract beginning a process known as labor?

    A.   Prostaglandins
    B.   Oxytocin
    C.   Estrogen
    D.   Follicle-stimulating hormone

102. What type of reproduction occurs when the female produces eggs which grow and develop without fertilization?

    A. Sexual
    B. Incomplete metamorphosis
    C. Parthenogenesis
    D. Complete metamorphosis

103. Which of the following is *not* a mechanisms by which the aging process may occur?

    A. Gene repression
    B. Genetic drift
    C. Accretion defects
    D. Depletional defects

104. What type of behaviors are genetically programmed and are coded for in the genes and do *not* have to be learned?

    A. Operant learning
    B. Classical conditioning
    C. Imitation
    D. Innate

105. Which behavior is a type of aggression that is often called "play fighting" where neither opponent is injured?

    A. Agnostic
    B. Defensive
    C. Dominance
    D. Territoriality

106. Scientists are trained not to ignore data that do not fit into their preconceived ideas or training. This characteristic is known as

    A. Researcher bias
    B. Experimental error
    C. Skepticism
    D. Tolerance of uncertainty

107. Which of the following scientists is credited with writing *The Canon of Medicine* that marks the beginning of experimental medicine and ushered the discovery of the contagious nature of infectious diseases?

    A. Thucydides
    B. Vesalius
    C. Avicenna
    D. Harvey

108. The unwanted mass that may come from the mass of the container or a maladjusted balance is which of the following?

    A. Scale
    B. Balance
    C. Tare
    D. Meniscus

109. What is the application of tools and knowledge to solve a problem?

   A.   Science
   B.   Mathematics
   C.   Technology
   D.   Creativity

110. The Clean Air Act of 1970 and Clean Water Act of 1972 placed restrictions on the release of pollutants into the environment and are examples of which of the following?

   A.   Technological response to a need
   B.   Scientific investigations
   C.   Social problem solved by political means
   D.   Economic response to a technological problem

111. What is *not* a strategy that is recommended by scientists to minimize or eliminate use and storage problems?

   A.   Increase the cost of storage.
   B.   Have consumers examine the long-term nature of the product.
   C.   Recommend that industries adopt a cradle-to-grave mentality about the processes that are used to make their product.
   D.   Everyone should read the directions and use products correctly and never over purchase.

112. Mendel's experiments yielded several principles of sexual reproduction that still apply today. Which is *not* one of the principles?

   A.   Mutation is a source of variation that changes the phenotypic ratio.
   B.   For each inherited character, each parent contributes one gene.
   C.   When an organism has two different alleles for a trait, one allele may be expressed and mask the effect of the other allele.
   D.   During the meiosis of a diploid organism, the paired alleles separate or segregate and randomly combine during gamete or sex cell formation.

113. In Mendelian inheritance patterns, if the genotypic ratio is 1:2:1, what is the expected phenotypic ratio?

   A.   1:2:1
   B.   1:3
   C.   3:1
   D.   4:0

114. Why is it easier for male offspring to be colorblind than female offspring?

   A.   There are more male colorblind individuals in the general population.
   B.   The colorblind gene is carried on the Y chromosome.
   C.   Females have to inherit the colorblindness gene from both parents.
   D.   The X chromosome is smaller than the Y chromosome.

115. Which of the following best exemplifies the condition whereby social needs are achieved by scientific and technological interaction to allow the human population to survive indefinitely in a changing world?

   A.   The emphasis on production shifts from quality to quantity.
   B.   Human populations are allowed to fluctuate with economics.
   C.   Extra funding is provided for pollution cleanup.
   D.   Renewable resources are favored over nonrenewable.

116. Which of the following is *not* a member of the class Mammalia?

    A.   You

    B.   Your dog

    C.   Your horse

    D.   Your parakeet

117. Which are more closely related?

    A.   Members of the same family

    B.   Members of the same class

    C.   Members of the same order

    D.   Members of the same kingdom

118. Which of the following are features that are possessed by some but not all of the members of the group?

    A.   Analogous structures

    B.   Homologous structures

    C.   Primitive characters

    D.   Derived characters

119. Which types of structures are perforated at the ends and have pores that allow the translocation of water and minerals from one tube into another?

    A.   Tracheids and vessels

    B.   Xylem and phloem

    C.   Vascular bundles

    D.   Sieve tubes and companion cells

120. The irregular dispersion of maple trees in a temperate deciduous forest is an example of which of the following?

    A.   Clustered dispersion

    B.   Even dispersion

    C.   Random dispersion

    D.   Ordered dispersion

121. Which of the following is a density-dependent limiting factor?

    A.   Competition

    B.   Weather

    C.   Natural disaster

    D.   Human interaction

122. Birds often following raiding army ants as they scour the forest floor. The birds eat the flying insects that are stirred up by the ants which remain unaffected. What type of relationship do the birds and army ants exemplify?

    A.   Mutualism

    B.   Commensalism

    C.   Competition

    D.   Parasitism

123. The proper use and maintenance of laboratory equipment is essential for laboratory safety. Which of the following is *not* recommended?

    A. Fire polish all glass tubing.
    B. Clean all glassware before each use to remove all residue.
    C. Never heat a closed container.
    D. Always pour water into acid.

124. Established safety and emergency procedures prevent problems and minimize teacher liability. Which of the following is *not* recommended?

    A. Know the location and limit the access to emergency gas, water, and electricity shut-off valves.
    B. Chemical splash safety glasses should be worn at all times by teachers, students, and visitors in the laboratory setting.
    C. Spill kits should be located in the nurse's office and the teacher should know how to use it.
    D. Contact the main office as soon as possible for any and all emergency events.

125. Commercial plant growers can mimic the seasons by adjusting the amount of darkness in a greenhouse to cause certain plants to bloom at special times of the year. The grower is using his or her knowledge of what characteristic of flowering plants to accomplish this phenomenon?

    A. Life history
    B. Photoperiod
    C. Abscisic acid
    D. Thigmotropism

126. Which of the following is *not* matched correctly?

    A. Auxins—inhibit bud production in stems
    B. Ethylene gas—ripening process
    C. Gibberellins—enlarge certain seedless fruit
    D. Cytokinins—plant dormancy

127. The pine tree produces both male and female cones which perform meiosis to produce spores. The spores mature and perform mitosis to produce the haploid sperm and eggs. This is the beginning of which of the following?

    A. Gametophyte generation
    B. Alternation of generations
    C. Sporophyte generation
    D. final stage of angiosperm reproduction

128. Which of the following is *not* one of the five main ways that plants reproduce vegetatively?

    A. Rhizomes
    B. Corms
    C. Seeds
    D. Bulbs

129. Secondary growth increases the amount of vascular tissue in a plant to compensate for the increased need of water and nutrients that extend beyond the capacity of the primary tissue. What causes secondary growth?

   A. Vascular cambium
   B. Lateral meristem
   C. Vascular bundle
   D. Cork cambium

130. Which biome is characterized by a short warm season that melts the very top layer of soil to create pools of water that cannot be absorbed by the permafrost layer beneath and thereby gives the appearance of a marshy plain?

   A. Tundra
   B. Taiga
   C. Savanna
   D. Temperate grassland

131. Which zone is the shallow, highly productive area connecting with the shore that reaps the benefit of nutrient runoff and aquatic plants abound?

   A. Benthic
   B. Littoral
   C. Limnetic
   D. Profundal

132. Which process removes carbon dioxide from the atmosphere as part of the geochemical cycle?

   A. Photosynthesis
   B. Transpiration
   C. Aerobic respiration
   D. Eutrophication

133. Which of the following does *not* have the same atomic number?

   A. Atoms of a different element
   B. Positive ions of a particular atom
   C. Negative charges from a single atom
   D. All elemental gold

134. Which group of elements exhibit chemical stability due to their filled valence electron energy levels?

   A. Inert elements
   B. Halogens
   C. Alkali metals
   D. Transition elements

135. Which cycle occurs in the stroma of the chloroplasts and is a series of enzyme-assisted biochemical reactions that ultimately produce a 3-carbon sugar?

A. Krebs'
B. Glycolysis
C. Calvin
D. Electron transport

136. Which scientist identified the process that cells use to convert sugars, fats, and proteins into energy, also called the Krebs' Cycle?

A. Hans Krebs
B. Rosalind Franklin
C. August Weisman
D. Alexander Fleming

137. Which of the following is *not* an invertebrate?

A. Arthropods
B. Mollusks
C. Crustaceans
D. Amphibians

138. Which enzyme catalyzes the first step of the Calvin Cycle by attaching an atmospheric carbon dioxide molecule to the 5-carbon sugar RuBP (ribulose biphosphate)?

A. ATPase
B. Ribulose polymerase
C. Nicotinamide adenine dinucleotidease
D. Rubisco (ribulose biphsophate carboxylase)

139. Which process is an enzyme-controlled, anaerobic reaction that occurs in the cytoplasm of a cell and requires two ATP molecules to begin but releases four ATP molecules for a net gain of two ATP molecules?

A. Photosynthesis
B. Glycolysis
C. Anaerobic respiration
D. Aerobic respiration

140. Which of the following is *not* part of the original cell theory?

A. All cells arise from pre-existing cells.
B. All living organisms are composed of one or more cells.
C. Cells are the basic unit of structure and function in organisms.
D. All cells are made of carbohydrates, proteins, and lipids.

Questions 141–142

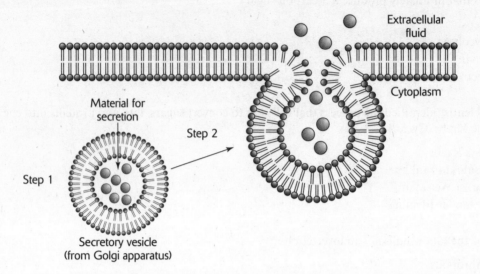

141. Which process is being demonstrated?

    A.   Diffusion
    B.   Osmosis
    C.   Exocytosis
    D.   Endocytosis

142. Which structure is labeled "A"?

    A.   Phosphoplipid bilayer
    B.   Cell wall
    C.   Epidermis
    D.   Dermis

143. Which of the following is *not* part of the nucleus?

    A.   rRNA
    B.   Nucleolus
    C.   Nuclear pore
    D.   Nuclear body

144. Which enzyme unzips and straightens the DNA molecule by breaking the hydrogen bonds that hold the complementary nitrogen bases (rungs of the ladder) together?

    A.   DNA polymerase
    B.   DNA helicases
    C.   DNA ligase
    D.   RNA polymerase

145. What makes up the "central dogma" of biology?

    A. Transcription and translation
    B. Natural selection and evolution
    C. Function determines structure; structure determines function
    D. Nutrients cycle, energy flows

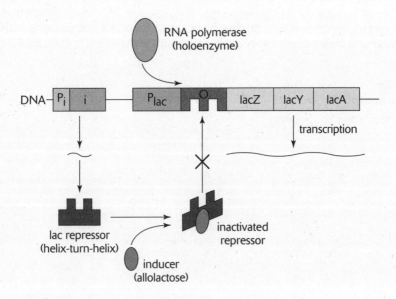

146. Which structure is labeled O?

    A. Operon
    B. Repressor
    C. Operator
    D. Regulatory gene

147. Which of the following is a recessive disorder caused by a single gene and is the most common fatal genetic disorder in the United States, causing the body to produce a thick mucus that clogs the lungs and blocks the pancreas from releasing digestive enzymes?

    A. Down syndrome
    B. Cystic fibrosis
    C. Hemophilia
    D. Turner syndrome

148. The California buckeye and a particular bee species have a mutualistic relationship. However, some introduced bee species are susceptible to the neurotoxin produced by the buckeye. The relationship between the mutual relationship between the buckeye and the bee species is probably due to which of the following?

    A. Convergent evolution
    B. Divergent evolution
    C. Gradualism
    D. Coevolution

149. Which of the following is *not* a type of prezygotic reproductive isolation?

    A. Territorial
    B. Seasonal
    C. Natural selection
    D. Behavioral

150. Which model was formulated when a researcher powered a mixture of amino acids with UV light and produced dipeptides and showed how short chains of amino acids in water form microspheres?

    A. Fox model
    B. Bubble model
    C. Miller-Urey model
    D. Oparin or Primordial Soup model

Biology Content Knowledge
Practice Test 2 Answer Key

1. C	31. A	61. A	91. D	121. A
2. A	32. A	62. D	92. D	122. B
3. D	33. B	63. B	93. D	123. D
4. A	34. B	64. A	94. D	124. C
5. B	35. D	65. C	95. B	125. B
6. C	36. D	66. B	96. A	126. D
7. A	37. B	67. C	97. C	127. A
8. D	38. D	68. D	98. D	128. C
9. B	39. A	69. C	99. A	129. B
10. A	40. C	70. A	100. C	130. A
11. D	41. A	71. C	101. B	131. B
12. C	42. D	72. B	102. C	132. A
13. D	43. D	73. D	103. B	133. A
14. B	44. B	74. B	104. D	134. A
15. A	45. C	75. C	105. A	135. C
16. C	46. C	76. B	106. D	136. A
17. C	47. A	77. A	107. C	137. D
18. B	48. C	78. C	108. C	138. D
19. C	49. C	79. D	109. C	139. B
20. D	50. A	80. D	110. C	140. D
21. A	51. B	81. B	111. A	141. C
22. D	52. D	82. A	112. A	142. A
23. D	53. C	83. D	113. C	143. D
24. C	54. A	84. B	114. C	144. B
25. D	55. D	85. A	115. D	145. A
26. A	56. A	86. C	116. D	146. C
27. B	57. B	87. C	117. A	147. B
28. C	58. D	88. B	118. D	148. D
29. C	59. C	89. D	119. A	149. C
30. D	60. C	90. A	120. C	150. A

Practice Test 2 Detailed Answers and Explanations

Praxis II Biology Content Knowledge (0235)

1. **C.** (ecology) Genetic variation will increase—not decrease—because of the new genome added to the population, making Choice A incorrect; no evidence exists that altruism will increase (Choice B); and diversity will increase—not decrease—as a new species is added to the population (Choice D).

2. **A.** (ecology) Territory and habitat (choices B and C) are the areas where the organisms reside; behavior patterns (Choice D) do not describe the full role.

3. **D.** (classical genetics and evolution) Embryological development is based solely on genetics; only Choice D attributes the development to genetics.

4. **A.** (classical genetics and evolution) The organisms differ greatly in their ancestry (Choice B) and evolution (Choice C). They did not coevolve, as indicated in Choice D.

5. **B.** (classical genetics and evolution) They did not coevolve (as indicated in Choice A); chickens and birds reproduce by internal fertilization (Choice C); and their life histories (Choice D) are vastly different.

6. **C.** (diversity of life) Releasing sperm (Choice A), gametogenesis (Choice D), and pollination (Choice B) involve sexual reproduction.

7. **A.** (diversity of life) The left ventricle (Choice B) and right atrium (Choice C) are part of the heart; the aorta (Choice D) is the main artery leading from the left ventricle.

8. **D.** (diversity of life) Plants and fungi have cell walls, are decomposers, and are eukaryotes, so Choice D is the only viable answer.

9. **B.** (diversity of life) Phloem tissue does not transport water, so choices A and D are incorrect; there is no root pressure so Choice C is incorrect.

10. **A.** (ecology) Increased atmospheric molecules decreases solar penetration, so Choice B incorrect; acid precipitation lowers the pH of surface water, making Choice C in correct; and phosphorus cycling (Choice D) is unchanged or perhaps increased by chemical weathering of acid precipitation.

11. **D.** (science, technology, and society) Self regulating, monitoring, and helping local groups are all good, but have not solved the problem in previous attempts.

12. **C.** (ecology) Sympatric speciation (Choice A) may occur later but not normally at the beginning of primary succession; secondary succession (Choice B) at least has soil to start with; and mutualism (Choice D) is a behavior between organisms that may occur once life has begun to colonize the newly formed area.

13. **D.** (diversity of life) An open circulatory system (Choice A) is associated with simpler animals; internal fertilization, digestive system, and food source (choices B and C) do not apply to metabolic rate.

14. **B.** (molecular and cellular biology) Both viroids and prions are found in nature, are harmful, and contain protein; the only difference listed is Choice B, viroids contain RNA.

15. **A.** (molecular and cellular biology) Hess' Law (Choice B) states that the heat (energy) requirement for any reaction is constant and independent of the manner in which the reaction tales place; the Second Law of Thermodynamics (Choice D) states that no natural reaction or process can occur unless it is accompanied by an increase in entropy; and bioenergetics (Choice C) is the expression of the energy flow through living systems.

16. **C.** (classical genetics and evolution) Incomplete dominance (Choice A) is true, but does not answer the question; evidence for gene linkage (Choice B) and multiple alleles (Choice D) is not provided.

17. **C.** (molecular and cellular biology) Viruses and viroids have the same characteristics except viroids cause Hepatitis D.

18. **B.** (molecular and cellular biology) The sugar phosphate backbone (Choice A) holds individual strands together, not the molecule; (Choice B) ATP energy does not hold the molecule together; and there is no measurable ionic attraction between the bases (Choice D).

19. **C.** (classical genetics and evolution) According to Darwin, only the most fit organisms survive to reproduce.

20. **D.** (basic principles) The number of seeds (Choice A) is a controlled variable; isopropyl alcohol (Choice B) was the independent variable; and corn seeds (Choice C) were incorrectly used as the control group.

21. **A.** (basic principles) The independent variable (application of isopropyl alcohol) was *not* confounded with the dependent variable (germination time) and *was* tested, making choices B and C incorrect; the germination time was measured in a consistent and objective manner so it was fair, making Choice D incorrect.

22. **D.** (basic principles) Isopropyl alcohol (Choice A) was the independent variable so it is plotted on the X axis; overall time (Choice B) was not a factor; and seed type (Choice C) was incorrectly used as the control-treatment group.

23. **D.** (basic principles) Soaking both containers (Choice A) with alcohol would eliminate the control group; corn seeds (Choice B) corn seeds are monocots the purpose of the experiment was to test the effect of isopropyl alcohol on the germination of weed seeds, not corn; measuring nongerminated seeds (Choice C) is acceptable, but it would not improve the experimental design.

24. **C.** (molecular and cellular biology) Polypeptides are made of protein (Choice A), but this does not answer the question. Different genes make different polypeptides, so Choice B is incorrect. Genes are not made of polypeptides, so Choice D is also incorrect.

25. **D.** (molecular and cellular biology) The central vacuole contains fluids and is usually the largest structure in a typical plant cell.

26. **A.** (molecular and cellular biology) The cell wall is the outermost covering of the cell.

27. **B.** (molecular and cellular biology) The Krebs' Cycle, glycolysis, and aerobic respiration occur mostly in the mitochondria, making choices A, C, and D incorrect; photosynthesis occurs in the chloroplasts.

28. **C.** (science, technology and society) Aluminum does not biodegrade in temperate climates, (b) it does not dissolve in water.

29. **C.** (ecology) Intraspecific competition (Choice A) does limit growth according to natural selection, but peaks and valleys still exist; excess food may increase the population, but it increases all populations so no net gain is noticed, making Choice B wrong. Predator-prey cycles (Choice D) are continual and cause temporary swings in populations.

30. **D.** (molecular and cellular biology) The daughter cells are nearly formed, which occurs during telephase. In prophase (Choice C) the cell is preparing to divide; metaphase (Choice B) occurs when the chromosomes align along the equatorial plate; the formation of the two cells is not obvious (Choice A) and has no anaphase.

31. **A.** (ecology) Climax communities are the endpoint of succession; primary succession (Choice B) begins without soil; a climax community is the end result of secondary succession (Choice C); tertiary succession (Choice D) is not found in the literature.

32. **A.** (molecular and cellular biology) Photosynthesis is inefficient converting light energy into chemical energy.

33. **B.** (classical genetics and evolution) The testcross is a standard mating to determine an unknown genotype and always involves a homozygous recessive individual. The test cross is the standard operation for determining an unknown genotype because the results identify the unknown genotype, other choices do not consistently provide this information.

34. **B.** (ecology) Nitrifying bacteria change unusable nitrogen into usable nitrogen; denitrifying bacteria do not recycle nutrients.

35. **D.** (classical genetics and evolution) A point mutation (Choice B) involves a single gene; a deletion (Choice A) is the loss of one or more genes; and a frame shift (Choice C) occurs when one or more bases are inserted or deleted.

36. **D.** (molecular and cellular biology) Choice D's genotype is the only one that includes all alleles.

37. **B.** (diversity of life) Operant conditioning (Choice C) is "trial and error"; habituation (Choice D) is the diminished response to a stimulus; and Choice A is a distracter that is not a correct response.

38. **D.** (basic principles) Students are to evacuate in the event of a major fire; the teacher extinguishes a minor fire, but this answer choice was not given.

39. **A.** (science, technology, and society) Relocating people (Choice B) may happen, but many will move against their will and that is only a part of the problem; without safeguards, allowing economics to drive the future (Choice C) may present environmental and social problems; and taxing for solutions to future problems (Choice D) is never popular.

40. **C.** (classical genetics and evolution) Analogous structures (Choice A) do not show any evolutionary connection; phenotypes (Choice B) are helpful, but prehistoric reconstructions are speculative, especially of prokaryotes; intelligent design (Choice D) is based on the Creationist Theory.

41. **A.** (molecular and cellular biology) The anticodon matches with the appropriate area on the codon to deliver a specific amino acid.

42. **D.** (diversity of life) Pepsinogen, a precursor to pepsin, is secreted by the chief cells in the mucosa of the stomach.

43. **D.** (diversity of life) Species level organization is the most specific.

44. **B.** (molecular and cellular biology) The cell membrane surrounds animal cells; cell walls (Choice A) are only in plants; ER and Golgi apparatus (choices C and D) are interior organelles.

45. **C.** (molecular and cellular biology) The nucleus (Choice A) contains the DNA and controls the activities of the cell; vacuoles (Choice B) mostly contain water and dissolved ions; and cytoplasm (Choice D) is the medium that suspends the organelles.

46. **D.** (molecular and cellular biology) Nuclear materials in prokaryote cells floats within the cytoplasm. A the nuclear membrane is a single layer; B cytoplasm does not have a membrane; C vacuoles are always single layer.

47. **A.** (molecular and cellular biology) Vacuoles are usually the largest organelle within a plant cell; choices B, C, and D are all present within a plant and animal cell.

48. **C.** (classical genetics and evolution) Codominance is not a blending, both alleles are expressed; incomplete dominance (Choice A) is a blending; sex-linked (Choice B) is gender specific; and dominant and recessive alleles (Choice D) is the "normal" inheritance pattern.

49. **C.** (molecular and cellular biology) Viruses, prions, and prokaryotes do not have a phospholipid bilayer.

50. **A.** (diversity of life) Geotropisms are plant growth patterns that are determined by gravity and plants hormones. B phototropism is the bending in response to light; C hydrotropism is a bending toward water; D hormone contraction is not a process.

51. **B.** (classical genetics and evolution) The Big Bang theory (Choice A) centers on the formation of the universe; uniformity and linear (choices C and D) are theories that project a smooth evolution.

52. **D.** (ecology) The meadow may or may not be the climax community (Choice A) for this area; there is no evidence of speciation (Choice B); and primary succession (Choice C) begins with an absence of soil.

53. **C.** (molecular and cellular biology) Schleiden and Schwann (choices A and B) developed the cell theory; Leuwenhoek (Choice D) invented the microscope.

54. **A.** (ecology) Immigration (Choice B) is a permanent movement; genetic drift (Choice D) references the flow of the gene pool; and territoriality (Choice C) is a protective behavior.

55. **D.** (science, technology, and society) Agricultural practices are more modernized but tend to follow social demand.

56. **A.** (diversity of life) Columnar (Choice B) refers to the shape of palisade cells; dermis (Choice C) is the protective covering; and stomata (Choice D) are the air holes on the underside of leaves.

57. **B.** (molecular and cellular biology) Lysosomes and vacuoles (choices A and C) are found in relatively stable numbers in all animal cells; chloroplasts (Choice D) are only found in plant cells.

58. **D.** (diversity of life) Darwin and Wallace (choices B and C) proposed natural selection; Whittaker (Choice A) proposed five categories of kingdoms.

59. **C.** (diversity of life) Evolutionary systematics (Choice A) weights degrees of importance to certain characters which produces a more subjective analysis of evolutionary relationships than cladistics; binomial nomenclature (Choice B) is a naming system; and phylogeny (Choice D) shows evolutionary relatedness.

60. **C.** (diversity of life) Plants were autotrophs before moving on dry land.

61. **A.** (diversity of life) Epithelial cells (Choice B) are usually cells that serve as a lining; phloem tissue (Choice C) is made of sieve tubes and companion cells; and palisade cells (Choice D) are photosynthetic cells found in the mesophyll of leaves or stems.

62. **D.** (molecular and cellular biology) The enzyme (Choice A) remains unchanged in the graphic; the substrate (Choice B) is converted into products; and no inhibitor (Choice C) is present.

63. **B.** (molecular and cellular biology) The active site is located on the enzyme; no enzyme-substrate mixture is formed.

64. **A.** (molecular and cellular biology) Enzymes are continually recycled with no structural change.

65. **C.** (diversity of life) Flowering plants are angiosperms.

66. **B.** (diversity of life) The node (Choice A) is the part of a stem where leaves, branches, or aerial roots may begin; (Choice C) the periole attaches the leaf to the stem, the leaf (Choice D) is the major photosynthetic part of the plant.

67. **C.** (diversity of life) Aves and reptiles (choices B and D) do have a double circulation system, as do you but amphibians (Choice C) were first; Porifera (Choice A) do not have a circulatory system.

68. **D.** (diversity of life) Capillaries deliver blood to veins.

69. **C.** (diversity of life) Leukocytes (Choice A) are WBCs; platelets (Choice B) help blood clotting; and basophils ophils (Choice D) function during allergic reactions to release histamines.

70. **A.** (diversity of life) A lysozyme is an enzyme that destroys the cell walls of most bacteria, so Choice D is incorrect. Antibodies are the blood plasma protein that bind with the receptor site and destroy the invading cell, making Choice B incorrect. Choice C is wrong because again, it is antibodies that are released into the bloodstream and flow to a site to destroy microbes.

71. **C.** (ecology) Humidity is very low in deserts because of the lack of moisture.

72. **B.** (diversity of life) Mollusks have two main methods of respiration: Gills are common in most aquatic mollusks and a primitive "lung" provides gaseous exchange in terrestrial mollusks, making choices A and D incorrect. Cnidarians and Porifera lack an organized internal transport system so they have to diffuse gases directly to/from the environment, Annelids and echinoderms (Choice C) respire directly through their skin.

73. **D.** (diversity of life) Unicellular organisms (Choice B) and aquatic invertebrates (Choice C) dilute ammonia with water and then excrete the ammonia directly into their environment; Porifera (Choice A) diffuse wastes directly into their environment.

74. **B.** (diversity of life) The epiglottis (Choice A) is the flap that prevents food from entering the air passages; Bowman's capsule (Choice C) is part of the nephron; and alveoli (Choice D) are the gaseous exchange part of the lung.

75. **C.** (diversity of life) Platyhelminthes have both a cephalic region and centralized nervous system. Unicellular animals (Choice D) do not have or need a nervous system. Cnidarians (Choice A) possess a "nerve network" throughout their body. Echinoderms (Choice B) have the first nerves, which are clusters of neurons acting as a team.

76. **B.** (diversity of life) Mechanorecptors detect deformation of the tissue through touch or stretch (Choice A) baroreceptors sense pressure; chemoreceptors (Choice C) sense chemicals; and photoreceptors (Choice D) are sensitive to light levels.

77. **A.** (molecular and cellular biology) Choices B, C, and D are all characteristics of prophase.

78. **C.** (molecular and cellular biology) Interphase (Choice A) is the functioning stage; during prophase (Choice B) the cell is preparing to divide; and during anaphase (Choice D) the cell is in the final stages before cytokinesis.

79. **D.** (diversity of life) Cell bodies do not scramble the nerve signal, so Choice D is correct.

80. **D.** (diversity of life) In an inactive neuron, sodium ions are actively transported out of the cell creating a positive charge outside of the cell and a negative charge in the cytoplasm inside the cell.

81. **B.** (diversity of life) As the myosin and actin fibers draw toward the center of the sarcomere, they drag the attached Z lines along with them. Moving the Z lines closer together contracts the sarcomere and thereby contracts the muscle or muscle fiber, the sliding filament describes part of the process.

82. **A.** (diversity of life) The pacemaker (Choice B) regulate the overall heartbeat; smooth muscle (Choice C) is not found within cardiac muscle; and Purkinje fibers (Choice D) relay the nervous signal to the ventricles.

83. **D.** (diversity of life) Porifera (Choice A) have spicules for support; an exoskeleton is a characteristic of arthropods (Choice B); and amphibians and reptiles (Choice C) have a strong bony skeleton.

84. **B.** (molecular and cellular biology) Both types of chlorophyll (choices A and C) are denatured due to cold weather leaving auxiliary pigments that are sensitive to other light waves; cytokinins (Choice D) are a type of plant hormone.

85. **A.** (molecular and cellular biology) Condensation reactions (Choice B) release water; hydrolysis (Choice C) is the splitting of water; and neutralization (Choice D) occurs between acids and bases.

86. **C.** (ecology) Under ideal conditions, populations growth is exponential, represented by a *J*-curve; (Choice A) moderate growth is relative, but is usually signified by a constant slope, (Choice B) an *S*-curve is typical of non-exponential growth, the interstate-curve (Choice D) is only found on interstate highways.

87. **C.** (diversity of life) Bones are living tissues that require a blood supply so they are surrounded by a periosteum, a fibrous sheet of connective tissue and blood vessels.

88. **B.** (diversity of life) The pancreas is both an exocrine and an endocrine gland. The exocrine portion of the pancreas secretes pancreatic juice into the small intestine. The endocrine portion of the pancreas secretes insulin. The bulbourethral (Choice A) is exocrine gland, and the ovaries and thymus (choices C and D) are both endocrine glands.

89. **D.** (diversity of life) LH (Choice A) stimulates the production of testosterone while FSH and testosterone (not testosterone alone, Choice C) stimulate sperm production in the seminiferous tubules; and estrogen (Choice B) is a female hormone.

90. **A.** (diversity of life) The fallopian tubes are the normal fertilization site, making Choice B incorrect; spermatogenesis occurs in the testes, making Choice C incorrect; and estrogen (Choice D) is secreted by the ovaries.

91. **D.** (diversity of life) Day 1 (Choice A): One cell becomes two cells = first cleavage. Day 2 (Choice B): Two cells become 4 cells = second cleavage. Choice C reflects what happens the next three days. On days 3–4, the existing 32 cells form into a solid ball of cells called a morula and on Day 5 the morula develops into a hollow fluid filled blastocyst = blastula stage. On days 6–7: The blastocyst attaches to the endometrium (implantation) and begins secreting human chorionic gonatotropin (HCG). HCG stimulates estrogen and progesterone to prevent menstrual flow, and causes morning sickness. Pregnancy tests detect the presence of HCG.

92. **D.** (diversity of life) Mammary glands are not found in amphioxus and lancelets.

93. **D.** (diversity of life) Fine hair develops during the second trimester.

94. **D.** (ecology) Temperate forests (choices A and B) are not dominated by grasslands; temperatures in the taiga biome (Choice C) are much colder than the savanna.

95. **B.** (classical genetics and evolution) Evolution does not respond to a predetermined goal (Choice A); acquired characteristics (Choice C) has not be proven; and stabilizing selection (Choice D) is a type of natural selection.

96. **A.** (molecular and cellular biology) Hydrolysis reactions (Choice B) split water; replacement reactions (Choice C) add switch or substitute reactants to form products; and degradation (Choice D) is the breakdown of a molecule into smaller units.

97. **C.** (diversity of life) The aorta transports blood after it has passed through the lungs and become oxygenated.

98. **D.** (ecology) The frog population has minimal effect on the squirrel and fox populations, making choices A and B incorrect; the plant population (Choice C) may actually decrease as more grasshoppers are available.

99. **A.** (molecular and cellular biology) The first trophic level (or producers) has the most available energy; the remaining choices represents trophic layers that derive their energy from the producers, the highest trophic level (in this case, the owl) has the least, approximately 10 percent of the usable energy is lost between trophic levels.

100. **C.** (ecology) The producers are the first level (Choice A); mice and squirrels are level 2 (Choice B); and the owl is at level 4 (Choice D).

101. **B.** (diversity of life) Prostaglandins (Choice A) increase the uterine contractions; estrogen (Choice C) plays many roles, but not this one; follicle stimulating hormone or FSH (Choice D) triggers the release of the eggs.

102. **C.** (diversity of life) Sexual reproduction (Choice A) results in fertilization; both types of metamorphosis (choices B and D) refer to life cycles.

103. **B.** (diversity of life) Genetic drift refers to the genetics of a population not the aging process.

104. **D.** (diversity of life) Choices A, B, and C are types of learned behavior.

105. **A.** (diversity of life) Defensive behavior (Choice B) is the tactics used to prepare for battle; in dominance (Choice C), the rank of an individual within a population confers the right to act condescendingly toward all beneath you while receiving the same treatment from those above you; and territoriality (Choice D) is signified when an individual or population reserves a particular location for their exclusive usage.

106. **D.** (basic principles) Researcher bias (Choice A) occurs when scientists become so convinced that their hypothesis is correct that they overlook a flaw or misread the data; skeptics (Choice C) are trained to treat new data with doubt; and experimental error (Choice B) is a mistake that happens during the experiment.

107. **C.** (basic principles) Thucydides (Choice A) proposed the immune system; Vesalius (Choice B) pioneered research into human anatomy; and Harvey (Choice D) described blood circulation.

108. **C.** (basic principles) Scales and balances (choices A and B) are instruments; the meniscus (Choice D) is the concave surface made by most liquids in a container.

109. **C.** (science, technology, and society) Science (Choice A) is the process in which facts and truth are determined; mathematics (Choice B) is the quantifying tool of science; and creativity (Choice D) is a part of technological innovation.

110. **C.** (science, technology, and society) The technological response (Choice A) and scientific investigations (Choice B) followed the legislation; the economic response (Choice D) raised prices.

111. **A.** (science, technology, and society) Increasing the cost is an economic response.

112. **A.** (classical genetics and evolution) Mendel did not know about mutations.

113. **C.** (classical genetics and evolution) The dominant allele in the heterozygote gives the same phenotype as the homozygous dominant, 3:1 indicates 3 dominant to 1 recessive; 1:3 indicates the reverse.

114. **C.** (classical genetics and evolution) The gene for colorblindness is carried only on the X chromosome, so males only need to inherit it from their mother.

115. **D.** (science, technology, and society) The concept of sustainability is designed to allow humans to live on this planet indefinitely. (Choices A, B, C) are partial answers that may have a positive effect but do not individually provide sustainability.

116. **D.** (diversity of life) Birds belong to the phylum Aves.

117. **A.** (diversity of life) Family is the most specific classification of those listed.

118. **D.** (diversity of life) Homologous and analogous (choices A and B) are found in all members of the same group; primitive characters (Choice C) are exhibited in all members.

119. **A.** (diversity of life) The structures in choices B, C, and D perform a different function than water transference: companion cells are phloem cells, which carry food; the vascular bundle is the xylem and phloem tissues, which are separate tissues that conduct food and water.

120. **C.** (ecology) Random dispersion is a chance event where there is no set pattern or regular spacing in random dispersion. (Choices A, B, D) are not the best examples of random dispersion, clustered dispersion indicates a large concentration in one area, with little or no concentration in another area, even and ordered distribution are usually the results of direct planting.

121. **A.** (ecology) All of the remaining foils are density-independent factors.

122. **B.** (ecology) A commensal relationship is one where one party is helped and the other is unaffected. (Choice A) mutualism occurs when both parties receive a benefit from their interaction, (Choice C) occurs when both parties are competing for a benefit, (Choice D) occurs when one party derives a benefit at the expense of the other party.

123. **D.** (basic principles) Never pour water into an acid; always pour acid into water. Pouring water into acid may cause the acid to splash back causing the possibility of injury; acid into water dilutes the acid.

124. **C.** (basic principles) Spill kits are to be located in each laboratory.

125. **B.** (diversity of life) Life history (Choice A) is a summary of the characteristics of an organism over time; abscisic acid (Choice C) is a plant hormone that prepares the plant for winter dormancy; and a thigmotropism (Choice D) is a plant's response to touch.

126. **D.** (diversity of life) Abscisic acid controls plant dormancy.

127. **A.** (diversity of life) Alternation of generations (Choice B) describes the reproductive life cycle of a plant; the sporophyte generation (Choice C) begins with the diploid zygote; and embryogenesis; pine trees are gymnosperms, (Choice D) the formation of haploid gametes would equate to the beginning of angiosperm reproduction.

128. **C.** (diversity of life) Seeds are a form of sexual reproduction.

129. **B.** (diversity of life) The vascular and cork cambium (choices A and D) grow as part of the lateral meristem; the vascular bundle (Choice C) is involved in primary growth.

130. **A.** (ecology) Temperate grasslands (Choice D) exist in warm and dry areas; taiga (Choice B) is a Russian word which loosely translated means for pine forest; and the Savanna (Choice C) is the great dry grasslands.

131. **B.** (ecology) The limnetic zone (Choice C) or euphotic or photic area connects to the littoral zone, but only includes the upper water layer. The limnetic zone receives enough light and nutrients to support photosynthesis. The profundal zone (Choice D), also known as the benthic zone (Choice A) or aphotic zone, only occurs in the deep water areas that do not receive enough light for photosynthesis to occur.

132. **A.** (ecology) Transpiration (Choice B) is the loss of water from leaves; aerobic respiration (Choice C) is energy production in mitochondria; and eutrophication (Choice D) is the over fertilization of waterways.

133. **A.** (molecular and cellular biology) Charges are not related to atomic number, atoms of the same element have the same atomic number.

134. **A.** (molecular and cellular biology) Inert elements do not need to add, share, or subtract valence electrons to become more energetically stable.

135. **C.** (molecular and cellular biology) The Krebs' Cycle and glycolysis (choices A and B) are involved in aerobic respiration; the electron transport system (Choice D) consists of a series of molecules that remove some of the energy from the excited electrons to create the energy-rich ATP and nictotinamide adenine dinucleotide (NADH) molecules.

136. **A.** (basic principles) Rosalind Franklin (Choice B) helped determine the structure of DNA; August Weisman (Choice C) identified sex cells; Alexander Fleming (Choice D) discovered penicillin.

137. **D.** (diversity of life) All foils have an exoskeleton instead of a backbone.

138. **D.** (molecular and cellular biology) The enzyme Rubisco (ribulose biphsophate carboxylase) catalyzes the first step of the Calvin Cycle by attaching an atmospheric carbon dioxide molecule to the 5-carbon sugar RuBP (ribulose biphosphate), (Choice A) ATPase is a class of enzymes that catalyze the decomposition of ATP to ADP; (Choice B) Ribulose polymerase represents a group of enzymes that catalyze programmed cell death and repair DNA, (Choice C) NADase catalyzes the breakdown of NAD.

139. **B.** (molecular and cellular biology) Photosynthesis (Choice A) occurs in the chloroplasts; anaerobic and aerobic respiration (choices C and D) occur after glycolysis.

140. **D.** (molecular and cellular biology) The biochemical components were not part of the cell theory.

141. **C.** (molecular and cellular biology) Diffusion (Choice A) is the random movement of molecules; osmosis (Choice B) is the movement of water; and endocytosis (Choice D) brings materials into the cell.

142. **A.** (molecular and cellular biology) The cell wall (Choice B) does not undergo exocytosis; the epidermis and dermis (choices C and D) are skin layers.

143. **D.** (molecular and cellular biology) Nuclear pores (Choice C) provide a selective passage way for substances to move from the nucleus into the cytoplasm; the nucleolus (Choice B) is a prominent sphere within the nucleus where ribosomal RNA (rRNA), Choice A, is synthesized.

144. **B.** (molecular and cellular biology) RNA polymerase (Choice D) matches or "reads" the nitrogen bases or gene sequence as it moves along the DNA strand in a 3' to 5' direction; DNA ligase (Choice C) is an enzyme that catalyzes the attachment of the strands back together to form the double-stranded DNA double helix; and DNA polymerase (Choice A) moves along the exposed DNA strands and adds complementary nucleotides to the exposed nitrogen bases according to the purine to pyrimidine base pairing rules (A-T, G-C).

145. **A.** (molecular and cellular biology) Protein synthesis occurs in two steps: transcription and translation. Transcription and translation make up the "central dogma" of biology: DNA→RNA→ protein, the remaining choices do not directly address these processes at a molecular level.

146. **C.** (molecular and cellular biology) An operon (Choice A) is a functional unit of prokaryote gene regulation in protein synthesis where as the operator (Choice C) is positioned to physically control the access to the genes; regulatory genes' (Choice D) code for proteins that regulate when genes start or stop coding for proteins that determine of affect a function; and a repressor (Choice B) is a protein that binds to an operator and turns "off" the function of the operon.

147. **B.** (classical genetics and evolution) Females with Turner syndrome (Choice D) have only one X chromosome, creating an XO genotype; hemophilia (Choice C) is a recessive sex-linked disorder that is only carried on the X chromosome; and most cases of Down syndrome (Choice A) are not a result of inheritance but an error in sex cell formation called nondisjunction resulting in the sperm or egg having an extra chromosome 21.

148. D. (classical genetics and evolution) Convergent evolution (Choice A) occurs when organisms of different ancestry develop structures that are similar in adaptation to their environment; divergent evolution (Choice B) is the process whereby two or more related species become more and more different in response to differing survival strategies in different environments; and gradualism (Choice C) is the belief that evolution is a gradual event that occurs continuously over long periods of time.

149. C. (classical genetics and evolution) Natural selection occurs after zygote formation.

150. A. (classical genetics and evolution) The Oparin or Primordial Soup model (Choice D) was developed by Oparin and Haldane in the 1920s and hypothesized that the early oceans were filled with a variety of organic molecules that joined together in a series of chemical reactions that were powered by energy from the sun, lightning, and volcanoes. The Miller-Urey model or Miller-Urey synthesis (Choice C) combined those gases that were thought to be present in the early atmosphere (water vapor, ammonia, hydrogen, methane, and nitrogen). Miller and Urey subjected this gaseous mixture to a spark to simulate lightning and analyzed the results. They found a mixture of amino acids, fatty acids, and hydrocarbons—the building blocks of life. The Bubble model (Choice B) was formulated by Louis Lerman who theorized that the gases that formed the early organic molecules were trapped in ocean bubbles. The bubbles formed by underwater volcanic eruptions would protect the ammonia and methane from the hazards of the damaging ultraviolet (UV) radiation.